INSTANT COOKING

INSTANT COOKING

fabulous food in no time at all

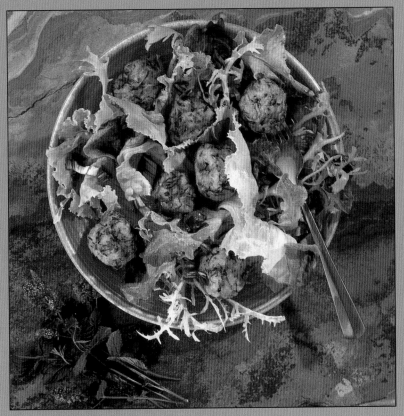

Editor: Jenni Fleetwood

LORENZ BOOKS

First published in 1999 by Lorenz Books

© Anness Publishing Limited 1999

Lorenz Books is an imprint of Anness Publishing Limited
Hermes House, 88–89 Blackfriars Road, London SE1 8HA

ISBN 1 85967 989 7

A CIP catalogue record for this book is available from the British Library

Publisher: Joanna Lorenz
Editor: Jenni Fleetwood
Project Editor: Felicity Forster
Recipes: Alex Barker, Carla Capalbo, Maxine Clark, Matthew Drennan,
Christine France, Sarah Gates, Shirley Gill, Carole Handslip, Patricia Lousada,
Norma McMillan, Sue Maggs, Sarah Maxwell, Janice Murfitt, Annie Nichols,
Angela Nilsen, Jenny Stacey, Liz Trigg, Hilaire Walden, Laura Washburn,
Steven Wheeler and Elizabeth Wolf-Cohen
Designers: Siân Keogh and Margaret Sadler
Jacket Designer: Simon Balley
Photographers: Karl Adamson, Edward Allwright, Steve Baxter, James Duncan,
Michelle Garrett, Amanda Heywood, Tim Hill and Don Last
Stylists: Madeleine Brehaut, Michelle Garrett, Hilary Guy and Fiona Tillett
Editorial Reader: Kate Henderson
Production Controller: Mark Fennell

Printed and bound in Italy

10 9 8 7 6 5 4 3 2 1

For all recipes, quantities are given in both metric and imperial measures, and where
appropriate, measures are also given in standard cups and spoons. Follow one set,
but not a mixture, because they are not interchangeable.

CONTENTS

INTRODUCTION

INTRODUCTION

The one ingredient none of us ever seems to have enough of is time. We live life in the fast lane, packing in a million and one activities between breakfast and bedtime. Even leisure – which sounds like it should be a laid-back proposition – has become a frenzied pursuit, as we struggle to find time for the exercise sessions we're told are essential for good health and vitality.

Faced with such demanding schedules, most of us – quite literally – put food on the back burner. We snatch sandwiches from petrol stations, fill our freezers with ready-prepared meals and can recite the telephone numbers of all our local takeaways. Good home-cooked meals are reserved for Saturdays or Sundays, and even then, there's no guarantee that every member of the family will be around to enjoy them.

So what's the answer? Accept the supermarket solution or fight back by finding a fail-safe collection of quick and easy dishes that can be prepared in next to no time? We'd advocate the latter, and to prove how easy it can be to cook delicious meals in under half an hour, we've produced this superb collection of simple and satisfying recipes.

Easy, effortless cooking takes a bit of planning, of course, but even there, we've taken the strain. Included in this book are menu plans, a step-by-step guide to time-saving techniques and suggestions for stocking the store cupboard, fridge and freezer with items that will make quick cooking a piece of cake – with instant icing, naturally!

Countdown to Cooking the Easy Way

Quick cooks are made, not born. Those people who walk in from work, fix a quick drink, disappear for 30 minutes and produce a marvellous meal weren't born with this knowledge. It takes practice, organization and a certain amount of expertise with a knife, can opener and whisk to whip up great grub in next to no time.

Pen and paper
A lot of unnecessary running around can be prevented by sitting down with pen and paper and drawing up a plan of action. Too often, ideas get the green light before realizing how much time and effort are needed to produce them. The first question to ask yourself is "How much time and energy do I have?" Be realistic – a lot of cooks come unstuck when they take on more than they can handle. Be kind to yourself and choose something you can cope with. You'll not only enjoy preparing the meal, you might even be composed enough to sit down and enjoy it.

Choosing your ingredients
Cooking becomes a pleasure when we can recognize and choose the finest ingredients to work with. Being able to see clearly what is good at a glance is one of the secrets of trouble-free cooking. Every item we shop

for has value associated with price, flavour and convenience. If price exceeds flavour, reconsider. If flavour is lost for the sake of convenience – powdered mashed potato, for instance – you should think again. The cook's ultimatum should be flavour and convenience at the right price.

Fresh herbs make a huge difference to quickly cooked meals. Fresh coriander has a wonderful flavour when stirred into a spicy dish at the end of cooking, basil is wonderful in sauces and salads, and snipped chives add the finishing touch to an omelette. Growing your own herbs isn't difficult, and not only provides you with an instant supply, but is also hugely rewarding.

Shopping

Shopping with a nose for flavour and freshness is the best way to fight through the consumer jungle and arrive home with quality produce. Choose well and give your cooking the head start that it deserves.

Fresh herbs or herb butter (prepared beforehand) add interest to simple dishes. Look for ready-washed vegetables to save time at home. Buy fish fillets that are already boned and skinned, and meat that is prepared for cooking. To enliven pasta and rice dishes, buy pesto and other flavoured sauces.

Do your shopping in one stop and try to write your list in accordance with the layout of the store. Back-tracking for the last few items on your list is no one's idea of fun. When even the simplest of meals is properly thought out, three-quarters of

the work is done. From your list you know exactly what you are cooking, what shopping you need and what you are going to do with the ingredients when you start to get to work in the kitchen.

Kitchen layout

Next, consider your kitchen. No matter how small or ill-equipped it may appear to an outsider, it's where you cook. You're probably stuck with the layout, but consider whether there are any simple changes that will make preparing food a lot easier. The cooker, main preparation area and sink should ideally be close together, and it helps to have the pots, pans and utensils you use most often within easy reach.

Pots and pans can hang from butcher's hooks or be placed on shelves. Put the ones you seldom

use in cupboards by all means, but keep your wok, favourite frying pan and saucepans where you can easily lay your hands on them. The same goes for utensils – drawers are alright for cake decorating sets and those doilies your Aunt Clara sent you, but spoons, spatulas and whisks will be much more useful in a jar next to the cooker.

It's always worth taking a few minutes to read a recipe through before you start. This should enable you to have all the necessary equipment to hand from the outset. For efficiency, keep knives sharp – this saves time when you have a lot of cutting or chopping to do.

It has to be said that some cooks are more organized in their kitchens than others. Some cooks clean and tidy up with near-surgical precision, while

others thrive in varying degrees of chaos. Cooking quickly depends on: a) knowing what you are doing, and b) being able to put your hands on what you need as you go. Most cooks work best of all in a relatively creative mess, where somehow everything comes together in the end. Whatever conditions you are comfortable with, make sure they are 'just so' before you begin cooking.

Storage of foods

When storing foods, separate sweet and savoury ingredients, except those that are used for both such as flour, eggs and sugar. Ingredients that are used often, including onions, garlic, olive oil and fruit make an attractive display in the kitchen if there is space.

Herbs and spices look great on a rack, but make sure they are not in direct sunlight, and check them frequently, discarding any you've had for

Right: A colourful selection of fresh produce, including root vegetables, green vegetables and salad ingredients.

Below: Simple ingredients such as pasta, vegetables and cheese make a quick and simple lunch or supper dish.

more than a few months. Herbs and spices rapidly lose flavour after opening and are best bought in small quantities. Like

perfume, they should be used, not saved for special occasions. Many cooks prefer to store spice jars on their sides in a shallow

drawer. This works well, as long as the drawer stays tidy and the contents are easily accessible.

Aromatics like onions can be kept in a basket on the work surface or suspended from a string. The same goes for garlic, although you may prefer to buy one bulb at a time and keep it close to your chopping board.

Maintaining your supplies

An essential item for any cook who aspires to being organized is a blackboard or whiteboard, on which any member of the household who spots supplies are running low can make a note. There's nothing more irritating than going to your well-stocked store cupboard and finding that someone has taken the noodles you'd earmarked for supper.

Really organized quick cooks also keep a list of supplies on the store-cupboard door. This enables them to see at a glance what's inside, and acts as a handy reminder of those wonton wrappers they bought on impulse a month ago, and still haven't quite got round to using.

Above: A wok is perfect for quick-cooking stir-fries and can also double as a steamer. Choose a heavy, non-stick wok for ease of cooking, and save time washing up, too.

in order. Watch TV cooks for time-saving tips – you may not be able to declare "Here's one I made earlier" but, with practice, you'll soon get the hang of keeping a watchful eye on several saucepans simultaneously. An electric timer – one of those simple battery-operated devices that sticks magnetically to the fridge – can be a huge help.

By using techniques like these you'll soon be whipping up speedy and appealing meals, even on the most hectic of days.

Above: A bowl of strawberries, crème fraîche and a ready-made flan case are all you need for an impromptu dessert.

Below: A delicious selection of fresh fruit is perfect for a quick snack.

Time management

Time management is a skill, like any other. If you are only cooking one dish, just follow the recipe. It will take you through the method step by step. However, if you want to serve accompaniments, you'll need to slot those in, along with the preparation of a pudding, if you are feeling really brave. Taking a few seconds to sort out the sequence really does pay, as does the time-honoured advice of setting out all the ingredients

Above: A good *batterie de cuisine* makes for efficiency in a kitchen where fast cooking is a priority.

Right: A heavy, non-stick frying pan allows food to spread over a large area and cook quickly and evenly.

Store-cupboard Ingredients

A well-stocked store cupboard is the secret of a quick cook's success, and when planning a kitchen it is worth thinking seriously about storage space. Ingredients you use frequently should be close at hand. Open shelves are often better than closed cupboards, and glass jars not only give you the opportunity to create a colourful display, they enable you to see at a glance when stocks are running low.

Arrowroot
Mixed with water, arrowroot is used to thicken sauces and glazes without destroying their clarity.

Baking powder
If you run out of self-raising flour, add baking powder to plain flour in the proportion of 5 ml/1 tsp to 115 g/4 oz/1 cup.

Bulgur wheat
A wholewheat grain that is steam-dried and cracked, this is a boon to the busy cook. Soak it in water, drain thoroughly, then squeeze tightly in a clean cloth to remove excess moisture. Mix with chopped vegetables, lemon juice and oil for a satisfying salad.

Cornflour
Made from maize, this light flour is mainly used for thickening, but is also sometimes mixed with plain flour for making extra-light sponge cakes.

Couscous
Pearl-like pellets of soaked semolina. Quick-cooking couscous is great for busy cooks.

Dried mushrooms
Full of flavour, dried mushrooms such as porcini need only a brief soaking in warm water before use.

Flour
White and wholemeal flour in both plain and self-raising versions are essentials. Keep in storage jars or tins in a cool, dry place.

Nuts
Useful for quick puddings, toppings and decorations – a basic selection should include ground and flaked almonds, cashews, peanuts, pecans, pine nuts, pistachios and walnuts. Add flaked and desiccated coconut, plus a packet of dried coconut milk and a tablet of coconut cream.

Oatmeal
Useful for thickening soups and stews, and to add to crumble toppings.

Pizza mix
A real time-saver – use it for family-size pizzas, calzone or pizzettes.

Polenta
Italian cornmeal – look for quick-cook versions.

Skimmed milk powder
Quick cooks always keep a packet handy, to make custards and sauces when there's very little fresh milk in the house.

Stock cubes
Buy good quality beef, chicken, fish and vegetable stock cubes, plus a can or two of quality consommé for those occasions where flavour is paramount.

Sugar
Caster sugar is perfect for quick cooking, as it dissolves very easily. For the recipes in this book you'll also need granulated sugar, soft light and dark brown sugar, muscovado and icing sugar.

Tortillas
Look out for shrink-wrapped packets of tortillas. Take the tortillas out of the packet, wrap them in microwave-safe clear film, heat them for a few seconds in the microwave, then spread with salsa and fill with savoury mince, shredded lettuce, chopped tomatoes, sliced onion, avocado and grated cheese.

Right: Wooden shelves with hooks for hanging garlic, fresh herbs and a handy nutmeg grater are perfect for displaying favourite ingredients. Baskets of citrus and aromatics, a bowl of eggs and bottles of wine, oils and vinegars are practical as well as pretty.

Pasta, Rice and Lentils

Pasta and rice are ideal for instant meals, as they take very little time to cook and are extremely versatile. With the exception of lentils, dried pulses are less useful, as they must be soaked before long, slow cooking. Use canned beans and chickpeas instead.

Arborio rice
This rounded short-grain rice is used for risottos, as is carnaroli.

Basmati rice
Generally acknowledged to be one of the world's greatest grains, this has a distinctive, fragrant aroma.

Campanelle
Italian pasta tubes with delicate, frilled edges, these are particularly pretty.

Capellini
Also known as angel-hair pasta, capellini consists of extremely fine strands.

Cellophane noodles
These oriental noodles are made from ground mung beans, and are also known as bean thread, transparent or glass noodles. They must always be soaked in warm water before being cooked.

Egg noodles
Widely used throughout China, Japan, Malaysia and Thailand, these can be fresh, but are more often sold dried. Many types need only be soaked in boiling water before use, and are ideal for quick cooking.

Lentils
Red lentils cook quickly without soaking, so are perfect for fast-track meals. Puy lentils take a little longer.

Long-grain rice
For speed, use easy-cook white or brown long-grain rice. This has been treated and partially cooked so the grains rapidly become tender and remain separate.

Pasta bows (farfalle)
A popular pasta shape, which takes its Italian name from the butterflies it resembles.

Penne
These short, tubular pasta shapes make great quick comfort food as they are substantial and hold sauce well. Look out for quick-cooking varieties.

Rice noodles
Also called bahn trang, these are made from ground rice and water. They range in thickness from very thin to wide ribbons (sold in skeins) and sheets. Always rinse rice noodles in warm water and drain before use.

Soba noodles
Made from a mixture of buckwheat and wheat flour, these popular Japanese noodles are cooked in simmering water, then drained.

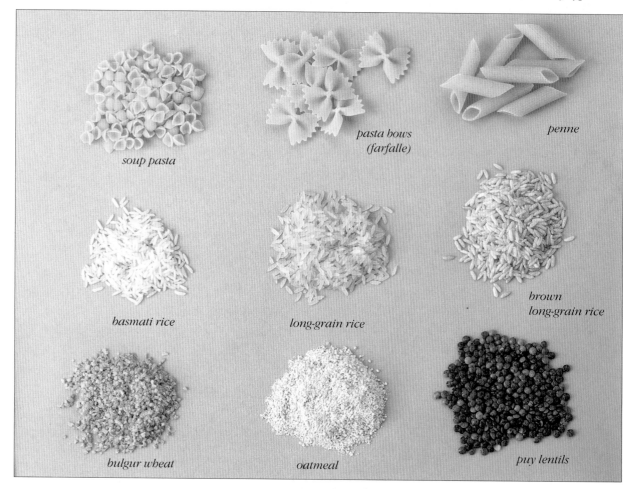

soup pasta

pasta bows (farfalle)

penne

basmati rice

long-grain rice

brown long-grain rice

bulgur wheat

oatmeal

puy lentils

Left: For speedy meals, make the most of pasta, rice, lentils and grains, such as bulgur wheat and oatmeal.

Somen noodles
Delicate, thin, white Japanese noodles made from wheat flour, these are usually sold dried, in bundles held together with a paper band.

Soup pasta
This is the collective term for a wide range of tiny shapes, which cook almost on contact when added to soups.

Spaghetti
The most popular form of pasta, spaghetti has long thin strands.

Tagliatelle
Italian flat, long ribbon noodles. The green version is flavoured with spinach.

Udon noodles
Wheat flour and water are used to make these Japanese noodles. They are usually round, but can be flat. The pre-cooked variety is best for quick cooking.

Vermicelli
Very fine pasta, this cooks rapidly. Italians make it from durum wheat, and there is also an oriental rice version.

Wild rice
Not a true rice, but the seed of an aquatic grass. The brown, long grains open when cooked. Wild rice is expensive, so is often mixed with long-grain rice. It makes an interesting accompaniment and is also widely used for salads.

Right: Dried noodles cook quickly. The picture shows (clockwise from top left): ribbon noodles, somen noodles, udon noodles, soba noodles, egg ribbon noodles, medium egg noodles, cellophane noodles, rice sheets, rice vermicelli, egg noodles and (centre) rice ribbon noodles.

Herbs and Spices

It's a myth that all herbs and spices need long, slow cooking to bring out their flavour: most fresh herbs and many spices are best added to dishes shortly before serving.

Basil
One of the most delicious fresh herbs, basil has an affinity for tomato, and is wonderful in salads and sauces.

Black peppercorns
For the best flavour, use black peppercorns freshly ground; the taste and aroma vanish quickly.

Caraway seeds
The warm, sweet flavour of caraway seeds makes them a great addition to braised cabbage.

Cardamom
Pods and ground cardamom add a warm, pungent flavour to curries and similar spicy dishes, while the black seeds are used in some desserts.

Cayenne
The finely ground powder from a fiery chilli. Use sparingly.

Chillies
Canny cooks use fresh chillies when they can get them, but keep a jar of bottled chillies and a packet of dried chillies for emergencies.

Chilli powder
Available in various strengths – mild chilli powder is a popular spice for quick cooking.

Chives
Snip fresh chives into omelettes, rice dishes or salads.

Cinnamon
Sticks add subtle flavour – try using one to stir hot chocolate – while ground cinnamon is a popular addition to cakes.

Coriander
The fresh herb has a wonderful flavour and is often used as an edible garnish. Ground coriander is deliciously warm and aromatic.

Cumin
Both seeds and ground cumin are valued for their warm, earthy flavour.

Curry powder and paste
Cooks with time on their hands roast and grind their own spices, but hurried hosts and hostesses find good-quality powders and pastes a real boon.

Five spice powder
A mixture of Szechuan pepper, cinnamon or cassia, cloves, fennel seeds and star anise, this is a popular Chinese spice.

Garam masala
A warm spice mix which is often sprinkled over a finished dish to enhance the flavours.

Garlic
Some quick cooks use garlic paste or minced garlic, but it takes only seconds to crush your own.

Ginger
Keep a ginger root in the freezer and grate it as needed. It will thaw as soon as it is added to a hot dish.

Herbes de Provence
A dried herb mixture of thyme, savory, rosemary, marjoram and oregano.

Mint
Fresh mint is marvellous in salads and chilled soups.

Mustard seeds
These pop when added to hot oil to release a wonderful nutty flavour.

Nutmeg
Keep whole nutmegs near the cooker and grate them as needed.

Oregano
This aromatic and highly flavoured herb is wonderful in tomato sauces and is traditionally sprinkled over the top of pizzas.

Paprika
A mild, sweet red powder, paprika adds colour.

Parsley
The clean, fresh taste of both curly parsley and the flat-leaf variety makes it a favourite herb.

Rosemary
Fresh rosemary is traditionally served with lamb but is also delicious with vegetables.

Saffron
The dried stigmas of a type of crocus, saffron is very expensive, but imparts a wonderful flavour and colour to food.

Sage
Wonderful with fried liver, sage has a strong flavour, so don't overdo it.

Salt
For seasoning, use sea-salt flakes or refined table salt.

Thyme
Fresh or dried, thyme is a popular herb. Whole sprigs can be used as a garnish.

Turmeric
This bright yellow powder is largely used for colouring. It has a pungent, bitter flavour and should be used sparingly.

saffron

red chilli flakes

coriander

mild chilli powder

fresh red chillies

chives

thyme

curly parsley

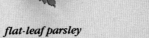

flat-leaf parsley

ground cumin

herbes de Provence

nutmeg

sage

rosemary

oregano

basil

black peppercorns

sea salt

The Bottle Store

Quick cooks keep favourite ingredients close at hand, creating a display of beautifully bottled oils and vinegars. Keep them out of direct sunlight, though, and store items like bottled capers and chillies in the fridge after opening.

Capers
The pickled flower buds of a bush native to the Mediterranean, capers have a strong, sharp flavour you either love or loathe. If you're a lover, try them with cottage cheese on a wholemeal sandwich, or add them to our recipe for quick Tomato Sauce.

Gherkins
These are small cucumbers, grown specifically for pickling. Use them in salads and cold sauces.

Green peppercorns
Pickled in brine, these are often used in steak sauces. They have an affinity with mustard.

Lemon and lime juice
Although it is preferable to use freshly squeezed lemon or lime juice in most recipes, bottled juices are very useful for those occasions when the fruit bowl is bare. Keep citrus juices in the fridge after opening and use as soon as possible.

Mayonnaise
It isn't difficult to make your own mayonnaise, but because the recipe uses raw egg yolks, the home-made product is not recommended for very young children or the elderly. Good-quality bought mayonnaise is very useful. Keep it in the fridge after opening.

Mustard
A little mustard will often bring out the flavour of other ingredients. In dressings, mustard is used as an emulsifier, helping to bring oil and vinegar together. As with oils, experiment to find your favourite type. A basic store cupboard should include both powdered and ready-made mustards, including a wholegrain variety and a mild Dijon type.

Oils
Keep the oils you use most often close to the cooker, but not so close that they will be affected by the heat. Exposure to bright sunlight is harmful to oils, especially olive oil, which is why the latter is often sold in green glass bottles. For general cooking, choose corn or sunflower oil, which can be heated to a high temperature without smoking. Sunflower oil is particularly useful for delicate dishes, as the flavour is not overpowering. Safflower oil has a higher concentration of polyunsaturated fatty acids than other oils. Olive oil is prized for its contribution to a healthy diet and is widely used in the recipes in this book. It tends to smoke at high temperatures, so use a light olive oil or a mixture of olive oil and sunflower oil for cooking. For salads, use virgin or extra-virgin oils.

Olives
Sold at different stages of ripeness (black olives are fully ripe), olives are ideal for quick meals. They are very good in salads, sauces and on pizzas.

Peanut butter
Although most often thought of as a spread, peanut butter is an important ingredient in Indonesian cooking. Satay sauce, which is superb with pork and pineapple kebabs, is a case in point.

Vinegars
It is important to use the recommended type of vinegar in a recipe. Flavours and strengths vary widely, depending on the base, which can be wine, beer or fruit juice. Red and white wine vinegars are widely used for dressings and marinades, while sherry vinegar is preferred when a more full-bodied flavour is required. Rice wine vinegar and cider vinegar are often less sour than other types, so are used to give sauces, stir-fries and dressings a tangy taste. One of the quick cook's best allies is good-quality balsamic vinegar. This dark Italian wine vinegar is rich and robust, but not harsh. A few drops, added to a sauce, will really boost the flavour. Malt vinegar is used for pickling, as a table condiment (with fish and chips, for instance), and is the traditional choice for mint sauce. Raspberry vinegar is mild and sweet. It is used in some dressings and can replace lemon juice on pancakes.

Wine
A dash or two gives a lift to soups and sauces – and has a similar effect on the cook! The recipes in this collection make judicious use of wine, spirits and liqueurs, but in most instances these can be omitted if preferred.

Italian olive oil

Spanish olive oil

lemon

Italian olive oil

French olive oil

Italian olive oil

hazelnut oil

safflower oil

walnut oil

groundnut oil

garlic oil

white wine vinegar

limes

olives

capers

mustard

Sauces and Pastes

When you want a speedy meal, take the tube. A wide range of sauces and pastes come in this handy form, ready for a quick squeeze whenever needed. Bottled sauces are very useful, too. They keep well, so it is worth buying and trying new varieties, and building up a versatile and tasty range of flavours.

Anchovy paste
Sold in tubes, anchovy paste is useful for adding a subtle flavour to a sauce to be served with fish. For a more robust taste, use pounded salted or drained canned anchovies. Look out for anchovy essence, too.

Carbonara sauce
Although your own version will be much better, a jar or two of the ready-made sauce will prove useful when you need to make a meal in double-quick time. Add sautéed fresh mushrooms or more bacon to make it go further.

Garlic paste
Squeeze it from the tube whenever you need it. Alternatively, buy a jar of chopped garlic – a great time-saver.

Horseradish sauce
Creamed horseradish sauce is the classic accompaniment to roast beef, but also tastes wonderful in a prawn cocktail.

Mushroom paste
Some Italian delicatessens sell this delicious delicacy. Mix a generous spoonful with some crème fraîche to make a quick pasta sauce. Mushroom ketchup is a very useful item in the quick cook's armoury – a small splash will intensify the flavour of any mushroom-based sauce, and will also add interest to a risotto, omelette or gravy.

Olive paste
Olive paste – tapenade – is available in jars and tubes, in both green and black varieties. The black is particularly tasty: toss a small amount with freshly cooked spaghetti for a superb treat. Tapenade is also very good with boiled new potatoes.

Pesto
The best option is to make your own, but fresh basil isn't always available. Look out for "fresh" pesto, sold in tubs in the chiller compartment of some supermarkets or health food shops. Third choice – but not necessarily an unacceptable option – is to buy pesto in the jar. Brands vary, so experiment until you find a good one. Red pesto is made from tomatoes and red peppers. It makes a delicious addition to soups and sauces, and can also be tossed with freshly cooked pasta.

Soy sauce
Soy sauce is famously used in stir-fries, but also gives cooked sauces and gravies a lift. Recipes in this book use both light and dark soy sauce, and kecap manis (sweet soy sauce). Other invaluable oriental sauces include Hoisin sauce, black bean sauce, oyster sauce and sweet chilli sauce.

Sun-dried tomatoes
For quick cooking, use the ones preserved in oil to deepen the flavour of tomato-based dishes.

Tabasco sauce
Hot chilli sauces like Tabasco are very useful for pepping up all manner of savoury dishes. Use them sparingly and stir them in well.

Tomato pasta sauce
Making your own pasta sauce only takes minutes, but when you are really pressed for time, it can be very handy to have a jar or two of ready-made sauce. Spice it up by stirring in pounded anchovies or olives, and a sprinkling of chopped fresh herbs. A splash of red wine, vermouth or balsamic vinegar can improve a bought sauce considerably.

Tomato purée
Concentrated tomato purée comes in tubes and cans and is absolutely invaluable for enriching the flavour of soups, sauces, drinks and bakes. Look out for sun-dried tomato paste, which has an excellent flavour and less dominant colour.

Tomatoes, canned
No self-respecting store cupboard should be without these. The range is extensive, so choose chopped or whole tomatoes, as you prefer. Passata, sold in jars and cans, is pulped tomato that has been strained to remove the seeds.

Worcestershire sauce
An old friend that is easily overlooked in the host of newer sauces that crowd supermarket shelves. Add a few drops of Worcestershire to sauces, gravies and meat dishes for instant flavour, but avoid using it in strict vegetarian cooking as it contains anchovies.

mushroom paste

salted anchovies

olive paste

tomato purée (paste)

carbonara sauce

chopped tomatoes

canned plum tomatoes

capers

tomato pasta sauce

fresh pesto

red pesto

pesto

sun-dried tomatoes in oil

chopped garlic

Dessert Ingredients

Instant puddings can be much more than a packet of powder whipped with water or milk. Add these extras to your basic dry stores and you'll have the makings of marvellous quick desserts.

Cakes
Foil-wrapped cakes with good keeping qualities can be easily transformed into simple puddings. Chocolate cake with liqueur, cherries, ice cream and cream makes a great sundae, while ginger cake and bananas with a brûlée topping is delicious.

Chocolate
Buy good-quality dark chocolate for quick puddings. Melted with cream, it makes an instant sauce for pancakes, ice cream or serving over profiteroles.

Cocoa powder
Use sugarless cocoa powder in drinks and desserts for a rich chocolate taste.

Dessert biscuits
Ratafias, langues de chat, cigarettes Russe and sponge fingers can be served with creamy desserts and are also useful as the basis of instant puddings. As a filling for nectarines, ratafias have no equal, while sponge fingers dipped in black coffee and brandy, then layered with whipped cream, make a marvellous dessert.

Eggs
Always buy eggs from a reputable supplier. Store in the fridge but bring to room temperature before using.

Essences
Vanilla essence is the most popular of these. Buy pure vanilla essence rather than a mere flavouring; the taste will be much better. Almond essence will also prove useful.

Fruit
Fresh fruit is the best and simplest sweet treat, but canned and dried fruit have an important part to play in the creation of quick puddings. Include canned peaches, apricots, pineapple rings and black cherries in your store-cupboard selection, and make sure you have packets of ready-to-use dried apricots, sultanas, raisins, currants, prunes and dates, as well as more exotic fruits like mango.

Instant coffee
Great for making mocha sauces and quick coffee whips. Use strong coffee for dipping sponge fingers when making tiramisù and similar desserts.

Jams and preserves
Keep a selection of good-quality jams in small pots for filling cakes, making quick fruit sauces and glazes. Croissants spread with ricotta and strawberry jam taste heavenly when barbecued.

Marshmallows
Marshmallows melted with cream make a quick fondue for dipping fruit kebabs. Alternatively, stir some crème de menthe into the mixture, pour it into a biscuit crust and leave it in the fridge until set. Decorate the pie with shaved chocolate before serving.

Marzipan
Use to fill apples for baking in the microwave – or mix with biscuit crumbs as a filling for peaches.

Meringues
Shop around for good-quality meringues and store them in an airtight jar for impromptu puddings. Meringues can be sandwiched with whipped cream and served with chocolate sauce, broken and stirred into ice cream for a delectable bombe, or made into mini pavlovas with berry fruits and clotted cream.

Muesli
Much more than a breakfast food, muesli makes a good quick crumble topping. For the easiest-ever dessert, layer raspberries with muesli and natural or Greek yogurt.

Sponge flan cases
Just fill with fruit and whipped cream for instant sweet success.

The Vegetable Basket

Speedy cooks love vegetables. What other savoury ingredients look so beautiful, taste so good and cook so quickly? With only minutes to spare you can toss a salad or steam a medley of mangetouts, baby carrots and miniature corn cobs. Simply add a dressing or dipping sauce and you have a marvellous quick meal. The sheer variety and range of vegetables now available in our supermarkets and grocer's shops is dazzling, but for flavour, it is still best to seek out seasonal produce. Summer's sun-ripened vine tomatoes will be much tastier than those that have come from a cold store, and freshly dug new potatoes are not only full of flavour, but can be cleaned with very little effort, as the skins simply rub off under running water. Carrot batons, cauliflower and broccoli florets, sliced leeks, trimmed beans and ready-to-cook snap peas are all there for the taking, along with shiny peppers of every hue, cook-in-the-bag spinach, wild and cultivated mushrooms and every member of the onion family.

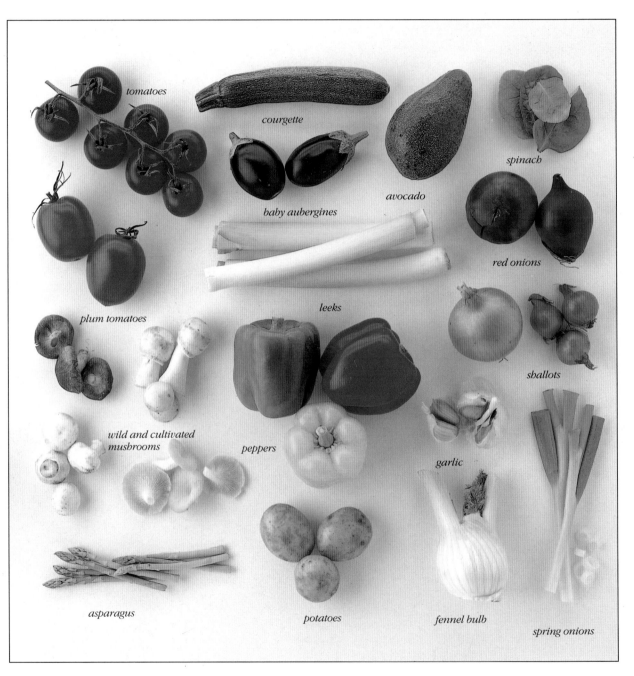

tomatoes

courgette

spinach

avocado

baby aubergines

red onions

plum tomatoes

leeks

shallots

wild and cultivated mushrooms

peppers

garlic

asparagus

potatoes

fennel bulb

spring onions

The Fruit Bowl

It is no coincidence that most of the desserts featured in this book are based upon fresh fruit. When nature has provided such a wide range of delicious sweet treats for our delectation, why look elsewhere? Fruit needs little or no preparation, looks luscious and actually promotes good health.

Fast cooks know that with a well-stocked fruit bowl, dessert will often take care of itself. A perfect pear, a bunch of grapes, a simple salad of kiwi fruit and orange segments – these are the sweetest solutions to the problem of what to serve when you don't have much time to make dessert.

The next step is a simple combination of two or more complementary types of fruit. Try chilled melon with wild strawberries, peaches with raspberries, or pineapple with lychees and oranges.

If you like hot fruit puddings, the good news for contemporary cooks is that you can produce delicious results in very little time. Grilling, frying and poaching are popular methods, and desserts like Caramelized Apples, Fruit Kebabs, and Pineapple Wedges with Rum Butter Glaze can be made while the dinner dishes are being cleared, giving your guests a brief respite before the meal's final flourish.

When shopping, choose fruit that is fresh, unblemished and ready to eat. Contrary to all those household hints that involve paper bags and chunks of apple, hard, unyielding fruit will seldom ripen satisfactorily at home.

Knowing just when a fruit is at its peak can be tricky, however. Most of us are familiar with apples and pears, but feel less confident when faced with exotic or unfamiliar fruit like papayas or cantaloupes. Some stores label some packs with the slogan 'ready to eat', but in the absence of this advice, here are a few tips:

Bananas should have no hint of green. A light mottling of brown indicates that the fruit is ready to eat, and will be easy to digest, but you should avoid any fruits that are bruised.

Citrus fruits are at their best in winter, when individual fruits feel heavy for their size. To persuade an orange or lemon to yield its juice, roll it on the work surface or work it firmly between the palms of your hands.

Mangoes are ready to eat when the skin has a red blush and sweet, perfumed aroma.

When it comes to choosing pineapples or melons, your nose is often your best judge. Ripe pineapples have a wonderful, sweet smell. Cantaloupes and similar melons, with a 'netted' rather than a hard, smooth skin, will have a lovely scent when ripe, and the skin will yield to the touch around the blossom end. Papayas become yellow-green when ripe, and yield gently to pressure in the hand.

Strawberries, raspberries and other berries are often sold in punnets. The fruit on top may look perfect, but it isn't easy to know what lies beneath. Check the bottom of the punnet – if it is at all soggy, leave it well alone.

For convenience, quick cooks keep cans of apricot halves, peach slices, pineapple chunks, red cherries and mandarin segments, plus dried fruits including apricots, mangoes and peaches, which can be poached, then puréed for instant whips.

Right: Fresh fruits can be used in both sweet and savoury salads. Ensure they are ripe and in peak condition.

lollo rosso

Salad Leaves

When time is short, nothing is swifter than a salad. Supermarkets speed the process still further by providing bags of crisp, washed leaves, so all the cook has to do is dress for dinner.

Batavian endive
Similar to escarole, but with a slightly sweeter, softer taste, Batavian endive is suited to most salads. With an underlying hint of bitterness, it stands up to a well-flavoured dressing.

Cos lettuce
With its faintly nutty taste, this is considered by many to have the finest flavour of all the salad leaves. It is the classic choice for Caesar salad.

Escarole
More robust than regular lettuce, escarole has a bitter flavour. It is best during the winter months. The bitterness is usually offset with a sweet dressing.

Frisée lettuce
Frisée or curly endive is a member of the chicory family. It has a clean, bitter taste and combines well with milder-flavoured salad leaves.

Iceberg lettuce
Compact and firm, this is a popular ingredient for salads, despite having little intrinsic flavour. Tops for texture, it can be torn or shredded, and is very versatile.

Lamb's lettuce
Also known as corn salad or maché, this has small, spoon-shaped leaves with a sweet, slightly nutty flavour.

Little gem
Little gem or sucrine is a small, sweet, compact lettuce that keeps well. The flavour resembles that of cos.

Lollo biondo
A loose-leafed lettuce with a curly edge, lollo biondo or green lollo has a mild flavour and goes well with stronger-tasting leaves.

Lollo rosso
Although this pretty, loose-leafed lettuce has lost a little of its star status, it is still hugely popular for its attractive red-tinged leaves and mild flavour.

Oakleaf lettuce
The dark colour and mild taste of these broad wavy leaves combine well with escarole and curly endive.

Rocket
The leaves have a peppery, slightly lemony taste and are often used to add zest and flavour to mixed salads.

Spinach
Young spinach leaves have a rich, sweet flavour and taste particularly good in a salad that includes crumbled, grilled bacon.

Watercress
Peppery and slightly pungent, watercress is extremely rich in vitamins. Scatter sprigs in salads or use to make sauces or soups.

Batavian endive

frisée lettuce

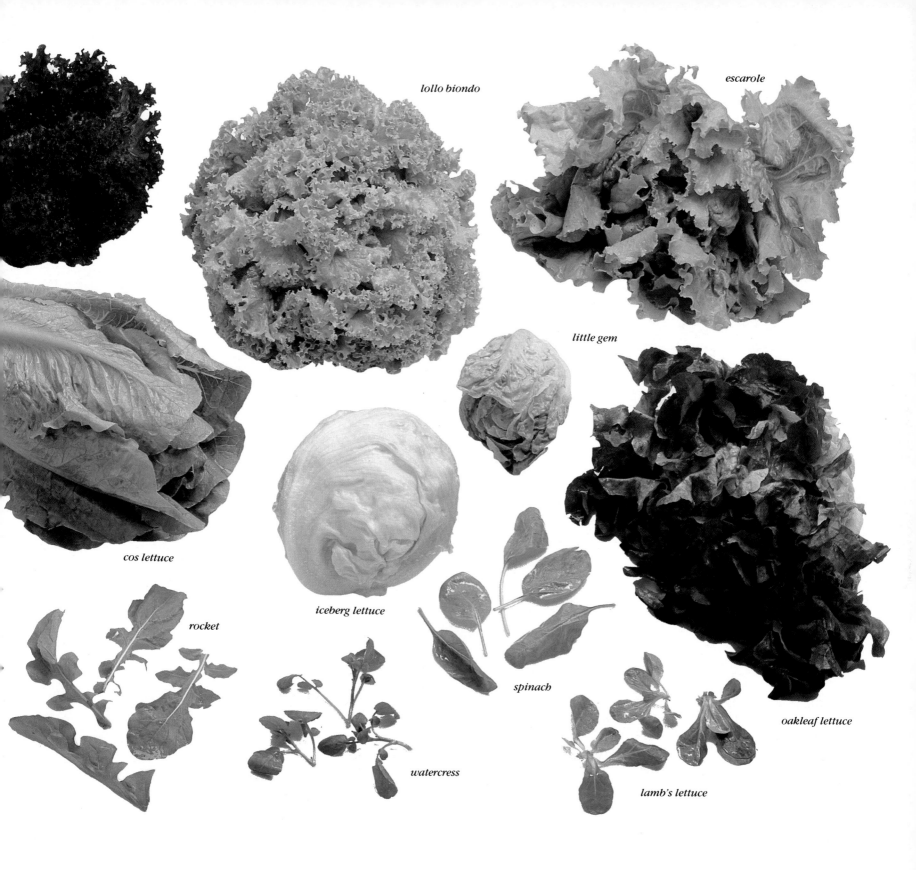

lollo biondo

escarole

little gem

cos lettuce

iceberg lettuce

rocket

spinach

watercress

lamb's lettuce

oakleaf lettuce

Meat and Fish

When the focus is on fast food, choose meats and fish that come ready-cooked, or can be sautéed or stir-fried swiftly and with as little fuss as possible. Choose lean, ready-trimmed portions and cut them into small, even-sized pieces for sautéeing or stir-frying.

Beef
Minced beef is the number one choice for quick cooking, with strips of steak coming a close second. Minced beef is the basis for burgers, pasta sauces, meatballs and chilli, while strips star in sizzling beef dishes, sukiyaki and stir-fries.

Chicken
Skinless, boneless chicken breasts are the best choice for the quick cook. Allow one per person unless you are cooking a stir-fry with plenty of vegetables, in which case one breast will stretch surprisingly and will certainly serve two. Smoked chicken is a good buy from the deli. Use it for sandwiches and in salads – it combines very well with fruit, especially melon.

Chorizo
This cured pork sausage comes from Spain and is flavoured with garlic and paprika. It goes well with canned chickpeas or butterbeans and is a popular pizza topping.

Crab
Dressed crab is ready to use. Try it as the basis of a sophisticated salad.

Ham
Cooked ham is ideal for quick snacks and salads. Don't automatically assume the most expensive choice on the deli counter is the best: shoulder often has a finer flavour than more costly crumbed ham. Smoked ham is delicious wrapped around asparagus.

Italian salami
Serve with ricotta salata or feta and black olives for a tasty tapa or snack.

Lamb
Buy lean, boneless lamb from the leg for stir-frying. It tastes particularly good with a fruity glaze.

Mixed seafood
It is the preparation that takes the time when it comes to seafood. Packets of mixed, prepared squid, mussels and prawns are great for fish soups and quick bakes.

Pancetta
Belly of pork, cured with salt and spices, this comes from Italy. Like bacon, which it resembles, it is available in both unsmoked and smoked forms and is generally sold thinly sliced. It used to be difficult to locate pancetta, but increased demand is making it more widely available. If you can't find it, use streaky bacon instead.

Parma ham
Also known as prosciutto crudo, this salted and air-dried ham is a delicacy. It is usually thinly sliced and served with figs or melon.

Pepperoni
A salami-type sausage, this is made from pork and beef, flavoured with fennel and red pepper. Thin slices of pepperoni are a favourite pizza topping.

Pork
For speed, choose fillet or pork steaks to make kebabs, stir-fries or seared specialities.

Prawns
Cooked prawns are perfect for quick meals. Just add mayonnaise or a seafood dressing. If using prawns in a composite dish, such as a risotto, take care not to let them overcook or they will toughen.

Sausages
Sausages are not just an ingredient – they're an industry. Every possible flavour is now available, so keep a few favourites in the freezer. Always thaw sausages thoroughly and make sure they are cooked through before serving. Chipolatas cook more quickly than regular sausages and make delicious popovers.

Smoked salmon
One of the swift cook's favourite ingredients, smoked salmon can be formed into cornets and filled with mousse or cream cheese, served simply in a salad, snipped into scrambled egg, used to top pizzettes or star in a sandwich.

pancetta

smoked chicken

smoked ham

sausages

chorizo

dressed crab

Parma ham

pepperoni

prawns

Italian salami

mixed seafood

minced beef

chicken

smoked salmon

Cheeses

Cheese is an excellent choice for the quick cook. Remove any rind and it is ready to use. There's a flavour for every occasion and every palate. Serve it solo, use it in salads or sandwiches, or team it with other ingredients. Whether hard or soft, cheese is equally at home in starters, main courses, sweets and even some soups.

Bavarian smoked cheese
With its distinctive, smoky flavour, this is a good choice for grilling. Try mixing it with Cheddar for a pizza topping with a difference.

Cheddar
Great for grating and grilling, this is arguably the world's most popular cheese. Flavours can vary from mild to extra mature. Cheddar is ideal for cooking as it melts without forming threads.

Dolcelatte
An Italian blue-veined cheese with a piquant flavour, Dolcelatte is semi-soft. Try crumbling it into a white sauce or serve it with apples or pears.

Edam
This ball-shaped Dutch cheese has a mild, nutty flavour which is particularly popular with children. Cubes of Edam alternating with pineapple chunks, red pepper squares and cucumber slices make delicious kebabs.

Feta
Preserved in brine, this crumbly cheese comes from Greece. It is wonderful in salads and has an affinity for tomatoes and olives. Try it baked, in filo pastry.

Goat's cheeses
These can be hard or soft, the latter being the most popular type. Sold in logs, rounds, pyramids or ovals, the soft cheeses range in flavour from fresh and creamy to strong and tangy, depending on the diet enjoyed by the goats. Goat's cheese is delicious with roasted vegetables.

Gorgonzola piccante
This cheese has a pleasantly sharp flavour, with a softish paste and blue-green veins. It makes a marvellous gratin with cauliflower and walnuts, and is good with all types of pasta, especially tagliatelle.

Gruyère
A hard cheese with a distinctive sweet and nutty taste, Gruyère is popular for cooking as it melts well.

Mozzarella
Good mozzarella should be very white, fairly elastic and moist when cut. It is often served in salads, but is also an excellent melting cheese – the prime choice for pizzas.

Oak-smoked Cheddar
This is just one of many Cheddar variants worth investigating. It

can be used in any recipe specifying a hard grating cheese.

Parmesan
Parmesan and pasta are an obvious pairing, but this wonderful cheese is also excellent in salads and on risottos. Buy fresh Parmesan in a chunk if possible and grate or shave it as needed.

Pecorino
An Italian sheep's milk cheese, this is used in much the same way as Parmesan. It has a distinctive, fairly strong flavour.

Red Leicester
This cheese has a mild flavour. The bright colour makes it a good choice for sauces. Mix it with mature Cheddar if you want to deepen the flavour.

Ricotta
The delicate flavour of this smooth, soft, Italian whey cheese makes it first choice for puddings and baked dishes.

Smoked mozzarella
This cheese has a creamy, smoky taste. Whether you prefer it to plain mozzarella is a matter of choice. Try it and see – it has the same excellent melting properties as the plain variety.

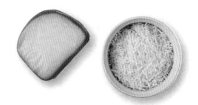

red Leicester

Gruyère

smoked mozzarella

Cheddar

oak-smoked Cheddar

goat's cheese

Gorgonzola

Parmesan

Edam

ricotta

mozzarella

Dolcelatte

Bavarian smoked cheese

Pecorino

feta

Quick Cookware

It isn't so much what cookware you have, but how you store it that is the main consideration for quick cooking. Have favourite pans and utensils close at hand – scrabbling in drawers wastes time and sparks stress.

Chopping boards

The jury is still out on whether plastic or wooden chopping boards are best. The important thing is to have separate boards for raw and cooked ingredients, and scrub them thoroughly after use.

Colanders and sieves

You need at least one metal colander and a sensibly sized sieve. A small sieve or tea strainer is useful for dusting icing sugar.

Saucepans

A few good-sized saucepans with well-fitting lids are a must. Buy the best quality you can afford, but don't necessarily plump for a boxed set. You may well end up with sizes you never use. Start with two or three reasonably sized pans, then double up on the size you use most. Choose heavy-based or non-stick pans that will be easy to clean – there isn't much point saving time cooking if you have to spend ages washing up afterwards. For quick cooking, you'll need several frying pans. A good wok is essential, as is a deep skillet with a lid and a pancake or crepe pan.

Knives

It pays to buy good-quality knives. A really sharp knife can halve your preparation time.

Knives are hugely personal possessions – every cook will have his or her favourites – but for most purposes a short, sharp vegetable knife, a flat-bladed cook's knife, a medium serrated knife and a bread knife will serve. Store knives in a block, if possible, or on a rack. In a drawer they are liable to get knocked and damaged.

Utensils

Store whisks, spoons and spatulas on a rack or in a jar on the work surface. It is useful to have both long and short-handled wooden spoons, and at least two whisks. Miniature whisks are handy for small quantities in cups. A reamer – a wooden utensil with a shaped end – is ideal for squeezing citrus fruits. Tongs are another essential item, but check before buying: you need a pair that is sturdy and easy to manipulate. You'll also need a fish slice, draining spoon, potato masher and one or two spatulas. Good-quality rubber spatulas are ideal for getting the last of the mixture out of a bowl, or scraping the sides of a food processor. For speed, it pays to buy a sturdy peeler. The type with a U-shaped handle and a blade across the top works fast and well.

wooden spatula

ladle

scissors

knives and peelers

vegetable knife

bread knife

whisks

slotted
spoon

serving
spoon

chopping
board

grater

colander

wok

saucepans

frying pan

TECHNIQUES AND BASIC RECIPES

Mastering a few simple techniques for food preparation will really speed up your cooking; making basic recipes in bulk is another great time-saver.

Peeling and Seeding Tomatoes

A simple and efficient way of preparing tomatoes.

1 Holding each tomato in turn, firmly (and keeping your fingers out of the way), cut a small cross on the bottom with a sharp knife.

2 Turn the tomato over and carefully cut out the core with the tip of the knife.

3 Immerse the tomato in boiling water for 10–15 seconds, then transfer to a bowl of cold water using a slotted spoon.

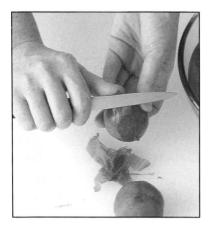

4 As soon as the tomato is cool enough to handle, lift it out and use the side of the knife blade to peel off the skin, which should be easy to remove.

5 Cut the tomato in half crosswise and squeeze out the seeds into a bowl. Discard the seeds.

6 Use a large knife to cut the peeled tomato into strips, then chop across the strips to make dice.

Chopping Onions

Uniform-sized dice make cooking easy. This method can't be beaten.

1 Peel the onion. Cut it in half with a large knife and set it cut-side down on a chopping board. Make lengthwise vertical cuts along the onion, cutting almost, but not quite, through to the root.

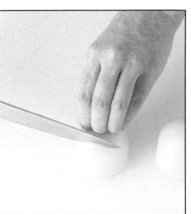

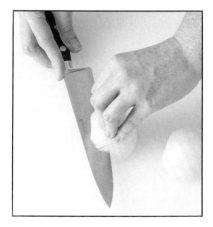

2 Using a cook's knife, make 2 horizontal cuts from the stalk end towards the root, cutting almost, but not completely through it, so that the onion remains sufficiently intact to be manageable.

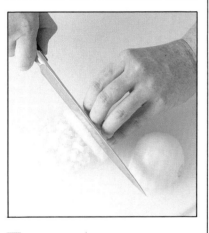

3 With the knife blade down, cut the onion neatly, first in one direction, then the other, so that it forms small, even dice. The size of the dice will be dictated by the recipe; small dice cook more quickly.

Slicing Onions

Use thin slices for sautéeing or to flavour oils for stir-frying, or use sweet onion slices in salads.

1 Peel the onion. Cut it in half with a large knife and set it cut-side down on a chopping board.

2 Using the tip of a sharp knife, cut out a triangular piece of the core from each half.

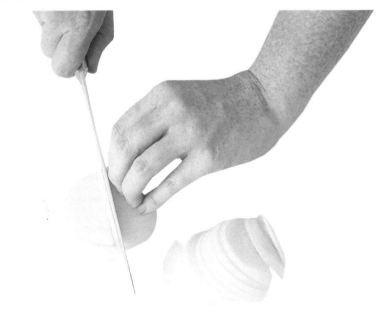

3 Holding the onion firmly (and keeping your fingers out of the way) cut across each half in vertical slices.

Shredding Cabbage

This method is useful for coleslaws, pickled cabbage or any cooked dish.

1 Put the cabbage on a board and hold it securely. Use a large cook's knife to cut the cabbage into quarters. If the knife is sharp, it should slide through the cabbage easily; if not, you may need to use a sawing action.

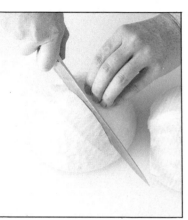

2 Place each quarter in turn on a chopping board. Rest it on one of the flat sides for safety, then use a sharp knife to cut out the core.

3 Holding the cabbage securely, slice across each quarter to form fine, even shreds. If the recipe requires the cabbage to be blanched, add the shreds to boiling water, cook for 1–2 minutes, then drain thoroughly.

Cutting Carrot Julienne

Julienne strips of any vegetable make decorative accompaniments, or can be used in stir-fries.

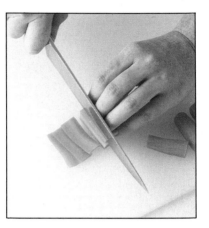

1 Peel the carrot and use a large knife to cut it into 5 cm/2 in lengths. Cut a thin sliver from one side of each piece so that it sits flat on the board.

2 Using a sharp cook's knife (or your favourite vegetable knife) cut the piece of carrot into thin lengthwise slices.

3 Stack the slices and cut through them to make fine strips.

Chopping Fresh Ginger

Fresh ginger imparts a clean, refreshing taste. Follow the instructions to chop finely.

1 Break off small knobs of ginger from the main root. Using a small, sharp knife, or a swivel-bladed peeler, remove the outer skin.

2 Slice the ginger flesh lengthwise and cut into strips.

3 Cut across the strips to form small, even dice.

COOK'S TIP
Root ginger can be frozen. Wrap the roots well and remove them from the freezer as and when you need them. Frozen ginger is very easy to grate and does not need to be peeled. Just add the frozen grated ginger to hot food; it will thaw on contact.

Chopping Chillies

Handle chillies with care. Always work in a well-ventilated area and keep away from your eyes.

1 Cut the chilli in half lengthwise and remove the core and seeds.

2 Cut it into lengthwise strips.

3 Cut across the strips to form small, even dice.

Stoning Olives

Using a stoner is the easiest way to remove the stone from an olive, but you can also use a sharp knife.

1 Put the olive in the stoner, pointed end uppermost.

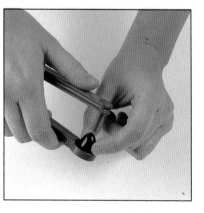

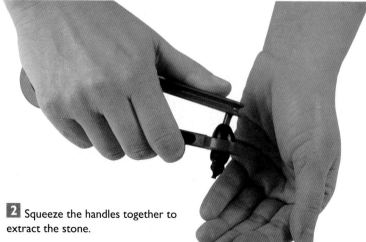

2 Squeeze the handles together to extract the stone.

COOK'S TIP
For speed, buy olives ready-stoned. It is also possible to obtain jars of sliced olives in brine, which are very handy for the quick cook.

Chopping Herbs

Use this method to chop herbs until they are as coarse or fine as you wish.

1 Strip the leaves from the stalk and pile them on a chopping board.

2 Using a sharp knife, cut the herbs into small pieces, holding the tip of the blade against the board and rocking the blade back and forth. A mezzaluna (a crescent-shaped blade with a handle at either end) does the job even more easily and efficiently.

Seasoning a Wok

If you are using a new wok or frying pan you will need to prepare it as follows to ensure the best results.

1 Heat the wok or frying pan with 30–45 ml/2–3 tbsp salt for about 15 minutes. Wipe out the salt. The wok is now ready for use.

2 To clean your wok, wipe out the inside with kitchen towels, where possible, keeping washing with detergent to a minimum. Seasoning a pan by the method described here will create a good non-stick surface.

Preparing Spring Onions

Spring onions can be used in stir-fries to flavour oil, as vegetables in their own right, or as decoration.

1 This technique can also be used for the larger green onions. Trim off the root of each spring onion with a sharp knife.

2 For an intense flavour, cut into matchsticks and stir-fry with vegetables of the same size.

3 Slice thinly to stir-fry with crushed garlic to flavour the cooking oil.

COOK'S TIP
Spring onion green can be used as decoration. If it is young and tender, snip it as you would chives. Long pieces can be blanched in boiling water, dried, and used to tie carrot julienne in bundles for garnishing.

Speedy Stir-frying

Stir-frying takes very little actual cooking time, often no more than a matter of minutes. For this reason it is important that all the ingredients are prepared ahead of time – washed, peeled or grated as required, and cut to approximately the same shape and size, to ensure even cooking.

1 Always heat the wok (or frying pan, if using) for a few minutes before adding the oil or any other ingredients.

2 If adding oil, swirl the oil into the wok and allow it to heat up before adding the next ingredients.

3 When adding the first ingredients, reduce the heat a little. This will ensure they are not overcooked or burnt by the time the remaining ingredients have been added to the wok.

4 Once all the ingredients have been added, quickly increase the heat, as this will allow the dish to cook in the least possible time. This ensures that the ingredients retain a crisp, fresh texture, and prevents them from becoming soggy or laden with oil.

5 Use a long-handled scoop or spatula to turn the ingredients as you stir-fry. This will allow the ingredients to cook evenly and quickly.

6 It may be easier to slice meat for stir-frying if it has been frozen slightly for an hour or so. By the time you have sliced it, the meat will have thawed.

Cooking Pasta

1 Throw the pasta into a large pan of boiling salted water. Stir once to prevent sticking. The addition of 15 ml/1 tbsp vegetable or olive oil will help to stop the water boiling over and prevent the pasta from sticking. Do not cover or the water will boil over.

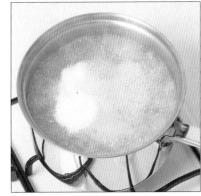

2 Quickly bring the pasta back to a rolling boil and boil until al dente (literally 'to the tooth') – the pasta should be just firm to the bite. It should not have a hard centre or be very floppy.

COOKING TIMES FOR FRESH AND DRIED PASTA

Calculate the cooking time from the moment the water returns to the boil after the pasta has been added.

Unfilled pasta
Fresh: 2–3 minutes, though some very thin pasta is ready as soon as the water returns to the boil.
Dried: 8–12 minutes, but keep checking as this is only a guide.

Filled pasta
Fresh: 8–10 minutes.
Dried: 15–20 minutes.

Above: Cook unfilled pasta until al dente, or firm to the bite.

3 Quickly drain the pasta well, using a large colander or sieve.

4 Immediately rinse the pasta with boiling water to wash off any starch and to prevent it from sticking together. Toss the pasta in a little olive oil or butter, or dress immediately with sauce. Serve hot pasta straight away.

5 It is up to you whether you toss the pasta with the sauce before serving or serve it with the sauce on top.

Below: Filled pasta takes a little longer to cook than unfilled.

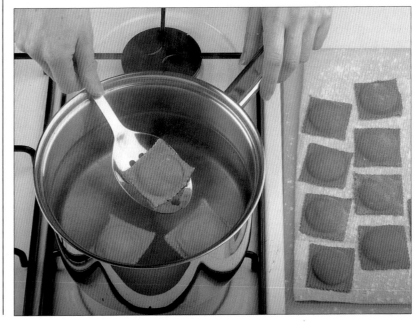

Scone Pizza Dough

The joy of using a scone mixture is that it is quick to make and uses store-cupboard ingredients.

MAKES
1 x 25 cm/10 in round
    pizza base
1 x 30 x 18 cm/12 x 7 in oblong
    pizza base

INGREDIENTS
115g/4 oz/1 cup self-raising
    flour
115 g/4 oz/1 cup self-raising
    wholemeal flour
pinch of salt
50 g/2 oz/1/4 cup butter, diced
about 150 ml/1/4 pint/2/3 cup
    milk

1 Mix together the flours and salt in a mixing bowl. Rub in the butter until the mixture resembles fine breadcrumbs.

2 Add the milk and mix with a wooden spoon to a soft dough.

3 Knead gently on a lightly floured surface until smooth. The dough is now ready to use.

Superquick Pizza Dough

If you're really pressed for time, try a packet pizza dough mix. For best results roll out the dough to a 25–30 cm/10–12 in circle; this is slightly larger than stated on the packet, but it does produce a perfect thin, crispy base. For a deep-pan version use two packets.

MAKES
1 x 25–30 cm/10–12 in circle
4 x 13 cm/5 in round pizza
    bases
1 x 30 x 18 cm/12 x 7 in oblong
    pizza base

INGREDIENTS
1 x 150 g/5 oz packet pizza
    base mix
120 ml/4 fl oz/1/2 cup lukewarm
    water

1 Empty the contents of the packet into a mixing bowl.

2 Pour in the water and mix with a wooden spoon to a soft dough.

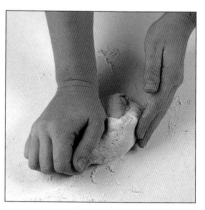

3 Turn the dough on to a lightly floured surface and knead for 5 minutes until smooth and elastic. The dough is now ready to use.

Using a Food Processor

For speed, make superquick pizza dough in a food processor; let the machine do the mixing and kneading.

Ready-made Pizza Bases

Fortunately for the busy cook it is now possible to buy fresh, frozen or long-life pizza bases from most supermarkets. Many are enriched with additional ingredients like cheese, herbs and onions. All you have to do is add your chosen topping and bake in the oven in the usual way. For a different pizza base, without having to make your own dough, try using French bread, pitta bread or muffins.

1 Put the pizza base mix in a food processor. Process briefly.

2 Measure the water into a jug. With the machine running, add the liquid and process until the dough forms a soft ball. Leave to rest for 2 minutes, then process for 1 minute more to knead the dough.

3 Put the dough on a lightly floured surface and roll it out to a large circle, or cut small rounds for pizzettes.

Tomato Sauce

Home-made tomato sauce can be used in a wide range of recipes and is an invaluable asset to the quick cook.

MAKES
about 250 ml/8 fl oz/1 cup

INGREDIENTS
15 ml/1 tbsp olive oil
1 onion, finely chopped
1 garlic clove, crushed
400 g/14 oz can chopped
    tomatoes
15 ml/1 tbsp tomato purée
15 ml/1 tbsp chopped fresh
    mixed herbs, such as parsley,
    thyme, basil and oregano
pinch of sugar
salt and black pepper

1 Heat the oil in a pan, add the onion and garlic, and gently fry for about 5 minutes until softened.

2 Add the tomatoes, tomato purée, herbs, sugar and seasoning.

3 Simmer, uncovered, stirring occasionally for 10–15 minutes or until the tomatoes have reduced to a thick pulp. Leave to cool.

Flavoured Oils

Brush these over pizza bases before adding the topping. They can also be used in salad dressings, or tossed with pasta.

CHILLI OIL
INGREDIENTS
150 ml/¼ pint/⅔ cup olive oil
10 ml/2 tsp tomato purée
15 ml/1 tbsp dried red chilli
    flakes

1 Heat the oil in a pan until very hot but not smoking. Stir in the tomato purée and chilli flakes. Leave to cool.

2 Pour the chilli oil into a small jar or bottle. Cover and store in the fridge for up to 2 months (the longer you keep it the hotter it gets).

GARLIC OIL
INGREDIENTS
3–4 whole garlic cloves
120 ml/4 fl oz/½ cup olive oil

1 Peel the garlic cloves and put them into a small jar or bottle.

2 Pour in the oil, cover, and keep in the fridge for up to 1 month.

Salad Dressing/Baste

A good salad dressing can double up as an effective baste for the grill and barbecue. This dressing is delicious with white meats or fish.

MAKES
105 ml/7 tbsp

INGREDIENTS
90 ml/6 tbsp olive oil
15 ml/1 tbsp white wine vinegar
5 ml/1 tsp French mustard
½ garlic clove, crushed
1 ml/¼ tsp sugar

1 Pour the oil and vinegar into a screw-topped jar.

2 Add the mustard, garlic and sugar.

3 Shake well, and use as a dressing or marinade for salad, meat and fish.

Mayonnaise

Although bought mayonnaise is fine for fast meals, it takes very little time to make your own. Make sure the egg yolks are at room temperature, and add the oil very gradually at the start. Home-made mayonnaise is made with raw egg yolks and may therefore be considered unsuitable for young children, pregnant mothers and the elderly.

MAKES
about 300 ml/½ pint/1¼ cups

INGREDIENTS
2 egg yolks
5 ml/1 tsp French mustard
150 ml/¼ pint/⅔ cup extra-
    virgin olive oil
150 ml/¼ pint/⅔ cup sunflower oil
10 ml/2 tsp white wine vinegar
salt and pepper

2 Add the olive oil a little at a time while the processor is running. When the mixture is thick, add the remainder of the oil in a slow, steady stream.

1 Place the egg yolks and mustard in a food processor and blend smoothly.

COOK'S TIP
Should mayonnaise separate during blending, add 30 ml/ 2 tbsp boiling water and beat until smooth. Store mayonnaise in the refrigerator for up to 1 week, sealed in a screw-topped jar.

3 Add the vinegar and season to taste with salt and pepper.

MENU PLANS

All of the recipes in this book can be prepared individually in 30 minutes or less, but they can also be combined with other dishes to provide a three-course meal. Below are some suggested menus, using different combinations of quick recipes from the book.

MENU 1

Butterfly Prawns, p. 74

Stir-fried Sweet and Sour Chicken, p. 149

Peach Melba, p. 406

MENU 2

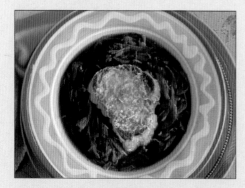

French Onion Soup, p. 59

Courgette Puffs with Salad and Balsamic Dressing, p. 236

Char-grilled Apples on Cinnamon Toasts, p. 374

MENU 3

Chilled Fresh Tomato Soup, p. 67

Veal Escalopes with Artichokes, p. 127

Red Berry Sponge Tart, p. 392

MENU 4

Creamy Parmesan and Cauliflower
Soup with Pasta Bows, p. 60

Grilled Snapper with Hot Mango
Salsa, p. 170

Chocolate Mousse on the Loose,
p. 408

MENU 5

Mini Spring Rolls, p. 78

Stir-fried Pork with Mustard, p. 134

Mango and Coconut Stir-fry, p. 380

MENU 6

Buckwheat Couscous with Goat's
Cheese and Celery, p. 112

Warm Stir-fried Salad, p. 266

Fruit Kebabs with Chocolate and
Marshmallow Fondue, p. 376

MENU 7

Sesame Seed Chicken Bites, p. 80

Indonesian Pork and Peanut Saté,
p. 142

Grilled Pineapple with Rum-custard
Sauce, p. 387

MENU 8

Asparagus Rolls with Herb Butter
Sauce, p. 224

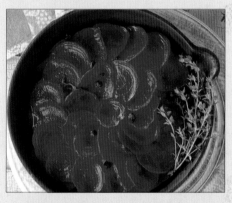

Beetroot and Celeriac Gratin, p. 231

Black Forest Sundae, p. 410

UNDER STARTER'S

You've arrived home **late** and your guests are due

in under an hour. Surely you haven't time to make

a starter? Oh **yes**, you have. The recipes

in this chapter have been especially

selected for the **ease** and

speed with which they can be

ORDERS

prepared. Crab and Egg Noodle Broth looks as

sophisticated as its name suggests, yet takes only

minutes to make. Butterfly Prawns take even less time

to prepare and are always popular, while crisp and

tender Deep-fried Florets with Tangy Thyme Mayonnaise is

the perfect choice for vegetarians.

Crab and Egg Noodle Broth

This delicious broth is an ideal solution when you are hungry and time is short, and you need something fast, nutritious and filling.

Serves 4

INGREDIENTS

75 g/3 oz fine egg noodles
25 g/1 oz/2 tbsp unsalted butter
1 small bunch spring onions, chopped
1 celery stick, sliced
1 medium carrot, peeled and cut
    into batons
1.2 litres/2 pints/5 cups chicken stock
60 ml/4 tbsp dry sherry
115 g/4 oz white crab meat, fresh
    or frozen
pinch of celery salt
pinch of cayenne pepper
10 ml/2 tsp lemon juice
1 small bunch coriander or flat-leaf
    parsley, to garnish

1 Bring a large saucepan of salted water to the boil. Toss in the egg noodles and cook according to the instructions on the packet. Cool under cold running water and leave immersed in water until required.

2 Heat the butter in another large pan, add the spring onions, celery and carrot, cover and soften the vegetables over a gentle heat for 3–4 minutes.

3 Add the chicken stock and sherry, bring to the boil and simmer for a further 5 minutes.

celery

egg noodles

crab meat

spring onions

coriander

4 Flake the crab meat between your fingers onto a plate and remove any stray pieces of shell.

5 Drain the noodles and add to the broth together with the crab meat. Season to taste with celery salt and cayenne pepper, and sharpen with the lemon juice. Return to a simmer.

6 Ladle the broth into shallow soup plates, scatter with roughly chopped coriander or parsley and serve.

Chicken Vermicelli Soup with Egg Shreds

This soup is very quick and easy – you can add all sorts of extra ingredients to vary the taste, using up any left-overs such as spring onions, mushrooms, prawns, chopped salami or herbs.

Serves 4–6

INGREDIENTS
3 large eggs
30 ml/2 tbsp chopped fresh coriander
  or parsley
1.5 litres/2½ pints/6¼ cups good
  chicken stock or canned consommé
100 g/4 oz/1 cup dried vermicelli or
  angel hair pasta
100 g/4 oz cooked chicken breast,
  sliced
salt and pepper

vermicelli

eggs   *chicken breast*

coriander

1 First make the egg shreds. Whisk the eggs together in a small bowl and stir in the coriander or parsley.

THAI CHICKEN SOUP

To make a Thai variation, use Chinese rice noodles instead of pasta. Stir 2.5 ml/ ½ tsp dried lemon grass, 2 small whole fresh chillies and 60 ml/4 tbsp coconut milk into the stock. Add four sliced spring onions and plenty of chopped fresh coriander.

2 Heat a small non-stick frying pan (skillet) and pour in 2–3 tbsp egg, swirling to cover the base evenly. Cook until set. Repeat until all the mixture is used up.

3 Roll each pancake up and slice thinly into shreds. Set aside.

4 Bring the stock to the boil and add the pasta, breaking it up into short lengths. Cook for 3–5 minutes until the pasta is almost tender, then add the chicken, salt and pepper. Heat through for 2–3 minutes, then stir in the egg shreds. Serve immediately.

Fresh Pea and Ham Soup

Frozen peas provide flavour, freshness and colour in this delicious winter soup, which is filling enough to make a light main course or a starter.

Serves 4

INGREDIENTS
115 g/4 oz small pasta shapes
30 ml/2 tbsp vegetable oil
1 small bunch spring onions, chopped
350 g/12 oz/3 cups frozen peas
1.2 litres/2 pints/5 cups chicken stock
225 g/8 oz raw unsmoked ham
   or gammon
60 ml/4 tbsp double cream
salt and freshly ground black pepper
warm crusty bread, to serve

ham

pasta

cream

peas

spring onions

1 Bring a large saucepan of salted water to the boil. Toss in the pasta and cook according to the instructions on the packet. Drain, cover with cold water and set aside until required.

2 Heat the vegetable oil in a large heavy saucepan and cook the spring onions until soft. Add the peas and stock, then simmer for 10 minutes.

3 Liquidize the soup in a blender and return to the saucepan. Cut the ham or gammon into short fingers and add it together with the pasta to the saucepan. Simmer for 2–3 minutes and season to taste. Stir in the cream and serve with the warm crusty bread.

VARIATION

Any pasta shapes can be used for this soup, although hoops or shells seem to work best of all.

Broccoli and Almond Soup

The creaminess of the toasted almonds combines perfectly with the slight bitterness of the taste of broccoli.

Serves 4–6

INGREDIENTS
50 g/2 oz/⅔ cup ground almonds
675 g/1½ lb broccoli
850 ml/1½ pints/3¾ cups vegetable stock or water
300 ml/½ pint/1¼ cups skimmed milk
salt and freshly ground black pepper

ground almonds

skimmed milk

broccoli

1 Preheat the oven to 180°C/350°F/Gas 4. Spread the ground almonds evenly on a baking sheet and toast in the oven for about 10 minutes, or until golden. Reserve ¼ of the almonds and set aside for the garnish.

2 Cut the broccoli into small florets and steam for 6–7 minutes or until tender.

3 Place the remaining toasted almonds, broccoli, stock or water and milk in a blender and blend until smooth. Season to taste.

4 Reheat the soup and serve sprinkled with the reserved toasted almonds.

French Onion Soup

In the time it takes to soften a few onions and brown some cheese on toast, this delicious soup appears on the table steaming hot and ready to eat. It makes a substantial starter or lunch dish.

Serves 4

INGREDIENTS
30 ml/2 tbsp vegetable oil
3 medium onions, sliced
900 ml/1½ pints/3¾ cups beef stock
4 slices French bread
butter, for spreading
115 g/4 oz/1 cup grated Gruyère,
   or Emmenthal cheese

onions

cheese

French bread

1 Heat the vegetable oil in a large frying pan and brown the onions over a steady heat, taking care they do not burn.

2 Transfer the browned onions to a large saucepan, cover with beef stock and simmer for 10 minutes.

3 Preheat the grill to a moderate temperature and toast the French bread on both sides. Spread one side with butter and top with grated cheese. Ladle the soup into four flameproof dishes, float the cheesy crusts on top and grill until crispy and brown.

Creamy Parmesan and Cauliflower Soup with Pasta Bows

A silky smooth, mildly cheesy soup which isn't overpowered by the cauliflower. It is an elegant dinner party soup served with the crisp melba toast.

Serves 6

INGREDIENTS
1 large cauliflower
1.1 litres/2 pints/5 cups chicken or vegetable stock
175 g/6 oz/1½ cups pasta bows (farfalle)
150 ml/5 fl oz/⅔ cup single (light) cream or milk
freshly grated nutmeg
pinch of cayenne pepper
60 ml/4 tbsp freshly grated Parmesan cheese
salt and pepper

MELBA TOAST
3–4 slices day-old white bread
freshly grated Parmesan cheese, for sprinkling
¼ tsp paprika

cauliflower

pasta bows

Parmesan cheese

nutmeg

1 Cut the leaves and central stalk away from the cauliflower and discard. Divide the cauliflower into florets (flowerets).

2 Bring the stock to the boil and add the cauliflower. Simmer for about 10 minutes or until very soft. Remove the cauliflower with a perforated spoon and place in a food processor.

3 Add the pasta to the stock and simmer for 10 minutes until tender. Drain, reserve the pasta, and pour the liquid over the cauliflower in the food processor. Add the cream or milk, nutmeg and cayenne to the cauliflower. Blend until smooth, then press through a sieve (strainer). Stir in the cooked pasta. Reheat the soup and stir in the Parmesan. Taste and adjust the seasoning.

4 Meanwhile make the melba toast. Pre-heat the oven to 180°C/350°F/gas mark 4. Toast the bread lightly on both sides. Quickly cut off the crusts and split each slice in half horizontally. Scrape off any doughy bits and sprinkle with Parmesan and paprika. Place on a baking sheet and bake in the oven for 10–15 minutes or until uniformly golden. Serve with the soup.

Red Onion and Beetroot Soup

This beautiful vivid ruby-red soup will look stunning at any dinner party.

Serves 4–6

INGREDIENTS
15 ml/1 tbsp olive oil
350 g/12 oz red onions, sliced
2 garlic cloves, crushed
275 g/10 oz cooked beetroot, cut into sticks
1.1 litres/2 pints/5 cups vegetable stock or water
50 g/2 oz/1 cup cooked soup pasta
30 ml/2 tbsp raspberry vinegar
salt and freshly ground black pepper
low-fat yogurt or fromage blanc, to garnish
snipped chives, to garnish

garlic

red onion

beetroot

pasta

chives

1 Heat the olive oil and add the onions and garlic.

2 Cook gently for about 20 minutes or until soft and tender.

COOK'S TIP
Try substituting cooked barley for the pasta to give extra nuttiness.

3 Add the beetroot, stock or water, cooked pasta shapes and vinegar and heat through. Season to taste.

4 Ladle into bowls. Top each one with a spoonful of yogurt or fromage blanc and sprinkle with chives.

Cauliflower, Flageolet and Fennel Seed Soup

The sweet, anise-liquorice flavour of the fennel seeds gives a delicious edge to this hearty soup.

Serves 4–6

INGREDIENTS

15 ml/1 tbsp olive oil
1 garlic clove, crushed
1 onion, chopped
10 ml/2 tsp fennel seeds
1 cauliflower, cut into small florets
2 × 400 g/14 oz cans flageolet beans, drained and rinsed
1.1 litres/2 pints/5 cups vegetable stock or water
salt and freshly ground black pepper
chopped fresh parsley, to garnish
toasted slices of French bread, to serve

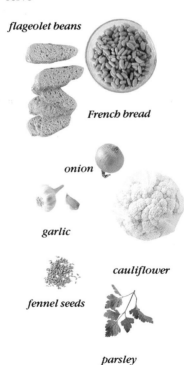

flageolet beans

French bread

onion

garlic

cauliflower

fennel seeds

parsley

1 Heat the olive oil. Add the garlic, onion and fennel seeds and cook gently for 5 minutes or until softened.

2 Add the cauliflower, half of the beans and the stock or water.

3 Bring to the boil. Reduce the heat and simmer for 10 minutes or until the cauliflower is tender.

4 Pour the soup into a blender and blend until smooth. Stir in the remaining beans and season to taste. Reheat and pour into bowls. Sprinkle with chopped parsley and serve with toasted slices of French bread.

Beetroot and Butter Bean Soup

This soup is a simplified version of borscht, and is prepared in a fraction of the time. Serve with a spoonful of sour cream and a scattering of chopped fresh parsley.

Serves 4

INGREDIENTS
30 ml/2 tbsp vegetable oil
1 medium onion, halved and sliced
5 ml/1 tsp caraway seeds
finely grated zest of ½ orange
250 g/9 oz cooked beetroot, grated
1.2 litres/2 pints/5 cups beef stock
   or rassol
1 × 400 g/14 oz can butter beans,
   drained
15 ml/1 tbsp wine vinegar
60 ml/4 tbsp sour cream
60 ml/4 tbsp chopped fresh parsley,
   to garnish

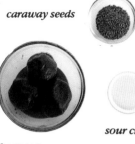
beetroot

caraway seeds

sour cream

onion

orange

butter beans

1   Heat the oil in a large saucepan and cook the onion, caraway seeds and orange zest until soft but not coloured.

2   Add the beetroot, stock or rassol, butter beans and vinegar and simmer for a further 10 minutes.

3   Divide the soup between four bowls, add a spoonful of sour cream to each and scatter with chopped fresh parsley.

COOK'S TIP

Rassol is a beetroot broth used to impart a strong beetroot colour and flavour. You are most likely to find it in Kosher food stores.

Baby Carrot and Fennel Soup

Sweet tender carrots find their moment of glory in this delicately spiced soup. Fennel provides an aniseed flavour without overpowering the carrots.

Serves 4

INGREDIENTS
50 g/2 oz/4 tbsp butter
1 small bunch spring onions, chopped
150 g/5 oz fennel bulb, chopped
1 celery stick, chopped
450 g/1 lb new carrots, grated
2.5 ml/½ tsp ground cumin
150 g/5 oz new potatoes, peeled
    and diced
1.2 litres/2 pints/5 cups chicken or
    vegetable stock
60 ml/4 tbsp double cream
salt and freshly ground black pepper
60 ml/4 tbsp chopped fresh parsley,
    to garnish

carrots

fennel bulb

celery

cream

spring onions

1 Melt the butter in a large saucepan and add the spring onions, fennel, celery, carrots and cumin. Cover and cook for 5 minutes until soft.

2 Add the potatoes and stock, and simmer for a further 10 minutes.

COOK'S TIP
For convenience, you can freeze the soup in portions before adding the cream, seasoning and parsley.

3 Liquidize the mixture in the pan with a hand-held blender. Stir in the cream and season to taste. Serve in individual bowls and garnish with chopped fresh parsley.

Succotash Soup Plate

Succotash is a North American Indian dish of corn and butter beans. Originally the dish was enriched with bear fat, although modern day succotash is finished with milk or cream. This version makes an appetizing and filling main course soup.

Serves 4

INGREDIENTS
50 g/2 oz/4 tbsp butter
1 large onion, chopped
2 large carrots, peeled and cut into
    short batons
900 ml/1½ pints/3¾ cups milk
1 vegetable stock cube
2 medium-sized waxy potatoes,
    peeled and diced
1 thyme sprig
225 g/8 oz/2 cups frozen sweetcorn
225 g/8 oz/3 cups frozen butter beans
    or broad beans
30 ml/2 tbsp chopped fresh parsley,
    to garnish

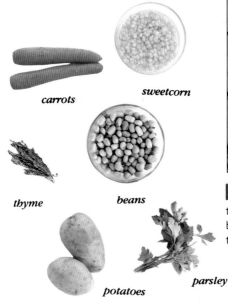

carrots

sweetcorn

thyme

beans

potatoes

parsley

1 Heat the butter in a large saucepan. Add the onion and carrots and cook over a gentle heat for 3–4 minutes, to soften without colouring.

2 Add the milk, stock cube, potatoes, thyme, sweetcorn and butter beans or broad beans. Simmer for 10 minutes until the potatoes are cooked through.

COOK'S TIP
Frozen sweetcorn and butter beans are best for flavour and convenience in this soup, although the canned variety may also be used.

3 Season to taste, ladle into soup plates and garnish with chopped fresh parsley.

Melon and Basil Soup

A deliciously refreshing, chilled fruit soup, just right for a hot summer's day.

Serves 4–6

INGREDIENTS
2 Charentais or rock melons
75 g/3 oz/⅓ cup caster sugar
175 ml/6 fl oz/¾ cup water
finely grated rind and juice of 1 lime
45 ml/3 tbsp shredded fresh basil
fresh basil leaves, to garnish

basil

caster sugar

lime

Charentais melon

1 Cut the melons in half across the middle. Scrape out the seeds and discard. Using a melon baller, scoop out 20–24 balls and set aside for the garnish. Scoop out the remaining flesh and place in a blender or food processor.

2 Place the sugar, water and lime zest in a small pan over a low heat. Stir until dissolved, bring to the boil and simmer for 2–3 minutes. Remove from the heat and leave to cool slightly. Pour half the mixture into the blender or food processor with the melon flesh. Blend until smooth, adding the remaining syrup and lime juice to taste.

3 Pour the mixture into a bowl, stir in the basil and chill. Serve garnished with basil leaves and melon balls.

COOK'S TIP
Add the syrup in two stages, as the amount of sugar needed will depend on the sweetness of the melon.

Chilled Fresh Tomato Soup

This effortless uncooked soup can be made in minutes.

Serves 4–6

INGREDIENTS

1.5 kg/3–3½ lb ripe tomatoes, peeled
  and roughly chopped
4 garlic cloves, crushed
30 ml/2 tbsp extra-virgin olive oil
  (optional)
30 ml/2 tbsp balsamic vinegar
freshly ground black pepper
4 slices wholemeal bread
low-fat fromage blanc, to garnish

wholemeal bread

garlic

fromage blanc

peppercorns

tomato

COOK'S TIP

For the best flavour, it is important to use only fully ripened, flavourful tomatoes in this soup.

1 Place the tomatoes in a blender with the garlic and olive oil if using. Blend until smooth.

2 Pass the mixture through a sieve to remove the seeds. Stir in the balsamic vinegar and season to taste with pepper. Chill quickly by adding several ice cubes or some crushed ice to the mixture, but take care not to dilute it too much.

3 Toast the bread lightly on both sides. Whilst still hot, cut off the crusts and slice in half horizontally. Place the toast on a board with the uncooked sides facing down and, using a circular motion, rub to remove any doughy pieces of bread.

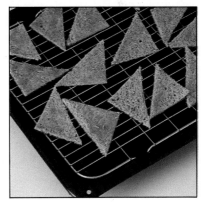

4 Cut each slice into 4 triangles. Place on a grill pan and toast the uncooked sides until lightly golden. Garnish each bowl of soup with a spoonful of fromage blanc and serve with the melba toast.

Deep-fried Florets with Tangy Thyme Mayonnaise

Cauliflower and broccoli make a sensational snack when coated in a beer batter and deep-fried. Serve with a tangy mayonnaise.

Serves 2–3

INGREDIENTS
175 g/6 oz cauliflower
175 g/6 oz broccoli
2 eggs, separated
30 ml/2 tbsp olive oil
250 ml/8 fl oz/1 cup beer
150 ml/5 oz/1¹/₄ cups plain flour
pinch of salt
30 ml/2 tbsp shredded fresh basil
vegetable oil for deep-frying
150 ml/¹/₄ pint/²/₃ cup good quality
  mayonnaise
10 ml/2 tsp chopped fresh thyme
10 ml/2 tsp grated lemon rind
10 ml/2 tsp lemon juice
sea salt, for sprinkling

basil

eggs

plain flour

mayonnaise

broccoli

beer

cauliflower

thyme

lemon

1 Break the cauliflower and broccoli into small florets, cutting large florets into smaller pieces. Set aside.

2 Beat the egg yolks, olive oil, beer, flour and salt in a bowl. Strain the batter if necessary, to remove any lumps.

3 Whisk the egg whites until stiff. Fold into the batter with the basil.

4 Heat the oil for deep-frying to 180°C/350°F or until a cube of bread, when added to the oil, browns in 30–45 seconds. Dip the florets in the batter and deep-fry in batches for 2–3 minutes until the coating is golden and crisp. Drain on kitchen paper.

5 Mix the mayonnaise, thyme, lemon rind and juice in a small bowl.

6 Sprinkle the florets with sea salt. Serve with the thyme and lemon mayonnaise.

Caponata

Caponata is a quintessential part of Sicilian antipasti and is a rich, spicy mixture of aubergine, tomatoes, capers and celery.

Serves 4

INGREDIENTS
60 ml/4 tbsp olive oil
1 large onion, sliced
2 celery sticks, sliced
450 g/1 lb aubergines, diced
5 ripe tomatoes, chopped
1 garlic clove, crushed
45 ml/3 tbsp red wine vinegar
15 ml/1 tbsp sugar
30 ml/2 tbsp capers
12 olives
pinch of salt
60 ml/4 tbsp chopped fresh parsley,
    to garnish
warm crusty bread, to serve
olives, to serve

celery

aubergines

onion   *tomatoes*   *olives*

capers

1 Heat half the oil in a large heavy saucepan. Add the onion and celery and cook over a gentle heat for about 3–4 minutes to soften.

2 Add the remainder of the oil with the aubergines and stir to absorb the oil. Cook until the aubergines begin to colour, then add the chopped tomatoes, garlic, vinegar and sugar.

3 Cover the surface of the vegetables with a circle of greaseproof paper and simmer for 8–10 minutes.

4 Add the capers and olives, then season to taste with salt. Turn the caponata out into a bowl, garnish with parsley and serve at room temperature with warm crusty bread and olives.

Grilled Green Mussels with Cumin

Large green shelled mussels have a more distinctive flavour than the more common small black variety. Keep the empty shells to use as individual salt and pepper holders for fishy meals.

Serves 4

INGREDIENTS
45 ml/3 tbsp fresh parsley
45 ml/3 tbsp fresh coriander
1 garlic clove, crushed
pinch of ground cumin
25 g/1 oz/2 tbsp unsalted butter, softened
25 g/1 oz/3 tbsp brown breadcrumbs
freshly ground black pepper
12 green mussels or 24 small mussels on the half-shell
chopped fresh parsley, to garnish

parsley

butter

garlic

bread

coriander

mussels

1 Chop the herbs finely.

2 Beat the garlic, herbs, cumin and butter together with a wooden spoon.

3 Stir in the breadcrumbs and freshly ground black pepper.

4 Spoon a little of the mixture onto each mussel and grill for 2 minutes. Serve garnished with chopped fresh parsley.

Crispy "Seaweed" with Flaked Almonds

This popular starter in Chinese restaurants is in fact usually made not with seaweed but spring greens! It is easy to make at home and the result is delicious.

Serves 4-6

INGREDIENTS
450 g/1 lb spring greens
groundnut oil, for deep-frying
1.5 ml/¼ tsp sea salt flakes
5 ml/1 tsp caster sugar
50 g/2 oz/½ cup flaked
  almonds, toasted

spring greens

almonds

groundnut oil

sea salt

sugar

COOK'S TIP

It is important to dry the spring greens thoroughly before deep-frying them, otherwise it will be difficult to achieve the desired crispness without destroying their vivid colour.

1 Wash the spring greens under cold running water and pat well with kitchen paper to dry thoroughly. Remove and discard the thick white stalks from the spring greens.

2 Lay several leaves on top of one another, roll up tightly and, using a sharp knife, slice as finely as possible into thread-like strips.

3 Half-fill a wok with oil and heat to 180°C/350°F. Deep fry the spring greens in batches for about 1 minute until they darken and crisp. Remove each batch from the wok as soon as it is ready and drain on kitchen paper.

4 Transfer the "seaweed" to a serving dish, sprinkle with the salt and sugar, then mix well. Garnish with the toasted flaked almonds scattered over.

Hot Spicy Crab Claws

Crab claws are used to delicious effect in this quick starter based on an Indonesian dish called *Kepiting Pedas*.

Serves 4

INGREDIENTS
12 fresh or frozen and thawed
  cooked crab claws
4 shallots, roughly chopped
2-4 fresh red chillies, seeded and
  roughly chopped
3 garlic cloves, roughly chopped
5 ml/1 tsp grated fresh
  root ginger
2.5 ml/½ tsp ground coriander
45 ml/3 tbsp groundnut oil
60 ml/4 tbsp water
10 ml/2 tsp sweet soy sauce
  (*kecap manis*)
10-15 ml/2-3 tsp lime juice
salt, to taste

shallots

crab claws

sweet soy sauce

garlic

coriander

red chillies

groundnut oil

lime

ginger

1 Crack the crab claws with the back of a heavy knife to make eating easier. Set aside. In a mortar, pound the chopped shallots with the pestle until pulpy. Add the chillies, garlic, ginger and ground coriander and pound until the mixture forms a coarse paste.

2 Heat the wok over a medium heat. Add the oil and swirl it around. When it is hot, stir in the chilli paste. Stir-fry for about 30 seconds. Increase the heat to high. Add the crab claws and stir-fry for another 3–4 minutes.

3 Stir in the water, sweet soy sauce, lime juice and salt to taste. Continue to stir-fry for 1–2 minutes. Serve at once, garnished with fresh coriander. The crab claws are eaten with the fingers, so provide finger bowls.

COOK'S TIP
If whole crab claws are unavailable look out for frozen ready-prepared crab claws. These are shelled with just the tip of the claw attached to the white meat. Stir fry for about two minutes until hot through.

Butterfly Prawns

Use raw prawns if you can because the flavour will be better, but if you substitute cooked prawns, cut down the stir-fry cooking time by one third.

Serves 4

INGREDIENTS

2.5 cm/1 in piece root ginger
350 g/12 oz raw prawns, thawed if
    frozen
50 g/2 oz/½ cup raw peanuts, roughly
    chopped
45 ml/3 tbsp vegetable oil
1 clove garlic, crushed
1 red chilli, finely chopped
45 ml/3 tbsp smooth peanut butter
15 ml/1 tbsp fresh coriander, chopped
fresh coriander sprigs, to garnish

FOR THE DRESSING

150 ml/¼ pint/⅔ cup natural
    low-fat yogurt
5 cm/2 in piece cucumber, diced
salt and freshly ground black pepper

diced cucumber

peanuts

coriander

prawn

chilli

1 To make the dressing, mix together the yogurt, cucumber and seasoning in a bowl, then leave to chill while preparing and cooking the prawns.

2 Peel the ginger, and chop it finely.

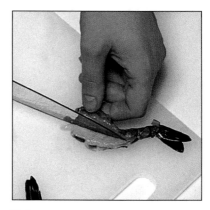

3 Prepare the prawns by peeling off the shells, leaving the tails intact. Make a slit down the back of each prawn and remove the black vein, then slit the prawn completely down the back and open it out to make a 'butterfly'.

4 Heat the wok and dry-fry the peanuts, stirring constantly until golden brown. Leave to cool. Wipe out the wok with kitchen towels.

5 Heat the wok, add the oil and when hot add the ginger, garlic and chilli. Stir-fry for 2–3 minutes until the garlic is softened but not brown.

6 Add the prawns, then increase the heat and stir-fry for 1–2 minutes until the prawns turn pink. Stir in the peanut butter and stir-fry for 2 minutes. Add the chopped coriander, then scatter in the peanuts. Garnish with coriander sprigs and serve with the cucumber dressing.

Chicken Goujons

Serve as a first course for eight people or as a filling main course for four. Delicious served with new baby potatoes and a green salad.

Serves 8

INGREDIENTS

4 boned and skinned chicken breasts
175 g/6 oz/3 cups fresh breadcrumbs
5 ml/1 tsp ground coriander
10 ml/2 tsp ground paprika
2.5 ml/½ tsp ground cumin
45 ml/3 tbsp plain flour
2 eggs, beaten
oil, for deep-frying
salt and freshly ground black pepper
lemon slices, to garnish
sprigs of fresh coriander, to garnish

FOR THE DIP

300 ml/½ pint/1¼ cups Greek yogurt
30 ml/2 tbsp lemon juice
60 ml/4 tbsp chopped fresh coriander
60 ml/4 tbsp chopped fresh parsley

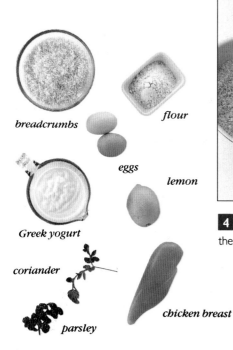

breadcrumbs

flour

eggs

lemon

Greek yogurt

coriander

parsley

chicken breast

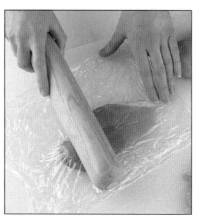

1 Divide the chicken breasts into two natural fillets. Place them between two sheets of clear film and, using a rolling pin, flatten each one to a thickness of 5 mm/¼ in.

2 Cut into diagonal 2.5 cm/1 in strips.

3 Mix the breadcrumbs with the spices and seasoning. Toss the chicken fillet pieces (goujons) into the flour, keeping them separate.

4 Dip the fillets into the beaten egg and then coat in the breadcrumb mixture.

5 Thoroughly mix all the ingredients for the dip together, and season to taste. Chill until required.

6 Heat the oil in a heavy-based pan. It is ready for deep-frying when a piece of bread tossed into the oil sizzles on the surface. Fry the goujons in batches until golden and crisp. Drain on kitchen paper and keep warm in the oven until all the chicken has been fried. Garnish with lemon slices and sprigs of fresh coriander.

Mini Spring Rolls

Eat these light crispy parcels with your fingers. If you like slightly spicier food, sprinkle them with a little cayenne pepper before serving.

Makes 20

INGREDIENTS
1 green chilli
125 ml/4 fl oz/½ cup vegetable oil
1 small onion, finely chopped
1 clove garlic, crushed
75 g/3 oz cooked chicken breast
1 small carrot, cut into fine
    matchsticks
1 spring onion, finely sliced
1 small red pepper, seeded and cut
    into fine matchsticks
25 g/1 oz beansprouts
5 ml/1 tsp sesame oil
4 large sheets filo pastry
1 × size 4 egg white, lightly beaten
long chives, to garnish (optional)
45 ml/3 tbsp light soy sauce, to serve

spring onions

chilli

pepper

garlic

beansprouts

1 Carefully remove the seeds from the chilli and chop finely, wearing rubber gloves to protect your hands, if necessary.

2 Heat the wok, then add 30 ml/2 tbsp of the vegetable oil. When hot, add the onion, garlic and chilli. Stir-fry for 1 minute.

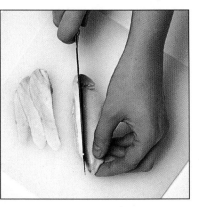

3 Slice the chicken thinly, then add to the wok and fry over a high heat, stirring constantly until browned.

4 Add the carrot, spring onion and red pepper and stir-fry for 2 minutes. Add the beansprouts, stir in the sesame oil and leave to cool.

COOK'S TIP

Be careful to avoid touching your face or eyes when deseeding and chopping chillies because they are very potent and may cause burning and irritation to the skin. Try preparing chillies under running water.

COOK'S TIP

Always keep filo pastry sheets covered with a dry, clean cloth until needed, to prevent them drying out.

5 Cut each sheet of filo into 5 short strips. Place a small amount of filling at one end of each strip, then fold in the long sides and roll up the pastry. Seal and glaze the parcels with the egg white, then chill uncovered for 15 minutes before frying.

6 Wipe out the wok with kitchen towels, heat it, and add the remaining vegetable oil. When the oil is hot, fry the rolls in batches until crisp and golden brown. Drain on kitchen towels and serve dipped in light soy sauce.

Sesame Seed Chicken Bites

Best served warm, these crunchy bites are delicious accompanied by a glass of chilled dry white wine.

Makes 20

INGREDIENTS
175 g/6 oz raw chicken breast
2 cloves garlic, crushed
2.5 cm/1 in piece root ginger, peeled and grated
1 × size 4 egg white
5 ml/1 tsp cornflour
25 g/1 oz/¼ cup shelled pistachios, roughly chopped
60 ml/4 tbsp sesame seeds
30 ml/2 tbsp grapeseed oil
salt and freshly ground black pepper

FOR THE SAUCE
45 ml/3 tbsp/¼ cup hoisin sauce
15 ml/1 tbsp sweet chilli sauce

TO GARNISH
root ginger, finely shredded
pistachios, roughly chopped
fresh dill sprigs

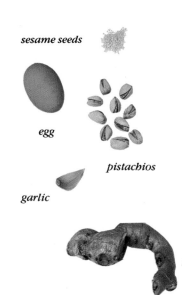

sesame seeds

egg

pistachios

garlic

ginger

1 Place the chicken, garlic, grated ginger, egg white and cornflour into the food processor and process them to a smooth paste.

2 Stir in the pistachios and season well with salt and pepper.

3 Roll into 20 balls and coat with sesame seeds. Heat the wok and add the oil. When the oil is hot, stir-fry the chicken bites in batches, turning regularly until golden. Drain on kitchen towels.

4 Make the sauce by mixing together the hoisin and chilli sauces in a bowl. Garnish the bites with shredded ginger, pistachios and dill, then serve hot, with a dish of sauce for dipping.

Welsh Rarebit Toasts

Welsh Rarebit is the gourmet's answer to cheese on toast. Serve as a tasty starter with drinks.

Serves 4

INGREDIENTS
200 ml/7 fl oz/scant 1 cup lager
60 ml/4 tbsp plain flour
10 ml/2 tsp mustard (powdered
   or ready-made)
2.5 ml/½ tsp celery salt
pinch of cayenne pepper
175 g/6 oz/1½ cups grated
   Cheddar cheese
6 thick slices white or wholemeal
   bread
3 celery sticks, to serve

Cheddar cheese

bread

flour

mustard

lager

1 Measure 50 ml/2 fl oz/¼ cup of the lager into a mixing bowl and combine with the flour, mustard, celery salt and cayenne pepper.

2 Bring the remaining lager to the boil in a heavy saucepan together with the cheese. Pour over the mixed ingredients and stir to blend evenly. Return to the saucepan and simmer gently, stirring continuously, to thicken.

3 Preheat a moderate grill and toast the bread on both sides. Spread thickly with the mixture, then grill until golden brown and bubbly. Cut into fingers and serve with celery sticks.

COOK'S TIP
Welsh Rarebit mixture will keep in the refrigerator for up to a week and is perfect for a fast snack at any time of the day.

The whole point about snacks is that they must be **quick** and **easy** to make. When you get an attack of the munchies, the last thing you want to do is wait, so these recipes are really **rapid**. Protein-packed omelettes are ideal, but can be a little dull. Try our **exciting** variations: Tomato Omelette Envelopes, Spanish Omelette or Soufflé Omelette. Nobody said you couldn't cheat a little, so make the **most** of tacos, tortillas and baked goods such as croissants. With a lot of imagination and a little time, they can be transformed into astonishingly **tasty** treats.

SPEEDY SNACKS

Tomato Omelette Envelopes

Delicious chive omelettes, folded and filled with tomato and melting Camembert cheese.

Serves 2

INGREDIENTS
1 small onion
4 tomatoes
30 ml/2 tbsp vegetable oil
4 eggs
30 ml/2 tbsp snipped fresh chives
115 g/4 oz Camembert cheese,
  rinded and diced
salt and freshly ground black pepper

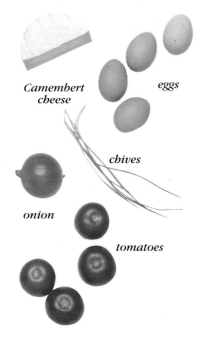

Camembert cheese

eggs

chives

onion

tomatoes

1 Cut the onion in half. Cut each half into thin wedges. Cut the tomatoes into wedges of similar size.

2 Heat 15 ml/1 tbsp of the oil in a frying pan. Cook the onion for 2 minutes over a moderate heat, then raise the heat and add the tomatoes. Cook for a further 2 minutes, then remove the pan from the heat.

3 Beat the eggs with the chives in a bowl. Add salt and pepper to taste. Heat the remaining oil in an omelette pan. Add half the egg mixture and tilt the pan to spread thinly. Cook for 1 minute.

4 Flip the omelette over and cook for 1 minute more. Remove from the pan and keep hot. Make a second omelette with the remaining egg mixture.

5 Return the tomato mixture to a high heat. Add the cheese and toss the mixture over the heat for 1 minute.

6 Divide the mixture between the omelettes and fold them over. Serve at once. Add crisp lettuce leaves and chunks of Granary bread, if liked.

COOK'S TIP
You may need to wipe the pan clean between the omelettes and reheat a little more oil.

Spanish Omelette

Spanish omelette belongs in every cook's repertoire and can vary according to what you have in store. This version includes soft white beans and is finished with a layer of toasted sesame seeds.

VARIATION
You can also use sliced cooked potatoes, any seasonal vegetables, baby artichoke hearts and chick-peas in a Spanish omelette.

Serves 4

INGREDIENTS
30 ml/2 tbsp olive oil
5 ml/1 tsp sesame oil
1 Spanish onion, chopped
1 small red pepper, deseeded
  and diced
2 celery sticks, chopped
1 × 400 g/14 oz can soft white
  beans, drained
8 eggs
45 ml/3 tbsp sesame seeds
salt and freshly ground black pepper
115 g/4 oz green salad, to serve

celery

red pepper

white beans

sesame oil

sesame seeds

eggs

1 Heat the olive and sesame oils in a 30 cm/12 in paella or frying pan. Add the onion, pepper and celery and cook to soften without colouring.

4 Stir the egg mixture with a flat wooden spoon until it begins to stiffen, then allow to firm over a low heat for about 6–8 minutes.

2 Add the beans and continue to cook for several minutes to heat through.

5 Preheat a moderate grill. Sprinkle the omelette with sesame seeds and brown evenly under the grill.

3 In a small bowl beat the eggs with a fork, season well and pour over the ingredients in the pan.

6 Cut the omelette into thick wedges and serve warm with a green salad.

Soufflé Omelette

This delectable soufflé omlette is light and delicate enough to melt in the mouth.

Serves 1

INGREDIENTS
2 eggs, separated
30 ml/2 tbsp cold water
15 ml/1 tbsp chopped fresh coriander
salt and freshly ground black pepper
7.5 ml/½ tbsp olive oil
30 ml/2 tbsp mango chutney
25 g/1 oz/¼ cup Jarlsberg cheese, grated

Jarlsberg

mango chutney

eggs

coriander

COOK'S TIP

A light hand is essential to the success of this dish. Do not overmix the egg whites into the yolks or the mixture will be heavy.

1 Beat the egg yolks together with the cold water, coriander and seasoning.

2 Whisk the egg whites until stiff but not dry and gently fold into the egg yolk mixture.

3 Heat the oil in a frying pan, pour in the egg mixture and reduce the heat. Do not stir. Cook until the omelette becomes puffy and golden brown on the underside (carefully lift one edge with a palette knife to check).

4 Spoon on the chutney and sprinkle on the Jarlsberg. Fold over and slide onto a warm plate. Eat immediately. (If preferred, before adding the chutney and cheese, place the pan under a hot grill to set the top.)

Omelette aux Fines Herbs

Eggs respond well to fast cooking and combine beautifully with a handful of fresh herbs. Serve with oven-ready chips and a green salad.

Serves 1

INGREDIENTS
3 eggs
30 ml/2 tbsp chopped fresh parsley
30 ml/2 tbsp chopped fresh chervil
30 ml/2 tbsp chopped fresh tarragon
15 ml/1 tbsp chopped fresh chives
15 ml/½ oz/1 tbsp butter
salt and freshly ground black pepper
350 g/12 oz oven-ready chips,
　　to serve
115 g/4 oz green salad, to serve
1 tomato, to serve

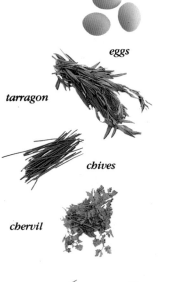

eggs

tarragon

chives

chervil

butter

parsley

1 Break the eggs into a bowl, season to taste and beat with a fork, then add the chopped herbs.

2 Heat an omelette or frying pan over a fierce heat, add the butter and cook until it foams and browns. Quickly pour in the beaten egg and stir briskly with the back of the fork. When the egg is two-thirds scrambled, let the omelette finish cooking for 10–15 seconds more.

3 Tap the handle of the omelette or frying pan sharply with your fist to make the omelette jump up the sides of the pan, fold and turn onto a plate. Serve with oven-ready chips, green salad and a halved tomato.

COOK'S TIP

From start to finish, an omelette should be cooked and on the table in less than a minute. For best results use free-range eggs at room temperature.

Filled Croissants

Croissants are very versatile and can be used with sweet or savoury fillings.

Makes 2

INGREDIENTS
2 croissants
knob of butter
2 eggs
salt and pepper
1 tablespoon double (heavy) cream
50 g/2 oz smoked salmon, chopped
1 sprig fresh dill, to garnish

croissants

smoked salmon

eggs

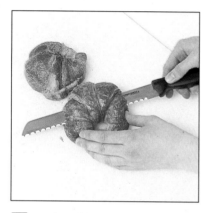

1 Preheat the oven to 180°C/350°F/gas mark 4. Slice the croissants in half horizontally and warm in the oven for 5–6 minutes.

2 Melt a knob of butter in a small pan. Beat the eggs in a bowl with seasoning to taste.

3 Add the eggs to the pan and cook for 2 minutes, stirring constantly.

4 Remove from the heat and stir in the cream and smoked salmon.

5 Spoon the smoked salmon mixture into the warmed croissants and garnish.

PEAR AND STILTON FILLING

Soften 100 g/4 oz Stilton cheese with a fork and mix in 1 peeled, cored and chopped ripe pear and 15 ml/1 tbsp chopped chives with a little black pepper. Spoon into a split croissant and bake in a preheated oven for 5 minutes.

Croque Monsieur

Probably the most popular snack food in France, this hot cheese and ham sandwich can be either fried or grilled.

Makes 2

INGREDIENTS
4 slices white bread
25 g/1 oz/2 tbsp softened butter
2 thin slices lean ham
50 g/2 oz Gruyère cheese,
  thinly sliced
1 sprig flat leaf parsley, to garnish

white bread

Gruyère cheese

ham

1 Spread the bread with butter.

2 Lay the ham on 2 of the buttered sides of bread.

3 Lay the Gruyère cheese slices on top of the ham and sandwich with the buttered bread slices. Press firmly together and cut off the crusts.

4 Spread the top with butter, place on a rack and cook for 2½ minutes under the grill preheated to a low to moderate temperature.

5 Turn the sandwiches over, spread the remaining butter over the top and return to the grill for a further 2½ minutes, until the bread is golden brown and the cheese is beginning to melt. Garnish with a sprig of flat leaf parsley.

COOK'S TIP

A flavoured butter can be used to complement a sandwich filling – for example, horseradish butter with beef, mustard butter with ham, lemon and dill butter with fish. To make these just beat the chosen flavouring into the softened butter with some seasoning. Other useful flavourings for butter are: anchovy or curry paste, garlic, herbs, Tabasco or chilli. These butters can also be used in open sandwiches.

Spiced Chicken Livers

Chicken livers can be bought frozen, but make sure that you defrost them thoroughly before using. Serve as a first course or light meal along with a mixed salad and garlic bread.

Serves 4

INGREDIENTS
350 g/12 oz chicken livers
115 g/4 oz/1 cup plain flour
2.5 ml/½ tsp ground coriander
2.5 ml/½ tsp ground cumin
2.5 ml/½ tsp ground cardamom seeds
1.25 ml/¼ tsp ground paprika
1.25 ml/¼ tsp ground nutmeg
90 ml/6 tbsp olive oil
salt and freshly ground black pepper
garlic bread, to serve

chicken livers

olive oil

flour

coriander

cardamom seeds

cumin

paprika

nutmeg

1 Dry the chicken livers on paper towels, removing any unwanted pieces. Cut the large livers in half and leave the smaller ones whole.

2 Mix the flour with all the spices and the seasoning.

3 Coat the first batch of livers with spiced flour, separating each piece. Heat the oil in a large frying pan and fry the livers in small batches. (This helps to keep the oil temperature high and prevents the flour from becoming soggy.)

4 Fry quickly, stirring frequently, until crispy. Keep warm and repeat with the remaining livers. Serve immediately with warm garlic bread.

Chilli Beef Tacos

A taco is a soft wheat or corn tortilla wrapped around a spicy warm savoury filling – you could describe it as a Mexican sandwich.

Makes 4

INGREDIENTS
15 ml/1 tbsp oil
1 small onion, chopped
2 garlic cloves, chopped
175 g/6 oz/¾ cup minced
    beef
7 ml/½ tbsp flour
200 g/7 oz can tomatoes
7 ml/½ tbsp Jalapeño peppers, finely
    chopped
salt
4 wheat or corn tortillas
45 ml/3 tbsp soured cream
½ avocado, peeled, stoned
    and sliced
1 tomato, sliced
Tomato Salsa, to serve (optional)

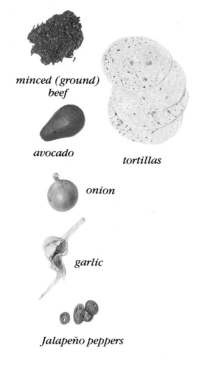

minced (ground)
beef

avocado

tortillas

onion

garlic

Jalapeño peppers

1 Heat the oil in a frying-pan (skillet), add the onion and fry until softened. Add the garlic and beef and cook, stirring so that the meat is broken up as it seals.

2 Stir in the flour, then add the canned tomatoes, peppers and salt to taste.

3 Heat the tortillas one at a time in a medium-hot lightly oiled pan.

4 Spread a spoonful of the meat mixture over each tortilla.

5 Top each tortilla with some soured cream and avocado and tomato slices. Roll up and eat immediately with Tomato Salsa if liked.

Stilton Burger

Slightly more up-market than the traditional burger, this tasty recipe contains a delicious surprise. The lightly melted Stilton cheese encased in a crunchy burger is absolutely delicious.

Serves 4

INGREDIENTS
450 g/1 lb/4 cups minced beef
1 onion, finely chopped
1 celery stick, chopped
5 ml/1 tsp dried mixed herbs
5 ml/1 tsp prepared mustard
50 g/2 oz/½ cup crumbled Stilton
    cheese
4 burger buns
salt and freshly ground black pepper

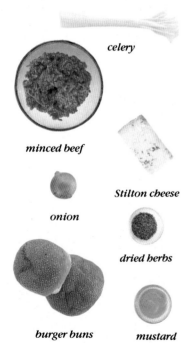

celery

minced beef

Stilton cheese

onion

dried herbs

burger buns   mustard

1 Place the minced beef in a bowl together with the onion and celery. Season well.

2 Stir in the herbs and mustard, bringing them together to form a firm mixture.

3 Divide the mixture into eight equal portions. Place four on a chopping board and flatten each one slightly.

4 Place the crumbled cheese in the centre of each.

5 Flatten the remaining mixture and place on top. Mould the mixture together encasing the crumbled cheese and shape into four burgers.

6 Grill under a medium heat for 10 minutes, turning once or until cooked through. Split the burger buns and place a burger inside each. Serve with salad and mustard pickle.

Fritters

A variation on beef patties, coated in batter and lightly fried, this tasty alternative need only be served with a light salad to provide a substantial snack.

Serves 4

INGREDIENTS
FOR THE PATTIES
225 g/8 oz/2 cups minced beef
1 onion, grated
10 ml/2 tsp chopped fresh oregano
50 g/2 oz/½ cup canned sweetcorn, drained
5 ml/1 tsp mustard
115 g/4 oz/2 cups fresh white breadcrumbs
oil for deep-frying
salt and freshly ground black pepper

FOR THE BATTER
115 g/4 oz/1 cup plain flour
60 ml/2 fl oz/¼ cup warm water
40 g/1½ oz/3 tbsp melted butter
60 ml/2 fl oz/¼ cup cold water
1 egg white

minced beef

onion

sweetcorn

butter

breadcrumbs

oregano

mustard

1 For the patties, place the minced beef in a bowl and mash with a fork. Add the onion, oregano, sweetcorn, mustard and breadcrumbs. Season well.

2 Form into eight round patties with lightly floured hands.

3 For the batter, sift the flour into a bowl and stir in the warm water and melted butter. Mix to a smooth batter with the cold water. Whisk the egg white until peaking and fold into the mixture.

4 Heat the oil for deep-frying to 160°C/325°F. Dip the patties into the batter to coat and fry two at a time in the oil. Drain on absorbent kitchen paper and serve with tomato pickle and green salad.

Nachos

The addition of minced beef to this traditional starter demonstrates the use of mince as an excellent extender, creating a filling, quick meal.

Serves 4

INGREDIENTS
225 g/8 oz/2 cups minced beef
2 red chillies, chopped
3 spring onions, chopped
175 g/6 oz nachos
300 ml/½ pint/1¼ cups soured cream
50 g/2 oz/½ cup freshly grated
   Cheddar cheese
salt and freshly ground black pepper

chilli

cheese

minced beef

nachos

cream

spring onions

1 Dry-fry the minced beef and chillies in a large pan for 10 minutes, stirring all the time.

2 Add the spring onions, season and cook for a further 5 minutes.

3 Arrange the nachos in four individual flameproof dishes.

4 Spoon on the minced beef mixture, top with soured cream and grated cheese. Grill under a medium heat for 5 minutes.

Sardines with Warm Herb Salsa

Plain grilling is the very best way to cook fresh sardines; served with this luscious herb salsa the only other essential item is fresh, crusty bread, to mop up the tasty juices.

Serves 4

12–16 fresh sardines
oil for brushing
juice of 1 lemon

FOR THE SALSA
15 ml/1 tbsp butter
4 spring onions, chopped
1 garlic clove, finely chopped
30 ml/2 tbsp finely chopped
   fresh parsley
30 ml/2 tbsp finely snipped
   fresh chives
30 ml/2 tbsp finely chopped
   fresh basil
30 ml/2 tbsp green olive paste
10 ml/2 tsp balsamic vinegar
rind of 1 lemon
salt and freshly ground black
   pepper

sardines
butter
green olive paste
balsamic vinegar
lemon
spring onions
parsley
basil
chives

1 To clean the sardines, use small scissors to slit them along the belly and pull out the innards. Wipe the fish with kitchen paper and then arrange on a grill rack.

2 Melt the butter and gently sauté the spring onions and garlic for about 2 minutes, shaking the pan occasionally, until softened but not browned.

3 Add the lemon rind and remaining ingredients and keep warm on the edge of the barbecue. Do not allow to boil.

4 Brush the sardines lightly with oil and sprinkle with lemon juice, salt and pepper. Cook for about 2 minutes on each side, over a moderate heat. Serve with the warm salsa and crusty bread.

Deep-fried Whitebait

A spicy coating on these fish gives this favourite dish a crunchy bite.

Serves 6

INGREDIENTS
115 g/4 oz/1 cup plain flour
2.5 ml/ ½ tsp curry powder
2.5 ml/ ½ tsp ground ginger
2.5 ml/ ½ tsp ground cayenne pepper
pinch of salt
1.1 kg/2½ lb fresh or frozen
   whitebait, thawed
vegetable oil for deep-frying
lemon wedges, to garnish

cayenne pepper

ground ginger

curry powder

lemon

whitebait

1 Mix together all the dry ingredients in a large bowl.

2 Coat the fish in the flour.

3 Heat the oil in a large, heavy-based saucepan until it reaches a temperature of 190°C/375°F. Fry the whitebait in batches for 2–3 minutes until the fish is golden and crispy.

4 Drain well on absorbent kitchen paper. Serve hot garnished with lemon wedges.

English Muffins with Sole, Spinach and Mushrooms

English muffins, frozen spinach and a few mushrooms form the beginning of this nourishing fish course. Any flatfish will do, although sole works best of all.

Serves 2

INGREDIENTS

115 g/4 oz/½ cup butter, plus extra
    for buttering muffins
1 medium onion, chopped
115 g/4 oz brown button mushrooms,
    sliced
2 fresh thyme sprigs, chopped
275 g/10 oz frozen leaf spinach,
    thawed
1.5 kg/3 lb sole or plaice to yield
    675 g/1½ lb skinned fillet
2 white English muffins, split
60 ml/4 tbsp crème fraîche
salt and freshly ground black pepper

1 Heat 50 g/2 oz/4 tbsp of the butter in a saucepan and add the onion. Cook over a gentle heat until soft but not coloured.

2 Add the mushrooms and thyme, cover and cook for a further 2–3 minutes. Remove the lid and increase the heat to drive off excess moisture.

English muffins

spinach

crème fraîche

thyme

sole

onion

3 Using the back of a large spoon, press the thawed frozen spinach in a sieve to extract the moisture.

4 Heat a further 25 g/1 oz/2 tbsp butter in a saucepan, add the spinach, heat through and season to taste.

5 Melt the remaining butter in a large frying pan, season the fillets and, with skin side uppermost, cook for 4 minutes, turning once.

COOK'S TIP

Approximately half of the weight of flatfish is bone, so if buying your fish whole, ask the fishmonger to give you the correct weight of boned fish.

6 Toast and butter the muffins. Divide the fillets between them, top with spinach and a layer of mushrooms, then finish with a spoonful of crème fraîche.

Tostadas with Refried Beans

A tostada is a crisp, fried tortilla used as a base on which to pile the topping of your choice – a variation on a sandwich and a very tasty snack popular in Mexico and South America.

Makes 6

INGREDIENTS
30 ml/2 tbsp oil
1 onion, chopped
2 garlic cloves, chopped
2.5 ml/½ tsp chilli powder
425 g/15 oz can borlotti or pinto beans, drained
150 ml/5 fl oz/⅔ cup chicken stock
15 ml/1 tbsp tomato purée
30 ml/2 tbsp chopped fresh coriander
salt and pepper
6 wheat or corn tortillas
45 ml/3 tbsp Tomato Salsa
30 ml/2 tbsp soured cream
50 g/2 oz/½ cup grated Cheddar cheese
fresh coriander leaves, to garnish

beans

onion

tortillas

garlic

chilli powder

tomato purée

Cheddar cheese　*coriander*

1 Heat the oil in a pan and fry the onion until softened.

2 Add the garlic and chilli powder and fry for 1 minute, stirring.

3 Mix in the beans and mash very roughly with a potato masher.

4 Add the stock, tomato purée (paste), chopped coriander and seasoning to taste. Mix thoroughly and cook for a few minutes.

5 Fry the tortillas in hot oil for 1 minute, turning once, until crisp, then drain on kitchen paper.

TOMATO SALSA

Makes about 300 ml/10 fl oz/1¼ cups

1 small onion, chopped
1 garlic clove, crushed
2 fresh green chillies, seeded and
   finely chopped, or 5 ml/1 tsp
   bottled chopped chillies
450 g/1 lb tomatoes, skinned and
   chopped
salt
30 ml/2 tbsp chopped fresh coriander

Stir all the ingredients together until
well mixed.

6 Put a spoonful of refried beans on
each tostada, spoon over some Tomato
Salsa, then some soured cream, sprinkle
with grated Cheddar cheese and garnish
with coriander.

Cucumber and Alfalfa Tortillas

Wheat tortillas are extremely simple to prepare at home. Served with a crisp, fresh salsa, they make a marvellous light lunch or supper dish.

Serves 4

INGREDIENTS
225 g/8 oz/2 cups plain flour
pinch of salt
45 ml/3 tbsp olive oil
100 ml–150 ml/4–5 fl oz/½–⅔ cup
   warm water
lime wedges, to garnish

FOR THE SALSA
1 red onion, finely chopped
1 fresh red chilli, seeded and finely
   chopped
30 ml/2 tbsp chopped fresh dill or
   coriander
½ cucumber, peeled and chopped
175 g/6 oz alfalfa sprouts

FOR THE SAUCE
1 large avocado, peeled and stoned
juice of 1 lime
25 g/1 oz/2 tbsp soft goat's cheese
pinch of paprika

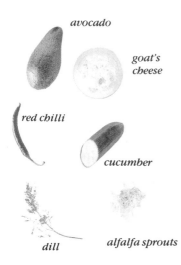

avocado

goat's cheese

red chilli

cucumber

dill   *alfalfa sprouts*

1 Mix all the salsa ingredients together in a bowl and set aside.

2 To make the sauce, place the avocado, lime juice and goat's cheese in a food processor or blender and blend until smooth. Place in a bowl and cover with clear film. Dust with paprika just before serving.

3 To make the tortillas, place the flour and salt in a food processor, add the oil and blend. Gradually add the water (the amount will vary depending on the type of flour). Stop adding water when a stiff dough has formed. Turn out onto a floured board and knead until smooth. Cover with a damp cloth.

4 Divide the mixture into 8 pieces. Knead each piece for a couple of minutes and form into a ball. Flatten and roll out each ball to a 23 cm/9 in circle.

5 Heat an ungreased heavy-based pan. Cook 1 tortilla at a time for about 30 seconds on each side. Place the cooked tortillas in a clean tea-towel and repeat until you have 8 tortillas.

6 To serve, spread each tortilla with a spoonful of avocado sauce, top with salsa and roll up. Garnish with lime wedges.

Pasta with Spinach and Anchovy Sauce

Deliciously earthy, this would make a good starter or light supper dish. Add some sultanas (golden raisins) to ring the changes!

Serves 4

INGREDIENTS

900 g/2 lb fresh spinach or 550 g/
   1¼ lb frozen leaf spinach, thawed
450 g/1 lb/4 cups angel hair pasta
salt
60 ml/4 tbsp olive oil
45 ml/3 tbsp pine nuts
2 garlic cloves, crushed
6 canned anchovy fillets or whole
   salted anchovies, drained and
   chopped
butter, for tossing the pasta

olive oil

pine nuts

spinach

anchovy fillets

garlic   *angel hair pasta*

1 Wash the spinach well and remove the tough stalks. Drain thoroughly. Place in a large saucepan with only the water that still clings to the leaves. Cover with a lid and cook over a high heat, shaking the pan occasionally, until the spinach is just wilted and still bright green. Drain.

2 Cook the pasta in plenty of boiling salted water according to the manufacturer's instructions.

3 Heat the oil in a saucepan and fry the pine nuts until golden. Remove with a perforated spoon. Add the garlic to the oil in the pan and fry until golden. Add the anchovies.

4 Stir in the spinach and cook for 2–3 minutes or until heated through. Stir in the pine nuts. Drain the pasta, toss in a little butter and turn into a warmed serving bowl. Top with the sauce and fork through roughly.

Cheese-stuffed Pears

These pears, with their scrumptious creamy topping, make a sublime dish when served with a simple salad.

Serves 4

INGREDIENTS
50 g/2 oz/¼ cup ricotta cheese
50 g/2 oz/¼ cup dolcelatte cheese
15 ml/1 tbsp honey
½ celery stick, finely sliced
8 green olives, pitted and roughly
    chopped
4 dates, stoned and cut into thin strips
pinch of paprika
4 ripe pears
150 ml/¼ pint/⅔ cup apple juice

honey

pear

apple juice

dates

dolcelatte

celery

olives

1 Preheat the oven to 200°C/400°F/ Gas 6. Place the ricotta in a bowl and crumble in the dolcelatte. Add the rest of the ingredients except for the pears and apple juice and mix well.

2 Halve the pears lengthwise and use a melon baller to remove the cores. Place in a ovenproof dish and divide the filling equally between them.

COOK'S TIP
Choose ripe pears in season such as Conference, William or Comice.

3 Pour in the apple juice and cover the dish with foil. Bake for 20 minutes or until the pears are tender.

4 Remove the foil and place the dish under a hot grill for 3 minutes. Serve immediately.

Sweet Potato Roulade

Sweet potato works particularly well as the base for this roulade. Serve in thin slices for a truly impressive dinner party dish.

Serves 6

INGREDIENTS

225 g/8 oz/1 cup low-fat soft cheese such as Quark
75 ml/5 tbsp low-fat yogurt
6–8 spring onions, finely sliced
30 ml/2 tbsp chopped brazil nuts, roasted
450 g/1 lb sweet potatoes, peeled and cubed
12 allspice berries, crushed
4 eggs, separated
50 g/2 oz/¼ cup Edam cheese, finely grated
salt and freshly ground black pepper
15 ml/1 tbsp sesame seeds

soft cheese

sesame seeds

sweet potato

yogurt

Edam

brazil nuts

spring onions

peppercorns

egg

I Preheat the oven to 200°C/400°F/ Gas 6. Grease and line a 33 × 25 cm/ 13 × 10 in Swiss roll tin with non-stick baking paper, snipping the corners with scissors to fit.

2 In a small bowl, mix together the soft cheese, yogurt, spring onions and brazil nuts. Set aside.

3 Boil or steam the sweet potato until tender. Drain well. Place in a food processor with the allspice and blend until smooth. Spoon into a bowl and stir in the egg yolks and Edam. Season to taste.

4 Whisk the egg whites until stiff but not dry. Fold ⅓ of the egg whites into the sweet potatoes to lighten the mixture before gently folding in the rest.

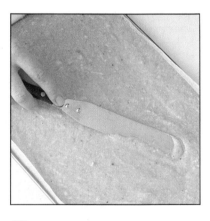

5 Pour into the prepared tin, tipping it to get the mixture right into the corners. Smooth gently with a palette knife and cook in the oven for 10–15 minutes.

COOK'S TIP

Choose the orange-fleshed variety of sweet potato for the most striking colour.

6 Meanwhile, lay a large sheet of greaseproof paper on a clean tea-towel and sprinkle with the sesame seeds. When the roulade is cooked, tip it onto the paper, trim the edges and roll it up. Leave to cool. When cool carefully unroll, spread with the filling and roll up again. Cut into slices to serve.

Buckwheat Couscous with Goat's Cheese and Celery

Couscous is made from cracked, partially cooked wheat, which is dried and then reconstituted in water or stock. It tastes of very little by itself, but carries the flavour of other ingredients very well.

Serves 4

INGREDIENTS
1 egg
30 ml/2 tbsp olive oil
1 small bunch spring onions, chopped
2 celery sticks, sliced
175 g/6 oz/1 cup couscous
75 g/3 oz/½ cup buckwheat
45 ml/3 tbsp chopped fresh parsley
finely grated zest of ½ lemon
25 g/1 oz/¼ cup chopped walnuts, toasted
150 g/5 oz strongly flavoured goat's cheese
salt and freshly ground black pepper
Cos lettuce leaves, to serve

buckwheat
celery
egg
goat's cheese
parsley
walnuts

1 Boil the egg for 10 minutes, cool, peel and set aside. Heat the oil in a saucepan and add the spring onions and celery. Cook for 2–3 minutes until soft.

2 Add the couscous and buckwheat and cover with 600 ml/1 pint/2½ cups of boiling salted water. Cover and return to a simmer. Remove from the heat and allow the couscous to soften and absorb the water for about 3 minutes. Transfer the mixture to a large bowl.

3 Grate the hard-boiled egg finely into a small bowl and add the chopped parsley, lemon zest and walnuts. Fold into the couscous, season, and crumble in the goat's cheese. Mix well and then turn out into a shallow dish. Serve warm with a salad of Cos lettuce.

VARIATION
Couscous is ideal as a filling for pitta breads when accompanied with crisp salad leaves.

Stuffed Garlic Mushrooms with a Parsley Crust

These garlic mushrooms are perfect for dinner parties, or you could serve them in larger portions as a light supper dish with a green salad. Try them stuffed with a healthy dose of freshly chopped parsley.

Serves 4

INGREDIENTS
350 g/12 oz large mushrooms,
   stems removed
3 garlic cloves, crushed
175 g/6 oz/¾ cup butter, softened
50 g/2 oz/1 cup fresh white
   breadcrumbs
50 g/2 oz/1 cup fresh parsley,
   chopped
1 egg, beaten
salt and cayenne pepper
8 cherry tomatoes, to garnish

1 Preheat the oven to 190°C/375°F/ Gas 5. Arrange the mushrooms cup side uppermost on a baking tray. Mix together the crushed garlic and butter in a small bowl and divide 115 g/4 oz/½ cup of the butter between the mushrooms.

parsley

butter   *egg*

garlic

mushrooms

breadcrumbs

2 Heat the remaining butter in a frying pan and lightly fry the breadcrumbs until golden brown. Place the chopped parsley in a bowl, add the breadcrumbs, season to taste and mix well.

3 Stir in the egg and use the mixture to fill the mushroom caps. Bake for 10–15 minutes until the topping has browned and the mushrooms have softened. Garnish with quartered tomatoes.

COOK'S TIP
If you are planning ahead, stuffed mushrooms can be prepared up to 12 hours in advance and kept in the fridge before baking.

MEAT

When the family's in a feeding **frenzy**, prove you can put a meal on the table in under half an hour with these **simple** and satisfying meat dishes. Stir-fries are the obvious solution – and you'll find some **wonderful** ways of using your wok to its full potential. Dishes like Sizzling Beef with

IN MINUTES

Celeriac Straw, Glazed Lamb, and Stir-fried Duck with Blueberries are **tasty** and **colourful** as well as being quick, while the grill offers equally **delicious** options such as Mexican Beef Burgers, Pork and Pineapple Satay, and Chicken Liver Kebabs.

Sizzling Beef with Celeriac Straw

The crisp celeriac matchsticks look like fine pieces of straw when cooked and have a mild celery-like flavour that is quite delicious.

Serves 4

INGREDIENTS
450 g/1 lb celeriac
150 ml/¼ pint/⅔ cup vegetable oil
1 red pepper
6 spring onions
450 g/1 lb rump steak
60 ml/4 tbsp beef stock
30 ml/2 tbsp sherry vinegar
10 ml/2 tsp Worcestershire sauce
10 ml/2 tsp tomato purée
salt and freshly ground black pepper

rump steak

celeriac

spring onions

pepper

1 Peel the celeriac and then cut it into fine matchsticks, using a cleaver.

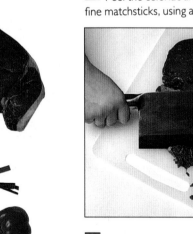

4 Chop the beef into strips, across the grain of the meat.

5 Heat the wok, and then add the remaining oil. When the oil is hot, stir-fry the chopped spring onions and red pepper for 2–3 minutes.

2 Heat the wok, then add two-thirds of the oil. When the oil is hot, fry the celeriac matchsticks in batches until golden brown and crispy. Drain well on kitchen towels.

3 Chop the red pepper and the spring onions into 2.5 cm/1 in lengths, using diagonal cuts.

6 Add the beef strips and stir-fry for a further 3–4 minutes until well browned. Add the stock, vinegar, Worcestershire sauce and tomato purée. Season well and serve with the celeriac straw.

Sukiyaki-style Beef

This Japanese dish is a meal in itself; the recipe incorporates all the traditional elements – meat, vegetables, noodles and beancurd. If you want to do it all properly, eat the meal with chopsticks, and a spoon to collect the stock juices.

Serves 4

INGREDIENTS
450 g/1 lb thick rump steak
200 g/7 oz Japanese rice noodles
15 ml/1 tbsp shredded suet
200 g/7 oz hard beancurd, cut
   into cubes
8 shitake mushrooms, trimmed
2 medium leeks, sliced into 2.5 cm/
   1 in lengths
90 g/3½ oz baby spinach, to serve

FOR THE STOCK
15 ml/1 tbsp caster sugar
90 ml/6 tbsp rice wine
45 ml/3 tbsp dark soy sauce
125 ml/4 fl oz/½ cup water

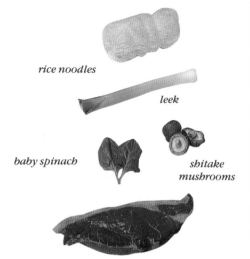

rice noodles

leek

baby spinach

shitake
mushrooms

rump steak

1 Cut the beef into thin slices.

2 Blanch the noodles in boiling water for 2 minutes. Strain well.

3 Mix together all the stock ingredients in a bowl.

4 Heat the wok, then add the suet. When the suet is melted, stir-fry the beef for 2–3 minutes until it is cooked, but still pink in colour.

5 Pour the stock over the beef.

6 Add the remaining ingredients and cook for 4 minutes, until the leeks are tender. Serve a selection of the different ingredients, with a few baby spinach leaves, to each person.

Tex-Mex Burgers in Tortillas

If you fancy a change from ordinary burgers in baps, try this easy Tex-Mex version. Serve with a crisp green salad.

Serves 4

500 g/1¹/₄ lb lean minced beef
1 small onion, finely chopped
1 small green pepper, seeded
  and finely chopped
1 garlic clove, crushed
oil for brushing
4 fresh tortillas
chopped fresh coriander, to
  garnish

FOR THE GUACAMOLE SAUCE
2 ripe avocados
1 garlic clove, crushed
2 tomatoes, chopped
juice of 1 lime or lemon
¹/₂ small green chilli, chopped
30 ml/2 tbsp chopped fresh
  coriander
salt and freshly ground black
  pepper

minced beef

green pepper

green chilli

lime   *coriander*

onion

garlic   *avocados*

oil

COOK'S TIP
The guacamole sauce should be made not more than about an hour before it's needed, or it will start to brown. If it has to be left to stand, sprinkle a little extra lime juice over the top and stir it in just before serving.

1 Mix together the minced beef, onion, pepper and garlic, and then season well with salt and pepper.

2 Using your hands, shape the mixture into four large, round burgers and brush them with oil.

3 For the guacamole sauce, cut the avocados in half, remove the stone and scoop out the flesh.

4 Mash the avocado flesh roughly and mix in the garlic, tomatoes, lime juice, chilli and coriander. Adjust the seasoning with salt and pepper.

5 Cook the burgers on a medium hot barbecue for 8–10 minutes, turning once, until golden brown.

6 When the burgers are almost cooked, heat the tortillas quickly on the barbecue for about 15 seconds each side and then place a spoonful of guacamole and a burger on each. Wrap the tortilla round the filling to serve, garnished with coriander.

Mexican Beef Burgers

Nothing beats the flavour and quality of a home-made burger. This version is from Mexico and is seasoned with cumin and fresh coriander.

Makes 4

INGREDIENTS
4 corn cobs
50 g/2 oz/1 cup stale white
   breadcrumbs
90 ml/6 tbsp milk
1 small onion, finely chopped
5 ml/1 tsp ground cumin
2.5 ml/½ tsp cayenne pepper
2.5 ml/½ tsp celery salt
45 ml/3 tbsp chopped fresh coriander
900 g/2 lb lean minced beef
4 sesame buns
60 ml/4 tbsp mayonnaise
4 tomato slices
½ iceberg lettuce or other leaves
   such as frisée or Webb's
salt and freshly ground black pepper
1 large packet corn chips,
   to serve

iceberg lettuce

minced beef

onion

tomatoes

sesame buns

white bread

1 Bring a large saucepan of water to the boil, add a good pinch of salt and cook the corn cobs for 15 minutes.

2 Combine the breadcrumbs, milk, onion, cumin, cayenne, celery salt and fresh coriander in a large bowl.

3 Add the beef and mix by hand until evenly blended.

4 Divide the mixture into four portions and flatten between sheets of clear film.

5 Preheat a moderate grill and cook for 10 minutes for medium burgers or 15 minutes for well-done burgers, turning once during the cooking time.

6 Split and toast the buns, spread with mayonnaise and sandwich the burgers with the tomato slices, lettuce leaves and seasoning. Serve with corn chips and the corn cobs.

COOK'S TIP
If planning ahead, freeze the burgers between sheets of greaseproof paper or clear film. Covered, they will keep well for up to twelve weeks. Defrost before cooking.

Black Pepper Beef Steaks with Red Wine Sauce

Every cook should know how to rustle up a pan-steak dinner with an impressive sauce to go with it. Black peppercorns follow the French tradition and combine well with the other bold flavours in the sauce.

Serves 4

INGREDIENTS

350 g/12 oz oven-ready chips or
 4 jacket potatoes
15 ml/1 tbsp black peppercorns
4 × 225 g/8 oz sirloin or rump steaks
15 ml/1 tbsp olive oil
chopped fresh parsley, to garnish
150 g/5 oz green salad, to serve

FOR THE RED WINE SAUCE

120 ml/4 fl oz/½ cup red wine
75 g/3 oz dark open-cap mushrooms,
 sliced
10 g/¼ oz dried morel mushrooms,
 soaked (optional)
300 ml/½ pint/1¼ cups beef stock
15 ml/1 tbsp cornflour
5 ml/1 tsp Dijon mustard
2.5 ml/½ tsp anchovy essence
 (optional)
10 ml/2 tsp red wine vinegar
25 g/1 oz/2 tbsp butter
salt and freshly ground black pepper

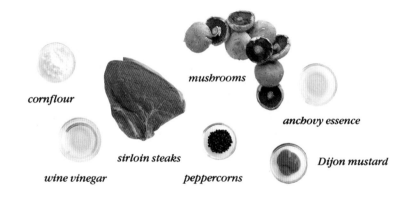

cornflour

mushrooms

anchovy essence

sirloin steaks

Dijon mustard

wine vinegar

peppercorns

1 Preheat the oven according to the instructions on the packet for oven-ready chips and cook. Alternatively, if you require jacket potatoes, cook in the microwave on high power (100%) for 8 minutes and then place in a preheated oven at 190°C/375°F/Gas 6 for a further 10 minutes. Crush the peppercorns using a pestle and mortar, or coarsely grind in a pepper mill. Coat both sides of the steak with the crushed peppercorns and brush lightly with olive oil.

2 Heat a heavy bare metal frying pan. Fry the steaks for 6–8 minutes for medium-rare or 12–16 minutes for well-done steaks, turning once throughout the cooking time.

3 Transfer the steaks to a plate, cover and keep warm. Pour off the excess fat from the frying pan, return to the heat and brown the sediment. To make the sauce, add the wine and stir with a flat wooden spoon to loosen the sediment.

4 Add the mushrooms to the frying pan with the dried morel, if using. Pour in the stock and cook briefly to soften.

5 Measure the cornflour, mustard and anchovy essence, if using, into a small bowl. Add 30 ml/2 tbsp of water and blend together to a smooth paste. Add to the frying pan, stirring continuously, and simmer to thicken.

COOK'S TIP

Non-stick frying pans are not suitable for making pan sauces. Only bare metal pans allow a rich sediment to form, which is essential to the flavour of a good sauce.

6 Add the vinegar to taste. Toss in the butter and swirl the contents in the pan with a circular motion until the butter has melted. Season to taste, return the steaks and heat through. Arrange the steaks on four plates, pour over the sauce and sprinkle with parsley. Serve with chips or baked potatoes and a green salad.

Spicy Beef

Promoting a fast-growing trend in worldwide cuisine, the wok is used in this recipe to produce a colourful and healthy meal.

Serves 4

INGREDIENTS
15 ml/1 tbsp oil
450 g/1 lb/4 cups minced beef
2.5 cm/1 in fresh root ginger, sliced
5 ml/1 tsp Chinese five-spice powder
1 red chilli, sliced
50 g/2 oz mangetout
1 red pepper, seeded and chopped
1 carrot, sliced
115 g/4 oz beansprouts
15 ml/1 tbsp sesame oil

pepper

mangetout

sesame oil

five-spice

beansprouts

minced beef

ginger

carrot

chilli

1 Heat the oil in a wok until almost smoking. Add the minced beef and cook for 3 minutes, stirring all the time.

2 Add the ginger, Chinese five-spice powder and chilli. Cook for 1 minute.

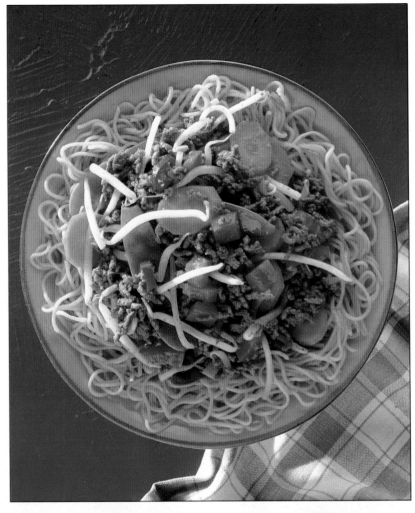

3 Add the mangetout, pepper and carrot and cook for a further 3 minutes, stirring continuously.

4 Add the beansprouts and sesame oil and cook for a final 2 minutes. Serve immediately with noodles.

Veal Escalopes with Artichokes

Artichokes are very hard to prepare fresh, so use canned artichoke hearts, instead – they have an excellent flavour and are simple to use.

Serves 4

INGREDIENTS
450 g/1 lb veal escalopes
1 shallot
115 g/4 oz smoked bacon,
    finely chopped
1 × 400 g/14 oz can of artichoke
    hearts in brine, drained and
    quartered
150 ml/¼ pint/⅔ cup veal stock
3 fresh rosemary sprigs
60 ml/4 tbsp double cream
salt and freshly ground black pepper
fresh rosemary sprigs, to garnish

veal escalopes

double cream

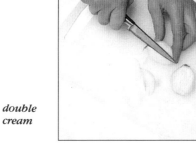

artichoke hearts

1 Cut the veal into thin slices.

2 Using a sharp knife, cut the shallot into thin slices.

3 Heat the wok, then add the bacon. Stir-fry for 2 minutes. When the fat is released, add the veal and shallot and stir-fry for 3–4 minutes.

4 Add the artichokes and stir-fry for 1 minute. Stir in the stock and rosemary and simmer for 2 minutes. Stir in the double cream, season with salt and pepper and serve garnished with sprigs of fresh rosemary.

Glazed Lamb

Lemon and honey make a classically good combination in sweet dishes, and this lamb recipe shows how well they work together in savoury dishes, too. Serve with a fresh mixed salad to complete this delicious dish.

Serves 4

INGREDIENTS
450 g/1 lb boneless lean lamb
15 ml/1 tbsp grapeseed oil
175 g/6 oz mangetout peas, topped
   and tailed
3 spring onions, sliced
30 ml/2 tbsp clear honey
juice of half a lemon
30 ml/2 tbsp fresh coriander, chopped
15 ml/1 tbsp sesame seeds
salt and freshly ground black pepper

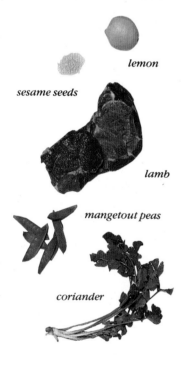

lemon

sesame seeds

lamb

mangetout peas

coriander

1 Using a sharp knife, cut the lamb into thin strips.

2 Heat the wok, then add the oil. When the oil is hot, stir-fry the lamb until browned all over. Remove from the wok and keep warm.

3 Add the mangetout peas and spring onions to the hot wok and stir-fry for 30 seconds.

4 Return the lamb to the wok and add the honey, lemon juice, coriander and sesame seeds, and season well. Bring to the boil and bubble for 1 minute until the lamb is well coated in the honey mixture.

Minted Lamb

Ask your butcher to remove the bone from a leg of lamb – it is sometimes called a butterfly leg of lamb – so that the meat can be sliced easily.

Serves 4

INGREDIENTS
450 g/1 lb boneless leg of lamb
30 ml/2 tbsp fresh mint, chopped
½ lemon
300 ml/½ pint/1¼ cups natural low-fat yogurt
15 ml/1 tbsp sunflower oil
salt and freshly ground black pepper
lemon wedges and fresh mint sprigs, to garnish

lemon

sunflower oil

mint

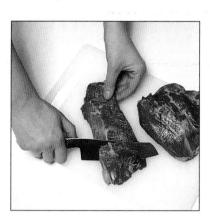

1 Using a sharp knife, cut the lamb into 6 mm/¼-in thick slices. Place in a bowl.

2 Sprinkle half the mint over the lamb, season well with salt and pepper and leave for 20 minutes.

3 Roughly cut up the lemon and place in the food processor. Process until finely chopped. Empty it into a bowl, then stir in the yogurt and remaining mint.

4 Heat the wok, then add the oil. When the oil is hot, add the lamb and stir-fry for 4–5 minutes until cooked. Serve with the yogurt dressing garnished with a lemon wedge and fresh mint sprigs.

Mixed Grill Skewers with Horseradish Butter

A hearty, classic selection of meats all cooked together on a skewer, drizzled with a delicious hot horseradish butter. Vary the meats as you like, but keep them all about the same thickness so they cook evenly.

Serves 4

4 small lamb noisettes, about
  2.5 cm/1 in thick
4 lamb's kidneys
4 streaky bacon rashers
8 cherry tomatoes
8 chipolata sausages
12–16 bay leaves

FOR THE HORSERADISH BUTTER:
30 ml/2 tbsp horseradish relish
45 ml/3 tbsp melted butter
salt and freshly ground black
  pepper

streaky bacon rashers

chipolata sausages

lamb's kidneys

lamb noisettes

melted butter

horseradish sauce

bay leaves

cherry tomatoes

COOK'S TIP
Try using your favourite mustard instead of horseradish, for a tangy mustard butter.

1 Trim any excess fat from the lamb noisettes. Halve the kidneys and remove the cores with scissors.

2 Cut each rasher of bacon in half across the middle and wrap each piece around a tomato or a half-kidney.

3 Thread the lamb, kidneys, tomatoes, chipolatas and bay leaves on to four long metal skewers.

4 Stir together the horseradish and butter until thoroughly mixed.

5 Brush a little of the horseradish butter over the meat and sprinkle with salt and pepper.

6 Cook on a medium-hot barbecue for 12–15 minutes, turning occasionally, until golden brown and thoroughly cooked. Serve with the remaining horseradish butter poured over.

Pan-fried Pork with Peaches and Green Peppercorns

When peaches are in season, consider this speedy pork dish, brought alive with green peppercorns.

Serves 4

INGREDIENTS

400 g/14 oz/2 cups long-grain rice
1 litre/1¾ pints/4 cups chicken stock
4 × 200 g/7 oz pork chops or
 loin pieces
30 ml/2 tbsp vegetable oil
30 ml/2 tbsp dark rum or sherry
1 small onion, chopped
3 large ripe peaches
15 ml/1 tbsp green peppercorns
15 ml/1 tbsp white wine vinegar
salt and freshly ground black pepper

onion

pork chops

dark rum

oil

green peppercorns

white wine vinegar

peaches

VARIATION

If peaches are not ripe when picked, they can be difficult to peel. Only tree ripened fruit is suitable for peeling. If fresh peaches are out of season, a can of sliced peaches may be used instead.

1 Cover the rice with 900 ml/1½ pints/3¾ cups chicken stock. Stir, bring to a simmer and cook uncovered for 15 minutes. Switch off the heat and cover for 5 minutes. Meanwhile, season the pork with a twist of black pepper. Heat a large bare metal frying pan and moisten the pork with 15 ml/1 tbsp oil. Cook for 12 minutes, turning once.

2 Transfer the meat to a warm plate. Pour off the excess fat from the pan and return to the heat. Allow the sediment to sizzle and brown, add the rum or sherry and loosen the sediment with a flat wooden spoon. Pour the pan contents over the meat, cover and keep warm. Wipe the pan clean.

3 Heat the remaining vegetable oil in the pan and soften the onion over a steady heat.

4 Cover the peaches with boiling water to loosen the skins, then peel, slice and discard the stones.

5 Add the peaches and peppercorns to the onion and coat for 3–4 minutes, until they begin to soften.

6 Add the remaining chicken stock and simmer briefly. Return the pork and meat juices to the pan, sharpen with vinegar, and season to taste. Serve with the rice.

Stir-fried Pork with Mustard

Fry the apples for this dish very carefully, because they will disintegrate if they are overcooked.

Serves 4

INGREDIENTS
500 g/1¼ lb pork fillet
1 tart apple, such as Granny Smith
40 g/1½ oz/3 tbsp unsalted butter
15 ml/1 tbsp caster sugar
1 small onion, finely chopped
30 ml/2 tbsp Calvados or
    other brandy
15 ml/1 tbsp Meaux or coarse-grain
    mustard
150 ml/¼ pint/⅔ cup double cream
30 ml/2 tbsp fresh parsley, chopped
salt and freshly ground black pepper
flat-leaf parsley sprigs, to garnish

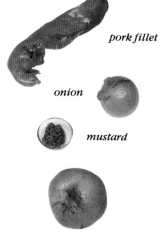

pork fillet

onion

mustard

apple

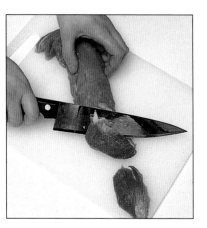

1 Cut the pork fillet into thin slices.

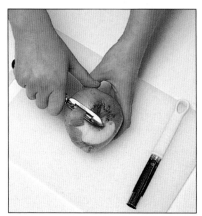

2 Peel and core the apple. Cut it into thick slices.

3 Heat the wok, then add half the butter. When the butter is hot, add the apple slices, sprinkle over the sugar, and stir-fry for 2–3 minutes. Remove the apple and set aside. Wipe out the wok with kitchen towels.

4 Heat the wok, then add the remaining butter and stir-fry the pork fillet and onion together for 2–3 minutes, until the pork is golden and the onion has begun to soften.

5 Stir in the Calvados or other brandy and boil until it is reduced by half. Stir in the mustard.

6 Add the cream and simmer for about 1 minute, then stir in the parsley. Serve garnished with sprigs of flat-leaf parsley.

Pork and Pineapple Satay

This variation on the classic satay has added pineapple, but keeps the traditional coconut and peanut sauce.

COOK'S TIP

If you cannot buy coconut milk, look out for creamed coconut in a block. Dissolve a 50 g/2 oz piece in 150 ml/¼ pint/⅔ cup boiling water and use as below.

Serves 4

500 g/1¼ lb pork fillet
1 small onion, chopped
1 garlic clove, chopped
60 ml/4 tbsp soy sauce
finely grated rind of ½ lemon
5 ml/1 tsp ground cumin
5 ml/1 tsp ground coriander
5 ml/1 tsp ground turmeric
5 ml/1 tsp dark muscovado sugar
225 g/8 oz can pineapple chunks, or 1 small fresh pineapple, peeled and diced
salt and freshly ground black pepper

FOR THE SATAY SAUCE
175 ml/6 fl oz/¾ cup coconut milk
115 g/4 oz/6 tbsp crunchy peanut butter
1 garlic clove, crushed
10 ml/2 tsp soy sauce
5 ml/1 tsp dark muscovado sugar

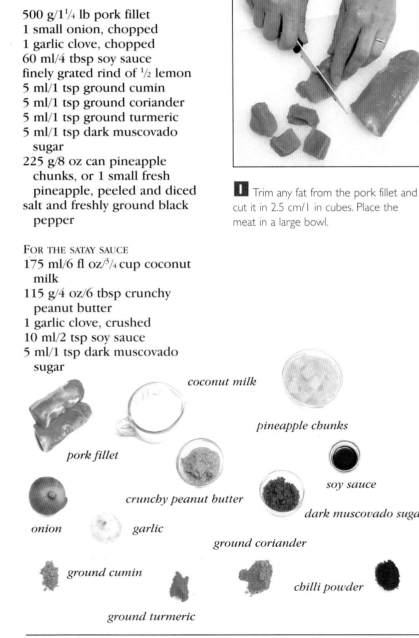

coconut milk

pineapple chunks

pork fillet

crunchy peanut butter

soy sauce

dark muscovado sugar

onion   garlic

ground coriander

ground cumin

chilli powder

ground turmeric

1 Trim any fat from the pork fillet and cut it in 2.5 cm/1 in cubes. Place the meat in a large bowl.

2 Place the onion, garlic, soy sauce, lemon rind, spices and sugar in a blender or food processor. Add two pieces of pineapple and process until the mixture is almost smooth.

3 Add the paste to the pork, tossing well to coat evenly. Thread the pieces of pork on to bamboo skewers, with the remaining pineapple.

4 For the sauce, pour the coconut milk into a small pan and stir in the peanut butter. Stir in the remaining sauce ingredients and heat gently over the barbecue, stirring until smooth and hot. Cover and keep warm on the edge of the barbecue.

5 Cook the pork and pineapple skewers on a medium-hot barbecue for 10–12 minutes, turning occasionally, until golden brown and thoroughly cooked. Serve with the satay sauce.

Sausage Popovers

This quick dish is always well received. The mashed potatoes and gravy make it a filling and tasty meal.

Serves 4

INGREDIENTS
900 g/2 lb floury potatoes
450 g/1 lb pork or beef sausages or
    chipolatas
1 × 400 g/14 oz can petit pois, to
    serve (optional)

FOR THE BATTER
3 eggs
300 ml/½ pint/1¼ cups whole milk
115 g/4 oz/1 cup plain flour
salt and freshly ground black pepper

FOR THE ONION GRAVY
30 ml/2 tbsp vegetable oil
1 medium onion, chopped
15 ml/1 tbsp plain flour
200 ml/7 fl oz/scant 1 cup chicken or
    beef stock
5 ml/1 tsp balsamic or red
    wine vinegar

onion

eggs   *flour*

sausages

1 Cut the potatoes into small pieces to reduce the cooking time. Bring them to the boil in salted water and cook for 15 minutes. Preheat the oven to 230°C/450°F/Gas 8 and partly cook the sausages or chipolatas for 5 minutes.

2 To make the batter, beat the eggs together with a good pinch of salt and a twist of black pepper in a bowl.

3 Add half of the milk and all of the flour and stir into a smooth batter. Pour in the remaining milk and combine evenly.

4 Arrange the partly cooked sausages in a shallow muffin tray.

5 Pour in the batter, transfer to the preheated oven and bake for 10 minutes until well risen and golden.

COOK'S TIP

When making risen batter dishes, it is important to put the mixture into a fiercely hot oven.

6 To make the onion gravy, heat the vegetable oil in a large saucepan and brown the onion for 3–4 minutes, then add the flour. Remove from the heat, gradually stir in the stock and sharpen with vinegar to taste. Mash the potatoes and serve with the popovers, gravy and petit pois if desired.

Wild Mushroom Rösti with Bacon and Eggs

Dried ceps or porcini mushrooms, commonly found in Italian delicatessens, are a good substitute for fresh. Cook them in a potato rösti and serve with bacon and a fried egg for breakfast or a lazy supper.

Serves 4

INGREDIENTS
675 g/1½ lb floury potatoes, peeled
10 g/¼ oz dried ceps or porcini
   mushrooms
2 fresh thyme sprigs, chopped
30 ml/2 tbsp chopped fresh parsley
60 ml/4 tbsp vegetable oil, for frying
4 × 115 g/4 oz gammon or
   unsmoked bacon
pinch of salt
4 eggs, to serve
1 bunch watercress, to serve

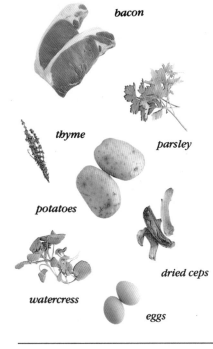

bacon

thyme

parsley

potatoes

dried ceps

watercress

eggs

COOK'S TIP

A large rösti can be made in a non-stick frying pan. Allow 12 minutes to cook. Half-way through the cooking time, invert the rösti on a large plate and slide back into the pan.

1 Bring the potatoes to the boil in a large saucepan of salted water and cook for 5 minutes.

2 Cover the mushrooms with boiling water to soften, then chop roughly.

3 Drain the potatoes, allow them to cool and grate them coarsely. Add the mushrooms, thyme and parsley and combine together well.

4 Heat 30 ml/2 tbsp of the oil in a frying pan, spoon in the rösti mixture in heaps and flatten. Fry for 6 minutes, turning once during cooking.

5 Preheat a moderate grill and cook the gammon or bacon slices until they sizzle at the edges.

6 Heat the remaining oil in a frying pan and fry the eggs as you like them. Serve the rösti together with the eggs and bacon and a watercress salad.

Indonesian Pork and Peanut Saté

These delicious skewers of pork are popular street food in Indonesia. They are quick to make and eat.

Serves 4

INGREDIENTS
400 g/14 oz/2 cups long-grain rice
450 g/1 lb lean pork
pinch of salt
2 limes, quartered, to garnish
115 g/4 oz green salad, to serve

FOR THE BASTE AND DIP
15 ml/1 tbsp vegetable oil
1 small onion, chopped
1 garlic clove, crushed
2.5 ml/½ tsp hot chilli sauce
15 ml/1 tbsp sugar
30 ml/2 tbsp soy sauce
30 ml/2 tbsp lemon or lime juice
75 ml/5 tbsp water
2.5 ml/½ tsp anchovy essence
   (optional)
60 ml/4 tbsp smooth peanut butter

lemon

lime

rice

peanut butter

pork

garlic

chilli sauce

1 In a large saucepan, cover the rice with 900 ml/1½ pints/3¾ cups of boiling salted water, stir and simmer uncovered for 15 minutes until the liquid has been absorbed. Switch off the heat, cover and stand for 5 minutes. Slice the pork into thin strips, then thread zig-zag fashion onto 16 bamboo skewers.

2 Heat the vegetable oil in a pan. Add the onion and cook over a gentle heat to soften without colouring for about 3–4 minutes. Add the next 6 ingredients and the anchovy essence, if using. Simmer briefly, then stir in the peanut butter.

3 Preheat a moderate grill, spoon a third of the sauce over the pork and cook for 6–8 minutes, turning once. Spread the rice out onto a serving dish, place the pork saté on top and serve with the dipping sauce. Garnish with quartered limes and serve with a green salad.

VARIATION

Indonesian saté can be prepared with lean beef, chicken or prawns.

Jambalaya

The perfect way to use up left-over cold meat —
Jambalaya is a fast, fortifying meal for a hungry family.

Serves 4

INGREDIENTS
45 ml/3 tbsp vegetable oil
1 medium onion, chopped
1 celery stick, chopped
½ red pepper, chopped
400 g/14 oz/2 cups long-grain rice
975 ml/1¾ pints/4 cups chicken
  stock
15 ml/1 tbsp tomato purée
3–4 shakes of Tabasco sauce
225 g/8 oz cold roast chicken or pork,
  thickly sliced
115 g/4 oz cooked sausage, such as
  chorizo or kabanos, sliced
75 g/3 oz/¾ cup frozen peas

roast chicken

peas

tomato purée

onion

sausages

celery

red pepper

rice

1 Heat the oil in a heavy saucepan and add the onion, celery and pepper. Cook to soften without colouring.

2 Add the rice, chicken stock, tomato purée and Tabasco sauce. Simmer uncovered for 10 minutes.

3 Stir in the cold meat, sausage and peas and simmer for a further 5 minutes. Switch off the heat, cover and leave to stand for 5 minutes more before serving.

VARIATION

You could also add cooked ham, smoked cod or haddock and fresh shellfish to a Jambalaya.

Chinese Duck in Pitta

This recipe is based on Chinese crispy duck but uses duck breast instead of whole duck. After 15 minutes' cooking, the duck breast will still have a pinkish tinge. If you like it well cooked, leave it in the oven for a further 5 minutes.

Makes 2

INGREDIENTS
1 duck breast, weighing about 175 g/
   6 oz
3 spring onions
7.5 cm/3 in piece cucumber
2 round pitta breads
30 ml/2 tbsp hoi-sin sauce
radish chrysanthemum and spring
   onion tassel, to garnish

pitta breads

cucumber

duck breast

hoi-sin sauce

spring onions (scallions)

1 Preheat the oven to 220°C/425°F/gas mark 7. Skin the duck breast, place the skin and breast separately on a rack and cook in the oven for 10 minutes.

2 Remove the skin from the oven, cut into pieces and return to the oven for a further 5 minutes.

3 Meanwhile, cut the spring onions and cucumber piece into fine shreds about 4 cm/1½ in long.

4 Heat the pitta bread in the oven for a few minutes until puffed up, then split in half to make a pocket.

5 Slice the duck breast thinly.

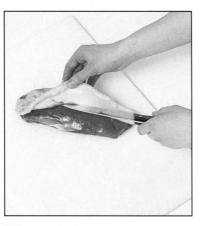

6 Stuff the duck breast into the pitta bread with a little spring onion, cucumber, crispy duck skin and some hoi-sin sauce. Serve garnished with a radish chrysanthemum and spring onion tassel.

Apricot Duck Breasts with Bean Sprout Salad

Duck is rich in fat, so it stays beautifully moist when cooked on a barbecue but any excess fat drains away.

Serves 4

4 plump duck breasts, with skin
1 small red onion, thinly sliced
115 g/4 oz/³/₄ cup ready-to-eat
  dried apricots
15 ml/1 tbsp clear honey
5 ml/1 tsp sesame oil
10 ml/2 tsp ground star anise
salt and freshly ground black
  pepper

FOR THE SALAD
¹/₂ head Chinese leaves, finely
  shredded
150 g/5 oz/2 cups bean sprouts
2 spring onions, shredded
15 ml/1 tbsp light soy sauce
15 ml/1 tbsp groundnut oil
5 ml/1 tsp sesame oil
5 ml/1 tsp clear honey

1 Place the duck breasts, skin-side down, on a board and cut a long slit down one side, cutting not quite through, to form a large pocket.

2 Tuck the slices of onion and the apricots inside the pocket and press the breast firmly back into shape. Secure with metal skewers.

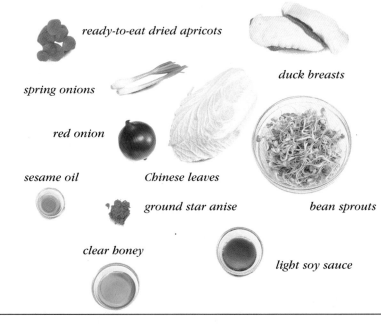

ready-to-eat dried apricots

duck breasts

spring onions

red onion

sesame oil   *Chinese leaves*

ground star anise   *bean sprouts*

clear honey

light soy sauce

3 Mix together the honey and sesame oil and brush over the duck, particularly the skin. Sprinkle over the star anise and season with salt and pepper.

4 To make the salad, mix together the shredded Chinese leaves, bean sprouts and spring onions.

COOK'S TIP

If you prefer not to eat the bean sprouts raw, they can be blanched first, by plunging them into boiling water for 1 minute. Drain and rinse in cold water.

5 Shake together all the remaining salad ingredients in a screw-topped jar. Season to taste with salt and pepper. Toss into the salad.

6 Cook the duck over a medium-hot barbecue for 12–15 minutes, turning once, until golden brown. The duck should be slightly pink in the centre.

Stir-fried Duck with Blueberries

Serve this conveniently quick dinner party dish with sprigs of fresh mint, which will give a wonderful fresh aroma as you bring the meal to the table.

Serves 4

INGREDIENTS

2 duck breasts, about 175 g/6 oz each
30 ml/2 tbsp sunflower oil
15 ml/1 tbsp red wine vinegar
5 ml/1 tsp sugar
5 ml/1 tsp red wine
5 ml/1 tsp *crème de cassis*
115 g/4 oz fresh blueberries
15 ml/1 tbsp fresh mint, chopped
salt and freshly ground black pepper
fresh mint sprigs, to garnish

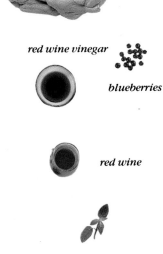

duck

red wine vinegar

blueberries

red wine

mint

1 Cut the duck breasts into neat slices. Season well with salt and pepper.

2 Heat the wok, then add the oil. When the oil is hot, stir-fry the duck for 3 minutes.

3 Add the red wine vinegar, sugar, red wine and *crème de cassis*. Bubble for 3 minutes, to reduce to a thick syrup.

4 Stir in the blueberries, sprinkle over the mint and serve garnished with sprigs of fresh mint.

Stir-fried Sweet and Sour Chicken

There are few cookery concepts that are better suited to today's busy lifestyle than the all-in-one stir-fry. This one has a South-east Asian influence.

Serves 4

INGREDIENTS
275 g/10 oz Chinese egg noodles
30 ml/2 tbsp vegetable oil
3 spring onions, chopped
1 garlic clove, crushed
2.5 cm/1 in fresh root ginger, peeled and grated
5 ml/1 tsp hot paprika
5 ml/1 tsp ground coriander
3 boneless chicken breasts, sliced
115 g/4 oz/1 cup sugar-snap peas, topped and tailed
115 g/4 oz baby sweetcorn, halved
225 g/8 oz fresh beansprouts
15 ml/1 tbsp cornflour
45 ml/3 tbsp soy sauce
45 ml/3 tbsp lemon juice
15 ml/1 tbsp sugar
45 ml/3 tbsp chopped fresh coriander or spring onion tops, to garnish

COOK'S TIP

Large wok lids are cumbersome and can be difficult to store in a small kitchen. Consider placing a circle of greaseproof paper against the food surface to keep cooking juices in.

I Bring a large saucepan of salted water to the boil. Add the noodles and cook according to the packet instructions. Drain, cover and keep warm.

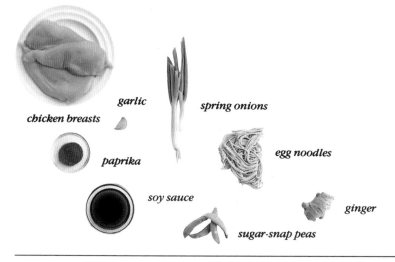

chicken breasts
garlic
spring onions
paprika
egg noodles
soy sauce
ginger
sugar-snap peas

2 Heat the oil. Add the spring onions and cook over a gentle heat. Mix in the next five ingredients, then stir-fry for 3–4 minutes. Add the next three ingredients and steam briefly. Add the noodles.

3 Combine the cornflour, soy sauce, lemon juice and sugar in a small bowl. Add to the wok and simmer briefly to thicken. Serve garnished with chopped coriander or spring onion tops.

Chicken Liver Stir-fry

The final sprinkling of lemon, parsley and garlic gives this dish a delightful fresh flavour and wonderful aroma.

Serves 4

INGREDIENTS
500 g/1¼ lb chicken livers
75 g/3 oz/6 tbsp butter
175 g/6 oz field mushrooms
50 g/2 oz chanterelle mushrooms
3 cloves garlic, finely chopped
2 shallots, finely chopped
150 ml/¼ pint/⅔ cup medium sherry
3 fresh rosemary sprigs
30 ml/2 tbsp fresh parsley, chopped
rind of 1 lemon, grated
salt and freshly ground pepper
fresh rosemary sprigs, to garnish
4 thick slices of white toast, to serve

1 Clean and trim the chicken livers to remove any gristle or muscle.

2 Season the livers generously with salt and freshly ground black pepper, tossing well to coat thoroughly.

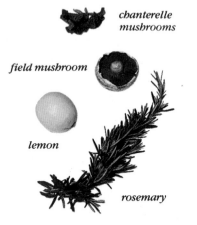

chanterelle
mushrooms

field mushroom

lemon

rosemary

3 Heat the wok and add 15 g/½ oz/ 1 tbsp of the butter. When melted, add the livers in batches (melting more butter where necessary but reserving 25 g/1 oz/ 2 tbsp for the vegetables) and flash-fry until golden brown. Drain with a slotted spoon and transfer to a plate, then place in a low oven to keep warm.

4 Cut the field mushrooms into thick slices and, depending on the size of the chanterelles, cut in half.

5 Heat the wok and add the remaining butter. When melted, stir in two-thirds of the chopped garlic and the shallots and stir-fry for 1 minute **until golden** brown. Stir in the mushrooms and continue to cook for a further 2 minutes.

6 Add the sherry, bring to the boil and simmer for 2–3 minutes until syrupy. Add the rosemary, salt and pepper and return livers to the pan. Stir-fry for 1 minute. Garnish with extra sprigs of rosemary, and serve sprinkled with a mixture of lemon, parsley and the remaining chopped garlic, with slices of toast.

Indonesian-style Satay Chicken

Use boneless chicken thighs to give a good flavour to these satays.

Serves 4

INGREDIENTS
50 g/2 oz/½ cup raw peanuts
45 ml/3 tbsp vegetable oil
1 small onion, finely chopped
2.5 cm/1 in piece root ginger, peeled
    and finely chopped
1 clove garlic, crushed
675 g/1½ lb chicken thighs, skinned
    and cut into cubes
90 g/3½ oz creamed coconut,
    roughly chopped
15 ml/1 tbsp chilli sauce
60 ml/4 tbsp crunchy peanut butter
5 ml/1 tsp soft dark brown sugar
150 ml/¼ pint/⅔ cup milk
1.2 ml/¼ tsp salt

creamed coconut

peanuts

chilli sauce

peanut butter

1 Shell and rub the skins from the peanuts, then soak them in enough water to cover, for 1 minute. Drain the nuts and cut them into slivers.

2 Heat the wok and add 5 ml/1 tsp oil. When the oil is hot, stir-fry the peanuts for 1 minute until crisp and golden. Remove with a slotted spoon and drain on kitchen towels.

3 Add the remaining oil to the hot wok. When the oil is hot, add the onion, ginger and garlic and stir-fry for 2–3 minutes until softened but not browned. Remove with a slotted spoon and drain on kitchen towels.

COOK'S TIP
Soak bamboo skewers in cold water for at least 2 hours, or preferably overnight, so they do not char when keeping the threaded chicken warm in the oven.

4 Add the chicken pieces and stir-fry for 3–4 minutes until crisp and golden on all sides. Thread on to pre-soaked bamboo skewers and keep warm.

5 Add the creamed coconut to the hot wok in small pieces and stir-fry until melted. Add the chilli sauce, peanut butter and cooked ginger and garlic, and simmer for 2 minutes. Stir in the sugar, milk and salt, and simmer for a further 3 minutes. Serve the skewered chicken hot, with a dish of the hot dipping sauce sprinkled with the roasted peanuts.

Glazed Chicken with Cashew Nuts

Hoisin sauce lends a sweet yet slightly hot note to this chicken dish, while cashew nuts add a pleasing contrast of texture.

VARIATION
Use blanched almonds instead of cashew nuts if you prefer.

Serves 4

INGREDIENTS
75 g/3 oz/¾ cup cashew nuts
1 red pepper
450 g/1 lb skinless and boneless
   chicken breasts
45 ml/3 tbsp groundnut oil
4 garlic cloves, finely chopped
30 ml/2 tbsp Chinese rice wine
   or medium-dry sherry
45 ml/3 tbsp hoisin sauce
10 ml/2 tsp sesame oil
5-6 spring onions, green parts
   only, cut into
   2.5 cm/1 in lengths

chicken

spring onion

red pepper

cashew nuts

Chinese rice wine

garlic

groundnut oil

hoisin sauce

sesame oil

1 Heat a wok until hot, add the cashew nuts and stir-fry over a low to medium heat for 1–2 minutes until golden brown. Remove and set aside.

2 Halve the pepper and remove the seeds. Slice the pepper and chicken into finger-length strips.

3 Heat the wok again until hot, add the oil and swirl it around. Add the garlic and let it sizzle in the oil for a few seconds. Add the pepper and chicken and stir-fry for 2 minutes.

4 Add the rice wine or sherry and hoisin sauce. Continue to stir-fry until the chicken is tender and all the ingredients are evenly glazed.

5 Stir in the sesame oil, toasted cashew nuts and spring onion tips. Serve immediately with rice or noodles.

Chicken Liver Kebabs

These may be barbecued outdoors and served with salads and baked potatoes or grilled indoors and served with rice and broccoli.

Serves 4

INGREDIENTS
115 g/4 oz rindless streaky bacon
 rashers
350 g/12 oz chicken livers
12 large (no need to pre-soak) stoned
 prunes
12 cherry tomatoes
8 button mushrooms
30 ml/2 tbsp olive oil

prunes

olive oil

tomatoes

mushrooms

bacon

chicken livers

1 Cut each rasher of bacon into two pieces, wrap a piece around each chicken liver and secure in position with wooden cocktail sticks.

2 Wrap the stoned prunes around the cherry tomatoes.

3 Thread the bacon-wrapped livers onto metal skewers with the tomatoes and prunes. Brush with oil. Cover the tomatoes and prunes with a strip of foil to protect them while grilling or barbecuing. Cook for 5 minutes on each side.

4 Remove the cocktail sticks and serve the kebabs immediately.

Chicken Teriyaki

A bowl of boiled rice is the ideal accompaniment to this Japanese-style chicken dish.

Serves 4

INGREDIENTS
450 g/1 lb boneless, skinless
    chicken breasts
orange segments and mustard and
    cress, to garnish

FOR THE MARINADE
5 ml/1 tsp sugar
15 ml/1 tbsp rice wine
15 ml/1 tbsp dry sherry
30 ml/2 tbsp dark soy sauce
rind of 1 orange, grated

orange

rice wine

soy sauce

chicken breast

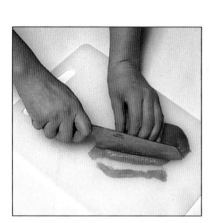

1 Finely slice the chicken.

2 Mix all the marinade ingredients together in a bowl.

COOK'S TIP
Make sure the marinade is brought to the boil and cooked for 4–5 minutes, because it has been in contact with raw chicken.

3 Place the chicken in a bowl, pour over the marinade and leave to marinate for 15 minutes.

4 Heat the wok, add the chicken and marinade and stir-fry for 4–5 minutes. Serve garnished with orange segments and mustard and cress.

Grilled Chicken with Pica de Gallo Salsa

This dish originates from Mexico. Its hot fruity flavours form the essence of Tex-Mex Cooking.

Serves 4

INGREDIENTS
4 chicken breasts
pinch of celery salt and cayenne
    pepper combined
30 ml/2 tbsp vegetable oil
corn chips, to serve

FOR THE SALSA
275 g/10 oz watermelon
175 g/6 oz canteloupe melon
1 small red onion
1–2 green chillies
30 ml/2 tbsp lime juice
60 ml/4 tbsp chopped fresh coriander
pinch of salt

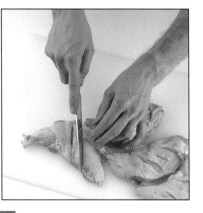

1 Preheat a moderate grill. Slash the chicken breasts deeply to speed up the cooking time.

2 Season the chicken with celery salt and cayenne, brush with oil and grill for about 15 minutes.

3 To make the salsa, remove the rind and as many seeds as you can from the melons. Finely dice the flesh and put it into a bowl.

green chillies

chicken breasts

red onion

lime

coriander

canteloupe melon

watermelon

4 Finely chop the onion, split the chillies (discarding the seeds which contain most of the heat) and chop. Take care not to touch sensitive skin areas when handling cut chillies. Mix with the melon.

5 Add the lime juice and chopped coriander, and season with a pinch of salt. Turn the salsa into a small bowl.

6 Arrange the grilled chicken on a plate and serve with the salsa and a handful of corn chips.

Thai Fried Rice

This hot and spicy dish is easy to prepare and makes a meal in itself.

VARIATION
Add 50 g/2 oz frozen peas to the chicken in step 3, if you wish.

Serves 4

INGREDIENTS

225 g/8 oz Thai jasmine rice
45 ml/3 tbsp vegetable oil
1 onion, chopped
1 small red pepper, seeded and cut into 2 cm/¾ in cubes
350 g/12 oz skinless and boneless chicken breasts, cut into 2 cm/¾ in cubes
1 garlic clove, crushed
15 ml/1 tbsp mild curry paste
2.5 ml/½ tsp paprika
2.5 ml/½ tsp ground turmeric
30 ml/2 tbsp Thai fish sauce (*nam pla*)
2 eggs, beaten
salt and ground black pepper
fried basil leaves, to garnish

rice

Thai fish sauce

chicken

curry paste

onion

egg

paprika

red pepper

turmeric

vegetable oil

1 Put the rice in a sieve and wash well under cold running water. Put the rice in a heavy-based pan with 1.5 litres/2½ pints/6¼ cups boiling water. Return to the boil, then simmer, uncovered, for 8–10 minutes; drain well. Spread out the grains on a tray and leave to cool.

2 Heat a wok until hot, add 30ml/2 tbsp of the oil and swirl it around. Add the onion and red pepper and stir-fry for 1 minute.

3 Add the chicken, garlic, curry paste and spices and stir-fry for 2–3 minutes.

4 Reduce the heat to medium, add the cooled rice, fish sauce and seasoning. Stir-fry for 2–3 minutes until the rice is very hot.

5 Make a well in the centre of the rice and add the remaining oil. When hot, add the beaten eggs, leave to cook for about 2 minutes until lightly set, then stir into the rice.

6 Scatter over the fried basil leaves and serve at once.

Stir-fried Turkey with Broccoli and Mushrooms

This is a really easy, tasty supper dish which works well with chicken too.

Serves 4

INGREDIENTS

115 g/4 oz broccoli florets
4 spring onions
5 ml/1 tsp cornflour
45 ml/3 tbsp oyster sauce
15 ml/1 tbsp dark soy sauce
120 ml/4 fl oz/½ cup
    chicken stock
10 ml/2 tsp lemon juice
45 ml/3 tbsp groundnut oil
450 g/1 lb turkey steaks, cut into
    strips, about 5 mm x 5 cm/
    ¼ x 2 in
1 small onion, chopped
2 garlic cloves, crushed
10 ml/2 tsp grated fresh
    root ginger
115 g/4 oz fresh shiitake
    mushrooms, sliced
75 g/3 oz baby sweetcorn,
    halved lengthways
15 ml/1 tbsp sesame oil
salt and ground black pepper
egg noodles, to serve

onion

broccoli

spring onion

oyster sauce   *turkey*   *mushrooms*

lemon

dark soy sauce

groundnut oil

garlic

baby sweetcorn

chicken stock

1 Divide the broccoli florets into smaller sprigs and cut the stalks into thin diagonal slices.

2 Finely chop the white parts of the spring onions and slice the green parts into thin shreds.

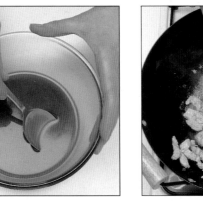

3 In a bowl, blend together the cornflour, oyster sauce, soy sauce, stock and lemon juice. Set aside.

4 Heat a wok until hot, add 30 ml/ 2 tbsp of the groundnut oil and swirl it around. Add the turkey and stir-fry for about 2 minutes until golden and crispy at the edges. Remove the turkey from the wok and keep warm.

5 Add the remaining groundnut oil to the wok and stir-fry the chopped onion, garlic and ginger over a medium heat for about 1 minute. Increase the heat to high, add the broccoli, mushrooms and sweetcorn and stir-fry for 2 minutes.

6 Return the turkey to the wok, then add the sauce with the chopped spring onion and seasoning. Cook, stirring, for about 1 minute until the sauce has thickened. Stir in the sesame oil. Serve immediately on a bed of egg noodles with the finely shredded spring onion scattered on top.

Fish is the **ideal** choice when time is short, as it needs little preparation and cooks very **quickly**. In fact, the biggest danger when it comes to preparing fish is overcooking, which ruins the **flavour** and texture. Cook it until the flesh turns opaque, but is still beautifully moist. When tested with the tip of a knife, the flesh should flake **easily**.

Some of the most **delicious** fish
dishes are also the **easiest**: try
Cajun-style Cod, Salmon Risotto
with Cucumber and Tarragon, or
Spiced Scallops in their Shells,
and find out why they call it fishing
for **compliments!**

FISH

Cajun-style Cod

This recipe works equally well with any firm-fleshed fish such as swordfish, shark, tuna or halibut.

Serves 4

INGREDIENTS

4 cod steaks, each weighing about
   175 g/6 oz
30 ml/2 tbsp natural low fat yogurt
15 ml/1 tbsp lime or lemon juice
1 garlic clove, crushed
5 ml/1 tsp ground cumin
5 ml/1 tsp paprika
5 ml/1 tsp mustard powder
2.5 ml/½ tsp cayenne pepper
2.5 ml/½ tsp dried thyme
2.5 ml/½ tsp dried oregano
new potatoes and a mixed salad,
   to serve

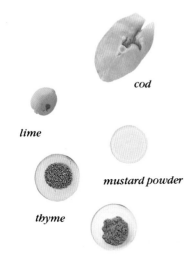

cod

lime

mustard powder

thyme

paprika

1 Pat the fish dry on absorbent kitchen paper. Mix together the yogurt and lime or lemon juice and brush lightly over both sides of the fish.

2 Mix together the garlic clove, spices and herbs. Coat both sides of the fish with the seasoning mix, rubbing in well.

COOK'S TIP

If you don't have a ridged grill pan, heat several metal skewers under a grill until red hot. Holding the ends with a cloth, press onto the seasoned fish before cooking to give a ridged appearance.

3 Spray a ridged grill pan or heavy-based frying pan with non-stick cooking spray. Heat until very hot. Add the fish and cook over a high heat for 4 minutes, or until the underside is well browned.

4 Turn over and cook for a further 4 minutes, or until the steaks have cooked through. Serve immediately accompanied with new potatoes and a mixed salad.

Thick Cod Fillet with Fresh Mixed-herb Crust

Mixed fresh herbs make this a delicious crust. Season well and serve with large lemon wedges.

Serves 4

INGREDIENTS
25 g/1 oz/2 tbsp butter
15 ml/1 tbsp fresh chervil
15 ml/1 tbsp fresh parsley
15 ml/1 tbsp fresh chives
175 g/6 oz/3 cups wholemeal
   breadcrumbs
4 × 225 g/8 oz thickly cut cod fillets,
   skinned
15 ml/1 tbsp olive oil
lemon wedges, to garnish
salt and freshly ground black pepper

1 Pre-heat the oven to 200°C/400°F/ Gas 6. Melt the butter and chop the herbs finely.

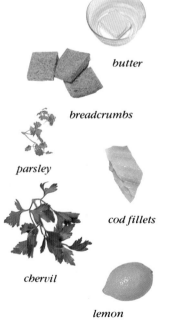

butter

breadcrumbs

parsley

cod fillets

chervil

lemon

2 Mix the butter with the breadcrumbs, herbs and seasoning.

3 Press a quarter of the mixture on top of each fillet. Place on a baking sheet and drizzle over the olive oil. Bake in the pre-heated oven for 15 minutes until the fish flesh is firm and the top turns golden. Serve garnished with lemon wedges.

Jamaican Spiced Cod Steaks with Pumpkin Ragout

Spicy hot from Kingston town, this fast fish dish is guaranteed to appeal. The term 'ragout' is taken from the old French verb *ragouter*, which means to stimulate the appetite.

Serves 4

INGREDIENTS
finely grated zest of ½ orange
30 ml/2 tbsp black peppercorns
15 ml/1 tbsp allspice berries or
   Jamaican pepper
2.5 ml/½ tsp salt
4 × 175 g/6 oz cod steaks
groundnut oil, for frying
new potatoes, to serve (optional)
45 ml/3 tbsp chopped fresh parsley,
   to garnish

FOR THE RAGOUT
30 ml/2 tbsp groundnut oil
1 medium onion, chopped
2.5 cm/1 in fresh root ginger, peeled
   and grated
450 g/1 lb fresh pumpkin, peeled,
   deseeded and chopped
3–4 shakes of Tabasco sauce
30 ml/2 tbsp soft brown sugar
15 ml/1 tbsp vinegar

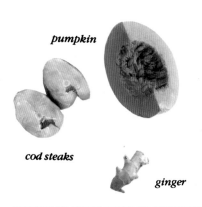

pumpkin

cod steaks

ginger

COOK'S TIP
This recipe can be adapted using any type of firm pink or white fish that is available, such as haddock, whiting, monkfish, halibut or tuna.

1 To make the ragout, heat the oil in a heavy saucepan and add the onion and ginger. Cover and cook, stirring, for 3–4 minutes until soft.

2 Add the chopped pumpkin, Tabasco sauce, brown sugar and vinegar, cover and cook over a low heat for 10–12 minutes until softened.

3 Combine the orange zest, peppercorns, allspice or Jamaican pepper and salt, then crush coarsely using a pestle and mortar. (Alternatively, coarsely grind the peppercorns in a pepper mill and combine with the zest and seasoning.)

4 Scatter the spice mixture over both sides of the fish and moisten with a sprinkling of oil.

5 Heat a large frying pan and fry the cod steaks for 12 minutes, turning once.

6 Serve the cod steaks with a spoonful of pumpkin ragout and new potatoes, if desired, and garnish the ragout with chopped fresh parsley.

Grilled Snapper with Hot Mango Salsa

A ripe mango provides the basis for a deliciously rich fruity salsa. The dressing needs no oil and features the tropical flavours of coriander, ginger and chilli.

Serves 4

INGREDIENTS
350 g/12 oz new potatoes
3 eggs
115 g/4 oz French beans, topped, tailed and halved
4 × 350 g/12 oz red snapper, scaled and gutted
30 ml/2 tbsp olive oil
175 g/6 oz mixed lettuce leaves, such as frisée or Webb's
2 cherry tomatoes
salt and freshly ground black pepper

FOR THE SALSA
45 ml/3 tbsp chopped fresh coriander
1 medium sized ripe mango, peeled, stoned and diced
½ red chilli, deseeded and chopped
2.5 cm/1 in fresh root ginger, grated
juice of 2 limes
generous pinch of celery salt

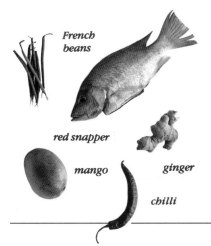

French beans

red snapper

mango   ginger

chilli

VARIATION
If fresh mangoes are unavailable, use the canned variety and drain well. Sea bream are also good served with the hot mango salsa.

1 Bring the potatoes to the boil in a large saucepan of salted water and simmer for 15–20 minutes. Drain.

2 Bring a second large saucepan of salted water to the boil. Put in the eggs and boil for 4 minutes, then add the beans and cook for a further 6 minutes, so that the eggs have had a total of 10 minutes. Remove the eggs from the pan, cool, peel and cut into quarters.

3 Preheat a moderate grill. Slash each snapper three times on either side moisten with oil and cook for 12 minutes, turning once.

4 To make the dressing, place the coriander in a food processor. Add the mango, chilli, ginger, lime juice and celery salt and process smoothly.

5 Moisten the lettuce leaves with olive oil, and distribute them between four large plates.

6 Arrange the snapper over the lettuce and season to taste. Halve the new potatoes and tomatoes, and distribute them with the beans and quartered hard-boiled eggs over the salad. Serve with the salsa dressing.

Red Snapper with Ginger and Spring Onions

This is a classic Chinese way of cooking fish. To partially cook and enhance the flavour of the spring onions and ginger, slowly pour hot oil over them.

Serves 2-3

INGREDIENTS
1 red snapper, about
   675-900 g/1½-2 lb, cleaned and
   scaled with head left on
1 bunch spring onions, cut into
   thin shreds
2.5 cm/1 in piece fresh root
   ginger, cut into thin shreds
1.5 ml/¼ tsp salt
1.5 ml/¼ tsp caster sugar
45 ml/3 tbsp groundnut oil
5 ml/1 tsp sesame oil
30-45 ml/2-3 tbsp light soy sauce
spring onion brushes, to garnish

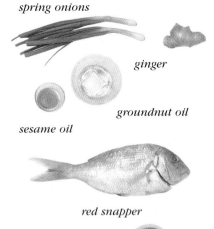

spring onions

ginger

groundnut oil

sesame oil

red snapper

light soy sauce

caster sugar

COOK'S TIP
If the fish is too big to fit inside the steamer, cut off the head and place it alongside the body – it can then be reassembled after it is cooked for serving.

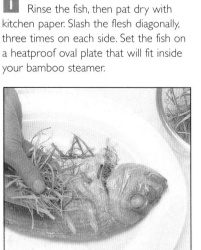

1 Rinse the fish, then pat dry with kitchen paper. Slash the flesh diagonally, three times on each side. Set the fish on a heatproof oval plate that will fit inside your bamboo steamer.

2 Tuck about one-third of the spring onions and ginger inside the body cavity. Place the plate inside the steamer, cover with its lid, then place in a wok.

3 Steam over a medium heat for 10–15 minutes until the fish flakes easily when tested with the tip of a knife.

4 Carefully remove the plate from the steamer. Sprinkle over the salt, sugar and remaining spring onions and ginger.

5 Heat the oils in a small pan until very hot, then slowly pour over the fish.

6 Drizzle over the soy sauce and serve at once, garnished with spring onion brushes.

Pan-fried Red Mullet with Lemon

This dish, which is spectacularly attractive and delicious, is also quick and easy to make.

Serves 4

INGREDIENTS
1 large bulb fennel
1 lemon
12 red mullet fillets, skin left intact
45 ml/3 tbsp fresh marjoram, chopped
45 ml/3 tbsp olive oil
225 g/8 oz lamb's lettuce
salt and freshly ground black pepper

FOR THE VINAIGRETTE
200 ml/7 fl oz/generous ¾ cup
    peanut oil
15 ml/1 tbsp white wine vinegar
15 ml/1 tbsp sherry vinegar
salt and freshly ground black pepper

FOR THE SAUCE
40 g/1½ oz black olives
15 g/½ oz/1 tbsp unsalted butter
25 g/1 oz/1 tbsp capers

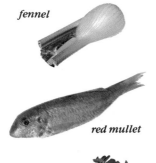

fennel

red mullet

marjoram

lamb's lettuce

1 Trim the fennel bulb and cut it into fine matchsticks. Peel the lemon. Remove any excess pith from the peel, then cut it into fine strips. Blanch the rind and refresh it immediately in cold water. Drain.

2 Make the vinaigrette by placing all the ingredients in a small bowl and lightly whisking until well mixed.

3 Sprinkle the red mullet fillets with salt, pepper and marjoram.

4 Heat the wok and add the olive oil. When the oil is very hot, add the fennel and stir-fry for 1 minute, then drain and remove.

5 Reheat the wok and, when the oil is hot, stir-fry the red mullet fillets, cooking them skin-side down first for 2 minutes, then flipping them over for 1 further minute. Drain well on kitchen towels and wipe the wok clean with kitchen towels.

6 For the sauce, cut the olives into slivers. Heat the wok and add the butter. When the butter is hot, stir-fry the capers and olives for 1 minute. Toss the lamb's lettuce in the dressing. Arrange the fillets on a bed of lettuce, topped with the fennel and lemon, and serve with the olive and caper sauce.

Fish Parcels

Sea bass is good for this recipe, but you could also use small whole trout, or white fish fillet such as cod or haddock.

Serves 4

4 pieces sea bass fillet or 4
  whole small sea bass, about
  450 g/1 lb each
oil for brushing
2 shallots, thinly sliced
1 garlic clove, chopped
15 ml/1 tbsp capers
6 sun-dried tomatoes, finely
  chopped
4 black olives, pitted and thinly
  sliced
grated rind and juice of
  1 lemon
5 ml/1 tsp paprika
salt and freshly ground black
  pepper

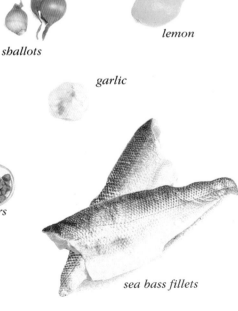
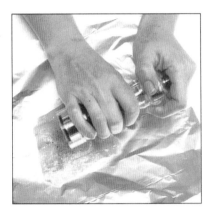
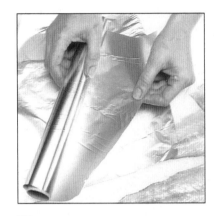

1 Clean the fish if whole. Cut four large squares of double-thickness foil, large enough to enclose the fish; brush with a little oil.

2 Place a piece of fish in the centre of each piece of foil and season well with salt and pepper.

3 Scatter over the shallots, garlic, capers, tomatoes, olives and grated lemon rind. Sprinkle with the lemon juice and paprika.

COOK'S TIP

These parcels can also be baked in the oven: place them on a baking sheet and cook at 200°C/400°F/Gas Mark 6 for 15–20 minutes.

4 Fold the foil over to enclose the fish loosely, sealing the edges firmly so none of the juices can escape. Place on a moderately-hot barbecue and cook for 8–10 minutes. Then open up the tops of the parcels and serve.

Sea Bass with Chinese Chives

Chinese chives are widely available in Oriental supermarkets but if you are unable to buy them, use half a large Spanish onion, finely sliced, instead.

Serves 4

INGREDIENTS
4 sea bass fillets, about 450 g/1 lb in all
5 ml/1 tsp cornflour
45 ml/3 tbsp vegetable oil
175 g/6 oz Chinese chives
15 ml/1 tbsp rice wine
5 ml/1 tsp caster sugar
salt and freshly ground pepper
Chinese chives with flowerheads,
   to garnish

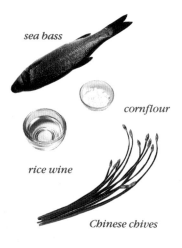

sea bass

cornflour

rice wine

Chinese chives

1 Remove the scales from the bass by scraping the fillets with the back of a knife, working from tail end to head end.

2 Cut the fillets into large chunks and dust them lightly with cornflour, salt and pepper.

3 Heat the wok, then add 30 ml/2 tbsp of the oil. When the oil is hot, toss the chunks of fish in the wok briefly to seal, then set aside. Wipe out the wok with kitchen towels.

4 Cut the Chinese chives into 5cm/2 in lengths and discard the flowers. Heat the wok and add the remaining oil, then stir-fry the Chinese chives for 30 seconds. Add the fish and rice wine, then bring to the boil and stir in the sugar. Simmer until the fish is cooked through. Serve hot, with some flowering Chinese chives, to garnish.

Smoked Haddock Fillets with Quick Parsley Sauce

Make any herb sauce with this method, making sure it is thickened and seasoned well to complement the smoky flavour of the fish.

Serves 4

INGREDIENTS

4 × 225 g/8 oz smoked haddock fillets
75 g/3 oz/6 tbsp butter, softened
25 g/1 oz/2 tbsp plain flour
300 ml/½ pint/1¼ cups milk
salt and freshly ground black pepper
60 ml/4 tbsp chopped fresh parsley

flour   *butter*

smoked haddock fillets

parsley

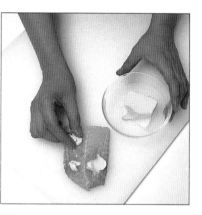

1 Smear the fish fillets on both sides with 50 g/2 oz/4 tbsp butter and pre-heat the grill.

2 Beat the remaining butter and flour together to make a thick paste.

3 Grill the fish for 10–15 minutes turning when necessary. Meanwhile, heat the milk until just below boiling point. Add the flour mixture in small knobs whisking constantly over the heat. Continue until the sauce is smooth and thick.

4 Stir in the seasoning and parsley and serve poured over the fillets.

Fillets of Pink Trout with Tarragon Cream Sauce

If you do not like the idea of cooking and serving trout on the bone, ask your fishmonger to fillet and skin the fish. Serve two fillets per person.

VARIATION
This recipe can also be made with salmon fillets and the dry sherry may be substituted with white wine.

Serves 4

INGREDIENTS
25 g/1 oz/2 tbsp butter
4 fresh trout, filleted and skinned
salt and freshly ground black pepper
new potatoes, to serve
runner beans, to serve

FOR THE CREAM SAUCE
2 large spring onions, white part
    only, chopped
½ cucumber, peeled, deseeded and
    cut into short batons
5 ml/1 tsp cornflour
150 ml/¼ pint/⅔ cup single cream
50 ml/2 fl oz/¼ cup dry sherry
30 ml/2 tbsp chopped fresh tarragon
1 tomato, chopped and deseeded

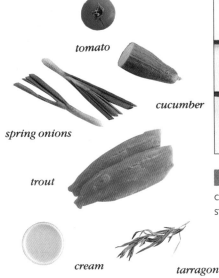

tomato

cucumber

spring onions

trout

cream

tarragon

1 Melt the butter in a large frying pan, season the fillets and cook for 6 minutes, turning once. Transfer to a plate, cover and keep warm.

2 To make the sauce, add the spring onions and cucumber to the pan, and cook over a gentle heat, stirring, until soft but not coloured.

3 Remove the pan from the heat and stir in the cornflour.

4 Return to the heat and pour in the cream and sherry. Simmer to thicken, stirring continuously.

5 Add the chopped tarragon and tomato, and season to taste.

6 Spoon the sauce over the fillets and serve with buttered new potatoes and runner beans.

Dover Sole in a Green Parsley Jacket

Quick to prepare and absolutely delicious, nothing compares with the rich sweetness of a Dover sole. Here, this fine fish sports a green parsley jacket trimmed with lemon and a hint of garlic.

Serves 2

INGREDIENTS
350 g/12 oz floury potatoes, peeled and finely chopped
300 ml/½ pint/1¼ cups milk, or as required
pinch of grated nutmeg
2 × Dover sole, skinned
25 g/1 oz/2 tbsp butter
salt and freshly ground black pepper
lemon wedges, to serve

FOR THE PARSLEY JACKET
25 g/1 oz/½ cup fresh parsley
25 g/1 oz crustless white bread, cubed
45 ml/3 tbsp milk
30 ml/2 tbsp olive oil
finely grated zest of ½ small lemon
1 small garlic clove, crushed

1 In a non-stick saucepan, cover the potatoes with the milk, add salt to taste, and the nutmeg, and bring to the boil. Simmer, uncovered, for 15 minutes until the potatoes have absorbed the milk. Mash, cover and keep warm.

Dover sole

lemon

parsley

2 To make the parsley jacket, chop the parsley in a food processor. Add the bread, milk, olive oil, lemon zest and garlic, then reduce to a fine paste.

3 Preheat a moderate grill. Season the sole, dot with butter and grill for 5 minutes. Turn and allow 2 minutes on the other side. Spread with the parsley mixture, return to the grill and continue to cook for a further 5 minutes. Serve with the mashed potatoes and wedges of lemon.

VARIATION
The same parsley mixture can be used to cover fillets of cod, haddock, whiting or silver hake.

Grilled Sea Bream with Fennel, Mustard and Orange

Sea bream is a revelation to anyone unfamiliar with its creamy rich flavour. The fish has a firm white flesh that partners well with a rich butter sauce, sharpened here with a dash of frozen orange juice concentrate.

Serves 2

INGREDIENTS
2 jacket potatoes
2 × 350g/12 oz sea bream, scaled and gutted
10 ml/2 tsp Dijon mustard
5 ml/1 tsp fennel seeds
30 ml/2 tbsp olive oil
50 g/2 oz watercress
175 g/6 oz mixed lettuce leaves, such as curly endive or frisée

FOR THE SAUCE
30 ml/2 tbsp frozen orange juice concentrate
175 g/6 oz/¾ cup unsalted butter, diced
salt and cayenne pepper

Dijon mustard

orange juice

cayenne pepper

lettuce

sea bream

COOK'S TIP

For speedy jacket potatoes, microwave small potatoes on 100% high power for 8 minutes, then crisp in a hot oven preheated to 200°C/400°F/Gas 6 for a further 10 minutes. Split, butter and serve.

1 Cook the potatoes according to the tip at the beginning of this recipe. Preheat a moderate grill. Slash the bream four times on either side. Combine the mustard and fennel seeds, then spread over both sides of the fish. Moisten with oil and grill for 12 minutes, turning once.

2 Place the orange juice concentrate in a bowl and heat over 2.5 cm/1 in of boiling water. Remove the pan from the stove, and gradually whisk the butter until creamy. Season, cover and set aside.

3 Moisten the watercress and lettuce leaves with the remaining olive oil, arrange the fish on two large plates and put the leaves to one side. Spoon over the sauce and serve with the potatoes.

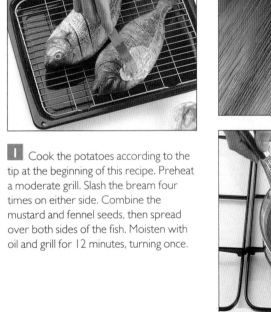

Salmon Risotto with Cucumber and Tarragon

Any rice can be used for risotto, although the creamiest ones are made with short-grain arborio and carnaroli rice. Fresh tarragon and cucumber combine well to bring out the flavour of the salmon.

Serves 4

INGREDIENTS
25 g/1 oz/2 tbsp butter
1 small bunch spring onions, white
   part only, chopped
½ cucumber, peeled, deseeded
   and chopped
400 g/14 oz/2 cups short-grain
   arborio or carnaroli rice
900 ml/1½ pints/3¾ cups chicken or
   fish stock
150 ml/¼ pint/⅔ cup dry white wine
450 g/1 lb salmon fillet, skinned
   and diced
45 ml/3 tbsp chopped fresh tarragon

salmon fillet

butter

cucumber

rice

tarragon

spring onions

1 Heat the butter in a large saucepan, and add the spring onions and cucumber. Cook for 2–3 minutes without colouring.

2 Add the rice, stock and wine, return to the boil and simmer uncovered for 10 minutes, stirring occasionally.

3 Stir in the diced salmon and tarragon. Continue cooking for a further 5 minutes, then switch off the heat. Cover and leave to stand for 5 minutes before serving.

VARIATION

Long-grain rice can also be used. Choose grains that have not been pre-cooked and reduce the stock to 750 ml/1¼ pints/3⅔ cups, per 400 g/14 oz/2 cups of rice.

Pickled Herrings with Beetroot and Apple Relish

Soused or pickled herrings are delicious with cooked beetroot. Serve with buttered rye bread and a sweet and sour apple relish.

Serves 4

INGREDIENTS
2 eggs
8 pickled herrings
250 g/9 oz cooked baby beetroot
fresh flat-leaf parsley, to garnish
4 slices buttered rye bread, to serve
150 ml/¼ pint/⅔ cup sour cream, to serve (optional)

FOR THE RELISH
30 ml/2 tbsp vegetable oil
2 large eating apples, peeled, cored and finely chopped
1 medium onion, chopped
15 ml/1 tbsp sugar
15 ml/1 tbsp cider vinegar
5 ml/1 tsp hot mustard
pinch of salt

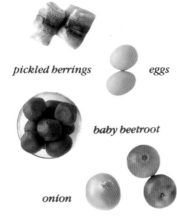

pickled herrings   *eggs*

baby beetroot

onion   *apples*

1 Bring a saucepan of water to the boil, gently lower in the eggs and cook for 10 minutes. Cool under running water and peel. Cut into quarters.

2 To make the relish, heat the oil in a saucepan and add the apple and onion. Cook over a gentle heat for 3–4 minutes without colouring. Add the sugar, vinegar and mustard, then season with salt.

COOK'S TIP
Choose full-flavoured green or red apples for the best results.

3 Divide the herrings between four plates. Slice the beetroot and arrange to one side with the relish. Decorate with egg quarters and garnish with parsley. Serve with buttered rye bread, and a spoonful of sour cream if you wish.

Thai Fish Stir-fry

This is a substantial dish: it is best served with chunks of fresh crusty white bread, for mopping up all the delicious, spicy juices.

Serves 4

INGREDIENTS

675 g/1½ lb mixed seafood (for
   example, red snapper, cod, raw
   prawn tails) filleted and skinned
300 ml/½ pint/1¼ cups coconut milk
15 ml/1 tbsp vegetable oil
salt and freshly ground black pepper

FOR THE SAUCE

2 large red chillies
1 onion, roughly chopped
5 cm/2 in piece root ginger, peeled
   and sliced
5 cm/2 in piece lemon grass, outer leaf
   discarded, roughly sliced
5 cm/2 in piece galingale, peeled
   and sliced
6 blanched almonds, chopped
2.5 ml/½ tsp turmeric
2.5 ml/½ tsp salt

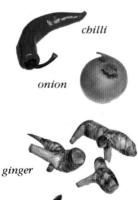

chilli

onion

ginger

prawn

1 Cut the filleted fish into large chunks. Peel the prawns, keeping their tails intact.

2 Carefully remove the seeds from the chillies and chop roughly, wearing rubber gloves to protect your hands if necessary. Then, make the sauce by putting the chillies and the other sauce ingredients in the food processor with 45 ml/3 tbsp of the coconut milk. Blend until smooth.

3 Heat the wok, then add the oil. When the oil is hot, stir-fry the seafood for 2–3 minutes, then remove.

4 Add the sauce and the remaining coconut milk to the wok, then return the seafood. Bring to the boil, season well and serve with crusty bread.

Spiced Scallops in their Shells

Scallops are excellent steamed. When served with this spicy sauce, they make a delicious yet simple starter. Each person spoons sauce on to the scallops before eating them.

Serves 4

INGREDIENTS
8 scallops, shelled (ask the fishmonger to reserve the cupped side of 4 shells)
2 slices fresh root ginger, shredded
½ garlic clove, shredded
2 spring onions, green parts only, shredded
salt and pepper

FOR THE SAUCE
1 garlic clove, crushed
15 ml/1 tbsp grated fresh root ginger
2 spring onions, white parts only, chopped
1-2 fresh green chillies, seeded and finely chopped
15 ml/1 tbsp light soy sauce
15 ml/1 tbsp dark soy sauce
10 ml/2 tsp sesame oil

scallops

ginger

spring onions

light soy sauce

garlic

green chilli

dark soy sauce

sesame oil

1 Remove the dark beard-like fringe and tough muscle from the scallops.

2 Place 2 scallops in each shell. Season lightly with salt and pepper, then scatter the ginger, garlic and spring onions on top. Place the shells in a bamboo steamer and steam for about 6 minutes until the scallops look opaque (you may have to do this in batches).

3 Meanwhile, mix together all the sauce ingredients and pour into a small serving bowl.

4 Carefully remove each shell from the steamer, taking care not to spill the juices, and arrange them on a serving plate with the sauce bowl in the centre. Serve at once.

Nasi Goreng

This dish is originally from Thailand, but can easily be adapted by adding any cooked ingredients you have to hand. Crispy prawn crackers make an ideal accompaniment.

Serves 4

INGREDIENTS
225 g/8 oz long grain rice
2 × size 3 eggs
30 ml/2 tbsp vegetable oil
1 green chilli
2 spring onions, roughly chopped
2 cloves garlic, crushed
225 g/8 oz cooked chicken
225 g/8 oz cooked prawns
45 ml/3 tbsp dark soy sauce
prawn crackers, to serve

rice

soy sauce

egg

chilli

prawns

1 Rinse the rice and then cook for 10–12 minutes in 500 ml/1 pint water in a saucepan with a tight-fitting lid. When cooked, refresh under cold water.

2 Lightly beat the eggs. Heat 15 ml/ 1 tbsp of oil in a small frying pan and swirl in the beaten egg. When cooked on one side, flip over and cook on the other side, remove from the pan and leave to cool. Cut the omelette into strips.

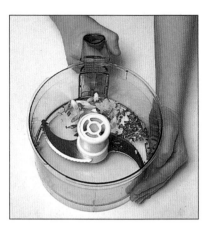

3 Carefully remove the seeds from the chilli and chop finely, wearing rubber gloves to protect your hands if necessary. Place the spring onions, chilli and garlic in a food processor and blend to a paste.

4 Heat the wok, and then add the remaining oil. When the oil is hot, add the paste and stir-fry for 1 minute.

5 Add the chicken and prawns.

6 Add the rice and stir-fry for 3–4 minutes. Stir in the soy sauce and serve with prawn crackers.

Spiced Prawns with Coconut

This spicy dish is based on *Sambal Goreng Udang*, which is Indonesian in origin. It is best served with plain boiled rice.

Serves 3-4

INGREDIENTS
2-3 fresh red chillies, seeded
  and chopped
3 shallots, chopped
1 lemon grass stalk, chopped
2 garlic cloves, chopped
thin sliver of dried shrimp paste
2.5 ml/½ tsp ground galangal
5 ml/1 tsp ground turmeric
5 ml/1 tsp ground coriander
15 ml/1 tbsp groundnut oil
250 ml/8 fl oz/1 cup water
2 fresh kaffir lime leaves
5 ml/1 tsp light brown soft sugar
2 tomatoes, peeled, seeded
  and chopped
250 ml/8 fl oz/1 cup coconut milk
675 g/1½ lb large raw prawns,
  peeled and deveined
squeeze of lemon juice
salt, to taste
shredded spring onions and
  flaked coconut, to garnish

1 In a mortar pound the chillies, shallots, lemon grass, garlic, shrimp paste, galangal, turmeric and coriander with a pestle until it forms a paste.

turmeric

red chillies

garlic

lemon grass

dried shrimp paste

prawns

coriander

galangal

groundnut oil

coconut milk

sugar

tomatoes

shallots

kaffir lime leaves

COOK'S TIP
Dried shrimp paste, much used in South-east Asia, is available from oriental stores.

2 Heat a wok until hot, add the oil and swirl it around. Add the spiced paste and stir-fry for about 2 minutes. Pour in the water and add the kaffir lime leaves, sugar and tomatoes. Simmer for 8-10 minutes until most of the liquid has evaporated.

3 Add the coconut milk and prawns and cook gently, stirring, for about 4 minutes until the prawns are pink. Taste and adjust the seasoning with salt and a squeeze of lemon juice. Serve at once, garnished with shredded spring onions and toasted flaked coconut.

Spicy Crab and Coconut

This spicy dish is delicious served with plain warm Naan bread.

Serves 4

INGREDIENTS

40 g/1½ oz dried unsweetened
  coconut flakes
2 cloves garlic
5 cm/2 in piece root ginger,
  peeled and grated
2.5 ml/½ tsp cumin seeds
1 small stick cinnamon
2.5 ml/½ tsp ground turmeric
2 dried red chillies
15 ml/1 tbsp coriander seeds
2.5 ml/½ tsp poppy seeds
15 ml/1 tbsp vegetable oil
1 medium onion, sliced
1 small green pepper, cut into strips
16 crab claws
fresh coriander sprigs, crushed,
to garnish
150 ml/¼ pint/⅔ cup natural low-fat
  yogurt, to serve

pepper

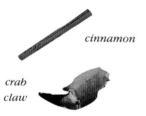

cumin seeds

cinnamon

*crab
claw*

1 Place the dried coconut, garlic, ginger, cumin seeds, cinnamon, turmeric, red chillies, coriander and poppy seeds into a food processor and process until well blended.

2 Heat the oil in the wok and fry the onion until soft, but not coloured.

3 Stir in the green pepper and stir-fry for 1 minute.

4 Remove the vegetables with a slotted spoon and heat the wok. Add the crab claws, stir-fry for 2 minutes, then briefly return all the spiced vegetables to the wok. Garnish with fresh coriander sprigs and serve with the cooling yogurt.

Steaming Mussels with a Spicy Dipping Sauce

In this recipe, the mussel juices are thickened with split red lentils and spiced with curry.

Serves 4

INGREDIENTS
75 ml/5 tbsp red lentils
2 loaves French bread
1.8 kg/4 lb/4 pints live mussels
75 ml/5 tbsp white wine

FOR THE DIPPING SAUCE
30 ml/2 tbsp vegetable oil
1 small onion, finely chopped
½ celery stick, finely chopped
1 large garlic clove, crushed
5 ml/1 tsp medium-hot curry paste

curry paste

French bread

garlic

red lentils

onion

celery

mussels

COOK'S TIP
Always buy mussels from a reputable supplier and ensure that the shells are tightly closed. Atlantic blue shell mussels are the most common and are farmed on ropes or poles in clean tidal waters. Small mussels are preferred for their sweet, tender flavour.

1 Soak the lentils in plenty of cold water until they are required. Preheat the oven to 150°C/300°F/Gas 2 and put the bread in to warm. Clean the mussels in plenty of cold water and pull off any stray beards. Discard any that are damaged.

2 Place the mussels in a large saucepan. Add the white wine, cover and steam the mussels for 8 minutes. Discard any that do not open after cooking.

3 Transfer the mussels to a colander over a bowl to collect the juices. Keep warm until required.

4 To make the dipping sauce, heat the vegetable oil in a second saucepan, add the onion and celery, and cook for 3–4 minutes to soften without colouring. Strain the mussel juices into a measuring jug to remove any sand or grit. There will be approximately 425 ml/15 fl oz/ 1⅔ cups of liquid.

5 Add the mussel juices to the saucepan, then add the garlic, curry paste and lentils. Bring to the boil and simmer for 10–12 minutes or until the lentils have fallen apart.

6 Turn the mussels out onto four serving plates and bring to the table with the dipping sauce, the warm French bread and a bowl to put the empty shells in.

Stir-fried Squid with Black Bean Sauce

If you cannot buy fresh squid you will find small or baby frozen squid, ready skinned, boned and with heads removed, at your local Oriental supermarket.

Serves 4

INGREDIENTS
1 large or 2 medium-sized squid
1 red chilli
10 ml/2 tsp peanut oil
1 clove garlic, crushed
30 ml/2 tbsp black bean sauce
60 ml/4 tbsp water
fresh parsley sprigs, to garnish
steamed rice, to serve

black bean sauce

garlic

squid

chillies

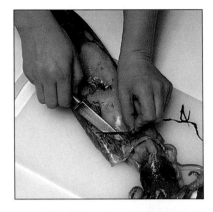

1 Carefully remove the skin from the squid and discard.

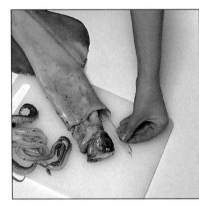

2 Cut off the head of each squid just below the eye, and discard.

3 Remove the bone from the squid and discard.

4 Cut the squid into bite-size pieces and score the flesh in a criss-cross pattern with a sharp knife.

5 Carefully deseed the chilli and chop it finely. Wear rubber gloves to protect your hands if necessary.

6 Heat the wok, then add the oil. When the oil is hot, add the garlic and cook until it starts to sizzle but does not colour. Stir in the squid and fry until the flesh starts to stiffen and turn white. Quickly stir in the black bean sauce, water and chilli. Continue stirring until the squid is cooked and tender (not more than a minute). Garnish with parsley sprigs and the tentacles and serve with steamed rice.

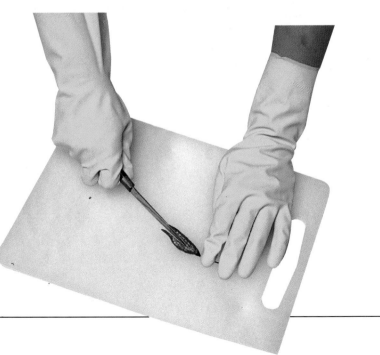

A repertoire of rapid vegetarian dishes is extremely useful,

not merely because **vegetarian** food is so

popular with everyone these days, but also for

those occasions when you've prepared a meat

meal, only to find out that one of your guests

is unable to **enjoy** it.

Being able to conjure up a **quick** and **delicious** alternative saves embarrassment and will earn you their respect and gratitude. **Classic** candidates would be Breaded Aubergine with Hot Vinaigrette, Creamy Cannellini Beans with Asparagus, or Red Pepper Polenta with Sunflower Salsa.

VIRTUAL VEGETARIAN

Risotto-stuffed Aubergines with Spicy Tomato Sauce

Aubergines are a challenge to the creative cook and allow for some unusual recipe ideas. Here, they are stuffed and baked with a cheese and pine nut topping.

Serves 4

INGREDIENTS
4 small aubergines
105 ml/7 tbsp olive oil
1 small onion, chopped
175 g/6 oz/scant 1 cup arborio rice
750 ml/1¼ pints/3⅔ cups
    vegetable stock
15 ml/1 tbsp white wine vinegar
8 fresh basil sprigs, to garnish

FOR THE TOPPING
25 g/1 oz/¼ cup freshly grated
    Parmesan cheese
15 g/½ oz/1 tbsp pine nuts

FOR THE TOMATO SAUCE
300 ml/½ pint/1¼ cups thick passata
    or tomato pulp
5 ml/1 tsp mild curry paste
pinch of salt

aubergines

onion

pine nuts

Parmesan cheese

passata

rice

COOK'S TIP
Don't be put off by the amount of oil aubergines absorb when cooking. Use olive oil and remember that good oils are low in saturated fat and are believed to fight against heart disease.

1 Preheat the oven to 200°C/400°F/Gas 6. Cut the aubergines in half lengthways and take out their flesh with a small knife. Brush with 30 ml/2 tbsp of the oil, place on a baking sheet and cook in the preheated oven for 6–8 minutes.

2 Chop the reserved aubergine flesh and heat the remainder of the olive oil in a medium saucepan. Add the aubergine flesh and the onion and cook over a gentle heat for 3–4 minutes until soft.

3 Add the rice, stir in the stock and simmer uncovered for a further 15 minutes. Stir in the vinegar.

4 Increase the oven temperature to 230°C/450°F/Gas 8. Spoon the rice into the aubergine skins, top with cheese and pine nuts, return to the oven and brown for 5 minutes.

5 To make the sauce, combine the passata or tomato pulp with the curry paste, heat through and add salt to taste.

6 Spoon the sauce onto four large serving plates and position two aubergine halves on each. Garnish with basil sprigs.

Creamy Cannellini Beans with Asparagus

Cannellini beans in a creamy sauce contrast with tender asparagus in this tasty toast topper.

Serves 2

INGREDIENTS

10 ml/2 tsp butter
1 small onion, finely chopped
1 small carrot, grated
5 ml/1 tsp fresh thyme leaves
400 g/14 oz can cannellini
  beans, drained
150 ml/¹/₄ pint/²/₃ cup single cream
115 g/4 oz young asparagus
  spears, trimmed
2 slices of fresh cut Granary bread
salt and freshly ground black pepper

Granary bread   *carrot*   *thyme*

asparagus spears   *butter*

single cream

onion   *cannellini beans*

parsley

1 Melt the butter in a pan. Add the onion and carrot and fry over a moderate heat for 4 minutes until soft. Add the thyme leaves.

2 Rinse the cannellini beans under cold running water. Drain thoroughly, then add to the onion and carrot. Mix lightly.

3 Pour in the cream and heat slowly to just below boiling point, stirring occasionally. Remove the pan from the heat and add salt and pepper to taste. Preheat the grill.

4 Place the asparagus spears in a saucepan. Pour over just enough boiling water to cover. Poach for 3–4 minutes until the spears are just tender.

5 Meanwhile, toast the bread under the grill until both sides are golden.

6 Place the toast on individual plates. Drain the asparagus and divide the spears between the slices of toast. Spoon the bean mixture over each portion and serve.

COOK'S TIP
Use your favourite variety of canned beans such as borlotti, haricot or flageolets.

Spring Vegetable Stir-fry

A colourful, dazzling medley of fresh and sweet young vegetables.

Serves 4

INGREDIENTS
15 ml/1 tbsp peanut oil
1 garlic clove, sliced
2.5 cm/1 in piece of fresh ginger root,
    finely chopped
115 g/4 oz baby carrots
115 g/4 oz patty pan squash
115 g/4 oz baby sweetcorn
115 g/4 oz French beans, topped and
    tailed
115 g/4 oz sugar-snap peas, topped
    and tailed
115 g/4 oz young asparagus, cut into
    7.5 cm/3 in pieces
8 spring onions, trimmed and cut into
    5 cm/2 in pieces
115 g/4 oz cherry tomatoes

FOR THE DRESSING
juice of 2 limes
15 ml/1 tbsp runny honey
15 ml/1 tbsp soy sauce
5 ml/1 tsp sesame oil

1 Heat the peanut oil in a wok or large frying pan.

2 Add the garlic and ginger and stir-fry over a high heat for 1 minute.

3 Add the carrots, patty pan squash, sweetcorn and beans and stir-fry for another 3–4 minutes.

4 Add the sugar-snap peas, asparagus, spring onions and cherry tomatoes and stir-fry for a further 1–2 minutes.

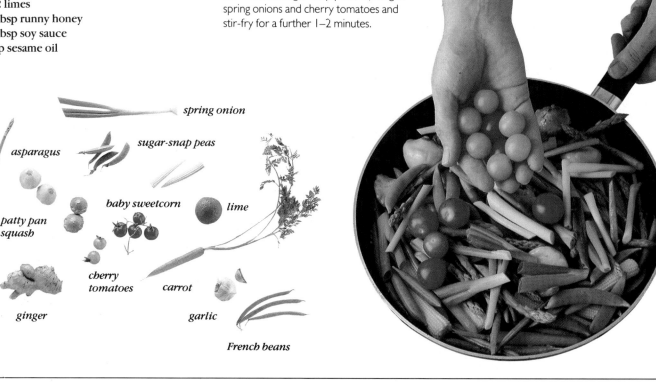

spring onion

asparagus

sugar-snap peas

patty pan squash

baby sweetcorn

lime

cherry tomatoes

carrot

ginger

garlic

French beans

5 Mix the dressing ingredients together and add to the pan.

6 Stir well then cover the pan. Cook for 2–3 minutes more until the vegetables are just tender but still crisp.

COOK'S TIP
Stir-fries take only moments to cook so prepare this dish at the last minute.

Stir-fried Chickpeas

Buy canned chickpeas and you will save all the time needed for soaking and then thoroughly cooking dried chickpeas. Served with a crisp green salad, this dish makes a filling vegetarian main course for two, or could be served in smaller quantities as a starter.

Serves 2–4 as an accompaniment

INGREDIENTS
30 ml/2 tbsp sunflower seeds
1 × 400 g/14 oz can chickpeas, drained
5 ml/1 tsp chilli powder
5 ml/1 tsp paprika
30 ml/2 tbsp vegetable oil
1 clove garlic, crushed
200 g/7 oz canned chopped tomatoes
225 g/8 oz fresh spinach, coarse stalks removed
salt and freshly ground black pepper
10 ml/2 tsp chilli oil

spinach

garlic

sunflower seeds

chickpeas

1 Heat the wok, and then add the sunflower seeds. Dry-fry until the seeds are golden and toasted.

2 Remove the sunflower seeds and set aside. Toss the chickpeas in chilli powder and paprika. Remove and reserve.

3 Heat the wok, then add the oil. When the oil is hot, stir-fry the garlic for 30 seconds, add the chickpeas and stir-fry for 1 minute.

4 Stir in the tomatoes and stir-fry for 4 minutes. Toss in the spinach, season well and stir-fry for 1 minute. Drizzle chilli oil and scatter sunflower seeds over the vegetables, then serve.

Gorgonzola, Cauliflower and Walnut Gratin

This cauliflower dish is covered with a bubbly blue cheese sauce topped with chopped walnuts and cooked under the grill.

Serves 4

INGREDIENTS
1 large cauliflower, broken into florets
25 g/1 oz/2 tbsp butter
1 medium onion, finely chopped
45 ml/3 tbsp plain flour
450 ml/¾ pint/scant 2 cups milk
150 g/5 oz Gorgonzola or other blue
    cheese, cut into pieces
2.5 ml/½ tsp celery salt
pinch of cayenne papper
75 g/3 oz/¾ cup chopped walnuts
pinch of salt
fresh parsley, to garnish
115 g/4 oz green salad, to serve

onion

butter *Gorgonzola*

walnuts

cauliflower

1 Bring a large saucepan of salted water to the boil and cook the cauliflower for 6 minutes. Drain and place in a flameproof gratin dish.

2 Heat the butter in a heavy saucepan. Add the onion and cook over a gentle heat to soften without colouring. Stir in the flour, then draw from the heat. Stir in the milk a little at a time until absorbed by the flour, stirring continuously. Add the cheese, celery salt and cayenne pepper. Simmer and stir to thicken.

3 Preheat a moderate grill. Spoon the sauce over the cauliflower, scatter with chopped walnuts and grill until golden. Garnish with the parsley and serve with a crisp green salad.

VARIATION

For a delicious alternative, substitute cauliflower with 1.1 kg/2½ lb fresh broccoli or combine both together.

Lemon and Ginger Spicy Beans

An extremely quick delicious meal, made with canned beans for speed. You probably won't need extra salt as canned beans tend to be already salted.

Serves 4

INGREDIENTS

5 cm/2 in piece fresh ginger root, peeled and roughly chopped
3 garlic cloves, roughly chopped
250 ml/8 fl oz/1 cup cold water
15 ml/1 tbsp sunflower oil
1 large onion, thinly sliced
1 fresh red chilli, seeded and finely chopped
¼ tsp cayenne pepper
10 ml/2 tsp ground cumin
5 ml/1 tsp ground coriander
½ tsp ground turmeric
30 ml/2 tbsp lemon juice
75 g/3 oz/⅓ cup chopped fresh coriander
1 × 400 g/14 oz can black-eyed beans, drained and rinsed
1 × 400 g/14 oz can aduki beans, drained and rinsed
1 × 400 g/14 oz can haricot beans, drained and rinsed
freshly ground black pepper

1 Place the ginger, garlic and 60 ml/4 tbsp of the cold water in a blender and mix until smooth.

2 Heat the oil in a pan. Add the onion and chilli and cook gently for 5 minutes until softened.

3 Add the cayenne pepper, cumin, ground coriander and turmeric and stir-fry for 1 minute.

4 Stir in the ginger and garlic paste from the blender and cook for another minute.

garlic
red chilli
aduki beans
ginger
ground coriander
black-eyed beans
ground turmeric
ground cumin
haricot beans
onion

5 Add the remaining water, lemon juice and fresh coriander, stir well and bring to the boil. Cover the pan tightly and cook for 5 minutes.

6 Add all the beans and cook for a further 5–10 minutes. Season with pepper and serve.

Bengali-style Vegetables

A hot dry curry using spices that do not require long slow cooking.

Serves 4

INGREDIENTS

¹/₂ medium cauliflower, broken into
  small florets
1 large potato, peeled and cut into
  2.5 cm/1 in dice
115 g/4 oz French beans, trimmed
2 courgettes, halved lengthways
  and sliced
2 green chillies
2.5 cm/1 in piece of fresh root
  ginger, peeled
120 ml/4 fl oz/¹/₂ cup natural yogurt
10 ml/2 tsp ground coriander
2.5 ml/¹/₂ tsp ground turmeric
25 g/1 oz/2 tbsp ghee
2.5 ml/¹/₂ tsp garam masala
5 ml/1 tsp cumin seeds
10 ml/2 tsp sugar
pinch each of ground cloves,
  ground cinnamon and
    ground cardamom
salt and freshly ground black pepper

1 Bring a large pan of water to the boil. Add the cauliflower and potato and cook for 5 minutes. Add the beans and courgettes and cook for 2–3 minutes.

2 Meanwhile, cut the chillies in half, remove the seeds and roughly chop the flesh. Finely chop the ginger. Mix the chillies and ginger in a small bowl.

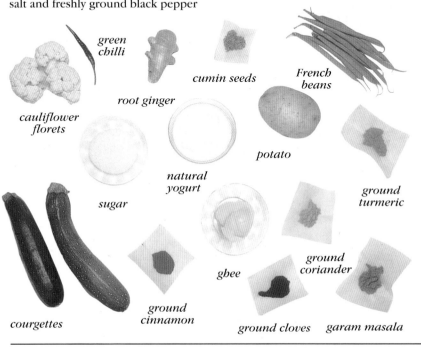

green chilli

cumin seeds

French beans

root ginger

cauliflower florets

natural yogurt

potato

sugar

ground turmeric

courgettes

ghee

ground coriander

ground cinnamon

ground cloves

garam masala

3 Drain the vegetables and tip them into a bowl. Add the chilli and ginger mixture, with the yogurt, ground coriander and turmeric. Season with plenty of salt and pepper and mix well.

4 Heat the ghee in a large frying pan. Add the vegetable mixture and cook over a high heat for 2 minutes, stirring from time to time.

5 Stir in the garam masala and cumin seeds and cook for 2 minutes.

6 Stir in the sugar and remaining spices and cook for 1 minute or until all the liquid has evaporated.

COOK'S TIP
If ghee is not available you can clarify your own butter. Melt 50 g/2 oz/¼ cup butter slowly in a small pan. Remove from the heat and leave for about 5 minutes. Pour off the clear yellow clarified butter, leaving the sediment in the pan.

Red Bean and Mushroom Burgers

Vegetarians, vegans and even meat-eaters can all enjoy these healthy, low-fat veggie burgers. With salad, pitta bread and Greek-style yogurt, they make a substantial meal.

COOK'S TIP

These burgers are not quite as firm as meat burgers, so handle them gently on the barbecue.

Serves 4

15 ml/1 tbsp olive oil
1 small onion, finely chopped
1 garlic clove, crushed
5 ml/1 tsp ground cumin
5 ml/1 tsp ground coriander
2.5 ml/¹/₂ tsp ground turmeric
115 g/4 oz/1¹/₂ cups finely
  chopped mushrooms
400 g/14 oz can red kidney
  beans
30 ml/2 tbsp chopped fresh
  coriander
wholemeal flour (optional)
olive oil for brushing
salt and black pepper
Greek-style yogurt, to serve

mushrooms

onion

wholemeal flour

red kidney beans

garlic

olive oil

coriander

cumin

turmeric

ground coriander

1 Heat the oil in a wide pan and fry the onion and garlic over a moderate heat, stirring, until softened. Add the spices and cook for a further minute, stirring continuously.

2 Add the mushrooms and cook, stirring, until softened and dry. Remove from the heat.

3 Drain the beans thoroughly and then mash them with a fork.

4 Stir into the pan, with the fresh coriander, mixing thoroughly. Season well with salt and pepper.

5 Using floured hands, form the mixture into four flat burger shapes. If the mixture is too sticky to handle, mix in a little flour.

6 Brush the burgers with oil and cook on a hot barbecue for 8–10 minutes, turning once, until golden brown. Serve with a spoonful of yogurt and a crisp green salad.

Mushroom and Okra Curry with Fresh Mango Relish

This simple but delicious curry with its fresh gingery mango relish is best served with plain basmati rice.

Serves 4

INGREDIENTS
4 garlic cloves, roughly chopped
2.5 cm/1 in piece of fresh ginger root, peeled and roughly chopped
1–2 red chillies, seeded and chopped
175 ml/6 fl oz/¾ cup cold water
15 ml/1 tbsp sunflower oil
5 ml/1 tsp coriander seeds
5 ml/1 tsp cumin seeds
5 ml/1 tsp ground cumin
2 green cardamom pods, seeds removed and ground
pinch of ground turmeric
1 × 400 g/14 oz can chopped tomatoes
450 g/1 lb mushrooms, quartered if large
225 g/8 oz okra, trimmed and cut into 1 cm/½ in slices
30 ml/2 tbsp chopped fresh coriander
basmati rice, to serve

FOR THE MANGO RELISH
1 large ripe mango, about 500 g/1¼ lb in weight
1 small garlic clove, crushed
1 onion, finely chopped
10 ml/2 tsp grated fresh ginger root
1 fresh red chilli, seeded and finely chopped
pinch of salt and sugar

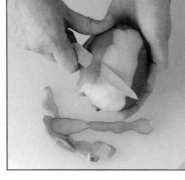

1 For the mango relish, peel the mango and cut off the flesh from the stone.

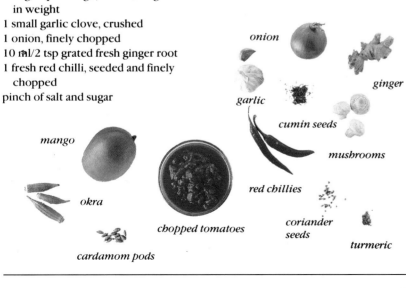

onion
garlic
ginger
cumin seeds
mango
mushrooms
okra
red chillies
chopped tomatoes
coriander seeds
cardamom pods
turmeric

2 In a bowl mash the mango flesh with a fork or pulse in a food processor, and mix in the rest of the relish ingredients. Set to one side.

3 Place the garlic, ginger, chilli and 45 ml/3 tbsp of the water into a blender and blend until smooth.

4 Heat the sunflower oil in a large pan. Add the whole coriander and cumin seeds and allow them to sizzle for a few seconds. Add the ground cumin, ground cardamom and turmeric and cook for 1 minute more.

5 Add the paste from the blender, the tomatoes, remaining water, mushrooms and okra. Stir to mix well and bring to the boil. Reduce the heat, cover, and simmer for 5 minutes.

6 Remove the cover, turn up the heat slightly and cook for another 5–10 minutes until the okra is tender. Stir in the fresh coriander and serve with rice and the mango relish.

Vedgeree with French Beans and Mushrooms

Crunchy French beans and mushrooms are the star ingredients in this vegetarian version of an old favourite.

Serves 2

INGREDIENTS

115 g/4 oz/³/₄ cup basmati rice
3 eggs
175 g/6 oz French beans, trimmed
50 g/2 oz/¹/₄ cup butter
1 onion, finely chopped
225 g/8 oz brown cap mushrooms,
   quartered
30 ml/2 tbsp single cream
15 ml/1 tbsp chopped fresh parsley

single cream   brown cap mushrooms   parsley

onion

butter

French beans

eggs

basmati rice

1 Wash the rice several times under cold running water. Drain thoroughly. Bring a pan of water to the boil, add the rice and cook for 10–12 minutes until tender. Drain thoroughly.

2 Meanwhile, half fill a second pan with water, add the eggs and bring to the boil. Simmer for 8 minutes. Drain the eggs, cool under cold water, then remove the shells.

3 While the eggs are cooking, cook the French beans in boiling water for 5 minutes. Drain, refresh under cold running water, then drain again.

4 Melt the butter in a large frying pan. Add the onion and mushrooms. Cook for 2–3 minutes over a moderate heat.

5 Add the French beans and rice to the onion mixture. Stir lightly to mix. Cook for 2 minutes. Cut the hard-boiled eggs in wedges and add them to the pan.

6 Stir in the cream and parsley, taking care not to break up the eggs. Reheat the kedgeree, but do not allow it to boil. Serve at once.

Nutty Rice and Mushroom Stir-fry

This delicious and substantial supper dish can be eaten hot or cold with salads.

Serves 4–6

INGREDIENTS

350 g/12 oz long grain rice
45 ml/3 tbsp sunflower oil
1 small onion, roughly chopped
225 g/8 oz field mushrooms, sliced
50 g/2 oz/½ cup hazelnuts,
   roughly chopped
50 g/2 oz/½ cup pecan nuts,
   roughly chopped
50 g/2 oz/½ cup almonds,
   roughly chopped
60 ml/4 tbsp fresh parsley, chopped
salt and freshly ground black pepper

rice

almonds

field mushroom

hazelnuts

pecan nuts

1 Rinse the rice, then cook for 10–12 minutes in 700–850 ml/1¼–1½ pints water in a saucepan with a tight-fitting lid. When cooked, refresh under cold water. Heat the wok, then add half the oil. When the oil is hot, stir-fry the rice for 2–3 minutes. Remove and set aside.

2 Add the remaining oil and stir-fry the onion for 2 minutes until softened.

3 Mix in the field mushrooms and stir-fry for 2 minutes.

4 Add all the nuts and stir-fry for 1 minute. Return the rice to the wok and stir-fry for 3 minutes. Season with salt and pepper. Stir in the parsley and serve.

Grilled Mixed Peppers with Feta and Green Salsa

Soft smoky grilled peppers make a lovely combination with the slightly tart salsa.

Serves 4

INGREDIENTS

4 medium peppers in different
    colours
45 ml/3 tbsp chopped fresh flat-leaf
    parsley
45 ml/3 tbsp chopped fresh dill
45 ml/3 tbsp chopped fresh mint
½ small red onion, finely chopped
15 ml/1 tbsp capers, coarsely chopped
50 g/2 oz/¼ cup Greek olives, pitted
    and sliced
1 fresh green chilli, seeded and finely
    chopped
60 g/4 tbsp pistachios, chopped
75 ml/5 tbsp extra-virgin olive oil
45 ml/3 tbsp fresh lime juice
115 g/4 oz/½ cup medium-fat feta
    cheese, crumbled
25 g/1 oz gherkins, finely chopped

olives
feta cheese
green chilli
mint
pistachios
peppers
gherkins
red onion

1 Preheat the grill. Place the whole peppers on a tray and grill until charred and blistered.

2 Place the peppers in a plastic bag and leave to cool.

COOK'S TIP
Feta cheese is quite salty so if preferred, soak in cold water and drain well before using.

3 Peel, seed and cut the peppers into even strips.

4 Mix all the remaining ingredients together, and stir in the pepper strips.

Red Pepper Polenta with Sunflower Salsa

This recipe is inspired by Italian and Mexican cookery. Cornmeal polenta is a staple food in Italy, served with brightly coloured vegetables. Mexican *Pipian* is made from sunflower seeds, chilli and lime.

Serves 4

INGREDIENTS
3 young courgettes
oil, for greasing
1.2 litres/2 pints/5 cups light
   vegetable stock
250 g/9 oz/2 cups fine polenta or
   cornmeal
1 × 200 g/7 oz can red peppers,
   drained and sliced
115 g/4 oz green salad, to serve

FOR THE SUNFLOWER SALSA
75 g/3 oz sunflower seeds, toasted
50 g/2 oz/1 cup crustless
   white bread
200 ml/7 fl oz/scant 1 cup
   vegetable stock
1 garlic clove, crushed
½ red chilli, deseeded and chopped
30 ml/2 tbsp chopped fresh coriander
5 ml/1 tsp sugar
15 ml/1 tbsp lime juice
pinch of salt

1 Bring a saucepan of salted water to the boil. Add the courgettes and simmer over a low heat for 2–3 minutes. Refresh under cold running water and drain. When they are cool, cut into strips.

2 Lightly oil a 23 cm/9 in loaf tin and line with a single sheet of greaseproof paper.

3 Bring the vegetable stock to a simmer in a heavy saucepan. Add the polenta in a steady stream, stirring continuously for about 2–3 minutes until thickened.

4 Partly fill the lined tin with the polenta mixture. Layer the sliced courgettes and peppers over the polenta. Fill the tin with the remaining polenta and leave to set for about 10–15 minutes. Polenta should be served warm or at room temperature.

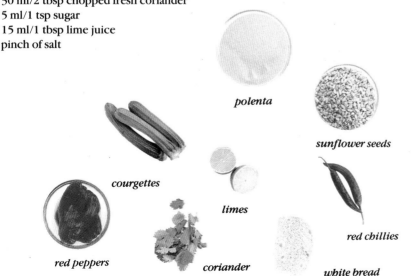

polenta

sunflower seeds

courgettes

limes

red chillies

red peppers

coriander

white bread

COOK'S TIP

Sunflower salsa will keep for up to 10 days in the refrigerator. It is delicious poured over a simple dish of pasta.

5 To make the salsa, reduce the sunflower seeds to a thick paste in a food processor. Add the remaining ingredients and combine thoroughly.

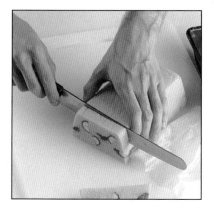

6 Turn the warm polenta out onto a board, remove the paper and cut into thick slices with a large wet knife. Serve with the salsa and a green salad.

Courgettes and Asparagus en Papillote

An impressive dinner party accompaniment, these puffed paper parcels should be broken open at the table by each guest, so that the wonderful aroma can be fully appreciated.

Serves 4

INGREDIENTS
2 medium courgettes
1 medium leek
225 g/8 oz young asparagus, trimmed
4 tarragon sprigs
4 whole garlic cloves, unpeeled
salt and freshly ground black pepper
1 egg, beaten

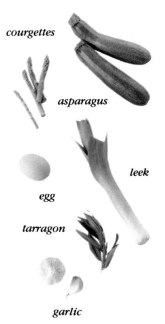

courgettes

asparagus

leek

egg

tarragon

garlic

1 Preheat the oven to 200°C/400°F/ Gas 6. Using a potato peeler slice the courgettes lengthwise into thin strips.

2 Cut the leek into very fine julienne strips and cut the asparagus evenly into 5 cm/2 in lengths.

3 Cut out 4 sheets of greaseproof paper measuring 30 × 38 cm/12 × 15 in and fold in half. Draw a large curve to make a heart shape when unfolded. Cut along the inside of the line and open out.

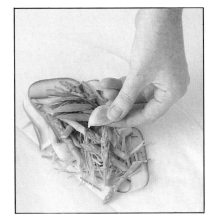

4 Divide the courgettes, asparagus and leek evenly between each paper heart, positioning the filling on one side of the fold line, and topping each with a sprig of tarragon and an unpeeled garlic clove. Season to taste.

COOK'S TIP

Experiment with other vegetables and herbs such as sugar-snap peas and mint or baby carrots and rosemary. The possibilities are endless.

5 Brush the edges lightly with the beaten egg and fold over.

6 Pleat the edges together so that each parcel is completely sealed. Lay the parcels on a baking tray and cook for 10 minutes. Serve immediately.

Breaded Aubergine with Hot Vinaigrette

Crisp on the outside, beautifully tender within, these aubergine slices taste wonderful with a spicy dressing flavoured with chilli and capers.

Serves 2

INGREDIENTS
1 large aubergine
50 g/2 oz/¹/₂ cup plain flour
2 eggs, beaten
115 g/4 oz/2 cups fresh
  white breadcrumbs
vegetable oil for frying
1 head radicchio
salt and freshly ground black pepper

FOR THE DRESSING
30 ml/2 tbsp olive oil
1 garlic clove, crushed
15 ml/1 tbsp capers, drained
15 ml/1 tbsp white wine vinegar
15 ml/1 tbsp chilli oil

aubergine

breadcrumbs

eggs

plain flour

radicchio

capers

white wine vinegar

garlic clove

COOK'S TIP
When serving a salad with a warm dressing use robust leaves that will stand up to the heat.

1 Top and tail the aubergine. Cut it into 5 mm/¹/₄ in slices. Set aside.

2 Season the flour with a generous amount of salt and black pepper. Spread out in a shallow dish. Pour the beaten eggs into a second dish, and spread out the breadcrumbs in a third.

3 Dip the aubergine slices in the flour, then in the beaten egg and finally in the breadcrumbs, patting them on to make an even coating.

4 Pour vegetable oil into a large frying pan to a depth of about 5 mm/¹/₄ in. Heat the oil, then fry the aubergine slices for 3–4 minutes, turning once. Drain on kitchen paper.

5 Heat the olive oil in a small pan. Add the garlic and the capers and cook over gentle heat for 1 minute. Increase the heat, add the vinegar and cook for 30 seconds. Stir in the chilli oil and remove the pan from the heat.

6 Arrange the radicchio leaves on two plates. Top with the hot aubergine slices. Drizzle over the vinaigrette and serve.

Asparagus Rolls with Herb Butter Sauce

For a taste sensation, try tender asparagus spears wrapped in crisp filo pastry. The buttery herb sauce makes the perfect accompaniment.

Serves 2

INGREDIENTS
4 sheets of filo pastry
50 g/2 oz/¹/₄ cup butter, melted
16 young asparagus spears, trimmed

FOR THE SAUCE
2 shallots, finely chopped
1 bay leaf
150 ml/¹/₄ pint/²/₃ cup dry white wine
175 g/6 oz butter, softened
15 ml/1 tbsp chopped fresh herbs
salt and freshly ground black pepper
snipped chives, to garnish

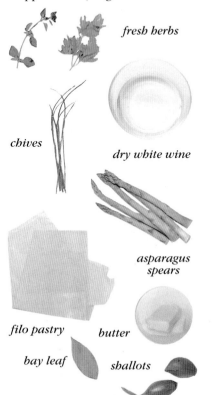

fresh herbs

chives

dry white wine

asparagus spears

filo pastry   *butter*

bay leaf   *shallots*

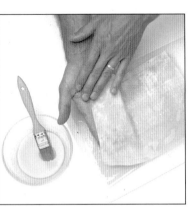

1 Preheat the oven to 200°C/400°F/ Gas 6. Brush each filo sheet with melted butter. Fold one corner of the sheet down to the bottom edge to give a wedge shape.

2 Lay 4 asparagus spears on top at the longest edge and roll up towards the shortest edge. Using the remaining filo and asparagus spears make 3 more rolls in the same way.

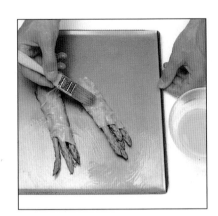

3 Lay the rolls on a greased baking sheet. Brush with the remaining melted butter. Bake in the oven for 8 minutes until golden.

4 Meanwhile, put the shallots, bay leaf and wine into a pan. Cover and cook over a high heat until the wine is reduced to about 45–60 ml/3–4 tbsp.

5 Strain the wine mixture into a bowl. Whisk in the butter, a little at a time, until the sauce is smooth and glossy.

6 Stir in the herbs and add salt and pepper to taste. Return to the pan and keep the sauce warm. Serve the rolls on individual plates with a salad garnish, if liked. Serve the butter sauce separately, sprinkled with a few snipped chives.

Deep-fried Courgettes with Chilli Sauce

Crunchy coated courgettes are great served with a fiery tomato sauce.

Serves 2

INGREDIENTS
15 ml/1 tbsp olive oil
1 onion, finely chopped
1 red chilli, seeded and finely diced
10 ml/2 tsp hot chilli powder
400 g/14 oz can chopped tomatoes
1 vegetable stock cube
50 ml/2 fl oz/¼ cup hot water
450 g/1 lb courgettes
150 ml/¼ pint/⅔ cup milk
50 g/2 oz/½ cup plain flour
oil for deep-frying
salt and freshly ground black pepper
thyme sprigs, to garnish

TO SERVE
lettuce leaves
watercress sprigs
slices of seeded bread

courgettes

chopped tomatoes

onion

red chilli

plain flour

stock cube

milk

chilli powder

1 Heat the oil in a pan. Add the onion and cook for 2–3 minutes. Add the chilli. Stir in the chilli powder and cook for 30 seconds.

2 Add the tomatoes. Crumble in the stock cube and stir in the water. Cover and cook for 10 minutes.

3 Meanwhile, top and tail the courgettes. Cut into 5 mm/¼ in slices.

4 Pour the milk into one shallow dish and spread out the flour in another. Dip the courgettes first in the milk, then into the flour, until well-coated.

5 Heat the oil for deep-frying to 180°C/350°F or until a cube of bread, when added to the oil, browns in 30–45 seconds. Add the courgettes in batches and deep-fry for 3–4 minutes until crisp. Drain on kitchen paper.

6 Place two or three lettuce leaves on each serving plate. Add a few sprigs of watercress and fan out the bread slices to one side. Season the sauce, spoon some on to each plate, top with the crisp courgettes and garnish with the thyme sprigs. Serve at once with salad and bread.

Stir-fried Spinach with Garlic and Sesame Seeds

The sesame seeds add a crunchy texture which contrasts well with the wilted spinach in this easy vegetable dish.

Serves 2

INGREDIENTS
225 g/8 oz fresh spinach, washed
25 ml/1½ tbsp sesame seeds
30 ml/2 tbsp groundnut oil
1.5 ml/¼ tsp sea salt flakes
2–3 garlic cloves, sliced

spinach

groundnut oil

garlic

sesame seeds

COOK'S TIP
Take care when adding the spinach to the hot oil as it will spit furiously.

1 Shake the spinach to get rid of any excess water, then remove the stalks and discard any yellow or damaged leaves. Lay several spinach leaves one on top of another, roll up tightly and cut crossways into wide strips. Repeat with the remaining leaves.

2 Heat a wok to a medium heat, add the sesame seeds and dry fry, stirring, for 1–2 minutes until golden brown. Transfer to a small bowl and set aside.

3 Add the oil to the wok and swirl it around. When hot, add the salt, spinach and garlic and stir-fry for 2 minutes until the spinach just wilts and the leaves are coated with the oil.

4 Sprinkle over the sesame seeds and toss well. Serve at once.

Spiced Coconut Mushrooms

Here is a simple and delicious way to cook mushrooms. They may be served alongside almost any Asian meal, such as stir-fried chicken or pork.

Serves 3-4

INGREDIENTS
30 ml/2 tbsp groundnut oil
2 garlic cloves, finely chopped
2 fresh red chillies, seeded and sliced into rings
3 shallots, finely chopped
225 g/8 oz brown-cap mushrooms, thickly sliced
150 ml/¼ pint/⅔ cup coconut milk
30 ml/2 tbsp chopped fresh coriander
salt and ground black pepper

red chillies

coconut milk

mushrooms

groundnut oil

coriander

garlic

1 Heat a wok until hot, add the oil and swirl it around. Add the garlic and chillies, then stir-fry for a few seconds.

2 Add the shallots and stir-fry for 2–3 minutes until softened. Add the mushrooms and stir-fry for 3 minutes.

3 Pour in the coconut milk and bring to the boil. Boil rapidly over a high heat until the liquid is reduced by half and coats the mushrooms. Taste and adjust the seasoning, if necessary.

4 Sprinkle over the coriander and toss gently to mix. Serve at once.

VARIATION
Use snipped fresh chives instead of coriander if you wish.

Masala Okra

Okra, or "ladies' fingers" are a popular Indian vegetable. In this recipe they are stir-fried with a dry, spicy masala to make a delicious side dish.

Serves 4

INGREDIENTS
450 g/1 lb okra
2.5 ml/½ tsp ground turmeric
5 ml/1 tsp chilli powder
15 ml/1 tbsp ground cumin
15 ml/1 tbsp ground coriander
1.5 ml/¼ tsp salt
1.5 ml/¼ tsp sugar
15 ml/1 tbsp lemon juice
15 ml/1 tbsp desiccated coconut
30 ml/2 tbsp chopped
    fresh coriander
45 ml/3 tbsp oil
2.5 ml/½ tsp cumin seeds
2.5 ml/½ tsp black mustard seeds
chopped fresh tomatoes, to garnish
poppadums, to serve

black mustard seeds   lemon juice   ground coriander   cumin seeds

ground cumin

chilli powder

sugar

ground turmeric   okra

desiccated coconut

salt   fresh coriander

COOK'S TIP

When buying okra, choose firm, brightly coloured pods that are less than 10 cm/4 in long.

1 Wash, dry and trim the okra. In a bowl, mix together the turmeric, chilli powder, cumin, ground coriander, salt, sugar, lemon juice, desiccated coconut and the fresh coriander.

2 Heat the oil in a large frying pan. Add the cumin seeds and mustard seeds and fry for about 2 minutes, or until they begin to splutter.

3 Add the spice mixture and continue to fry for 2 minutes.

4 Add the okra, cover, and cook over a low heat for 10 minutes, or until tender. Garnish with chopped fresh tomatoes and serve with poppadums.

Beetroot and Celeriac Gratin

Beautiful ruby-red slices of beetroot and celeriac make a stunning light accompaniment to any main course dish.

Serves 6

INGREDIENTS
350 g/12 oz raw beetroot
350 g/12 oz celeriac
4 thyme sprigs
6 juniper berries, crushed
salt and freshly ground black pepper
100 ml/4 fl oz/½ cup fresh orange
   juice
100 ml/4 fl oz/½ cup vegetable stock

celeriac

orange juice

beetroot

juniper berries

thyme

1 Preheat the oven to 190°C/375°F/ Gas 5. Peel and slice the beetroot very finely. Quarter and peel the celeriac and slice very finely.

2 Fill a 25 cm/10 in diameter, cast iron, ovenproof or flameproof frying pan with alternate layers of beetroot and celeriac slices, sprinkling with the thyme, juniper and seasoning between each layer.

3 Mix the orange juice and stock together and pour over the gratin. Place over a medium heat and bring to the boil. Boil for 2 minutes.

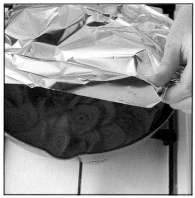

4 Cover with foil and place in the oven for 15–20 minutes. Remove the foil and raise the oven temperature to 200°C/ 400°F/Gas 6. Cook for a further 10 minutes.

Red Cabbage in Port and Red Wine

A sweet and sour, spicy red cabbage dish, with the added crunch of pears and walnuts.

Serves 6

INGREDIENTS

15 ml/1 tbsp walnut oil
1 onion, sliced
2 whole star anise
5 ml/1 tsp ground cinnamon
pinch of ground cloves
450 g/1 lb red cabbage, finely
   shredded
25 g/1 oz/2 tbsp dark brown sugar
45 ml/3 tbsp red wine vinegar
300 ml/½ pint/1¼ cups red wine
150 ml/¼ pint/⅔ cup port
2 pears, cut into 1 cm/½ in cubes
115 g/4 oz/½ cup raisins
salt and freshly ground black pepper
115 g/4 oz/½ cup walnut halves

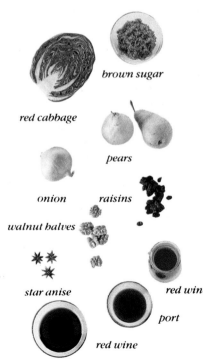

brown sugar

red cabbage

pears

onion   raisins

walnut halves

star anise

red wine vinegar

port

red wine

1 Heat the oil in a large pan. Add the onion and cook gently for about 5 minutes until softened.

2 Add the star anise, cinnamon, cloves and cabbage and cook for about 3 minutes more.

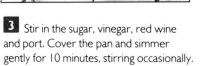

3 Stir in the sugar, vinegar, red wine and port. Cover the pan and simmer gently for 10 minutes, stirring occasionally.

4 Stir in the cubed pears and raisins and cook for a further 10 minutes or until the cabbage is tender. Season to taste. Mix in the walnut halves and serve.

Chinese Greens with Oyster Sauce

Here Chinese greens are prepared in a very simple way – stir-fried and served with oyster sauce. The combination makes a simple, quickly prepared, tasty accompaniment.

Serves 3-4

INGREDIENTS
450 g/1 lb Chinese greens
   (*pak choi*)
30 ml/2 tbsp groundnut oil
15–30 ml/1–2 tbsp oyster sauce

Chinese greens

groundnut oil

oyster sauce

VARIATION
You can replace the Chinese greens with Chinese flowering cabbage, which is also known by its Cantonese name *choi sam*. It has bright green leaves and tiny yellow flowers, which are also eaten along with the leaves and stalks. It is available from oriental grocers.

1 Trim the Chinese greens, removing any discoloured leaves and damaged stems. Tear into manageable pieces.

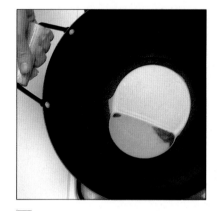

2 Heat a wok until hot, add the oil and swirl it around.

3 Add the Chinese greens and stir-fry for 2–3 minutes until the greens have wilted a little.

4 Add the oyster sauce and continue to stir-fry a few seconds more until the greens are cooked but still slightly crisp. Serve immediately.

SNAPPY SALADS

The sort of salad that used to be served as a **speedy** meal was often dreary in the extreme – a few lettuce leaves, some sad slices of cucumber and a wedge or two of tomato. Today's cooks are more **creative**, thanks to supermarkets and farm shops that stock a **superb** selection of salad greens and **fresh** young vegetables. The secret is in the assembly: a great salad first caresses the senses with its **good** looks, then satisfies the taste buds with its fabulous flavours. **Classic** combinations featured here include Rocket, Pear and Parmesan Salad, and Tomato and Feta Cheese Salad.

Courgette Puffs with Salad and Balsamic Dressing

This unusual salad consists of deep-fried courgettes, flavoured with mint and served warm on a bed of salad leaves with a balsamic dressing.

Serves 2

INGREDIENTS
450 g/1 lb courgettes
75 g/3 oz/1½ cups fresh white
  breadcrumbs
1 egg
pinch of cayenne pepper
15 ml/1 tbsp chopped fresh mint
oil for deep-frying
15 ml/1 tbsp/3 tbsp balsamic vinegar
45 ml/3 tbsp extra virgin olive oil
200 g/7 oz mixed salad leaves
salt and freshly ground black pepper

courgettes

white breadcrumbs

balsamic vinegar

mixed salad leaves

egg

mint

1 Top and tail the courgettes. Coarsely grate them and put into a colander. Squeeze out the excess water, then put the courgettes into a bowl.

2 Add the breadcrumbs, egg, cayenne, mint and seasoning. Mix well.

3 Shape the courgette mixture into balls, about the size of walnuts.

4 Heat the oil for deep-frying to 180°C/350°F or until a cube of bread, when added to the oil, browns in 30–40 seconds. Deep-fry the courgette balls in batches for 2–3 minutes. Drain on kitchen paper.

5 Whisk the vinegar and oil together and season well.

6 Put the salad leaves in a bowl and pour over the dressing. Add the courgette puffs and toss lightly together. Serve at once, while the courgette puffs are still crisp.

Rocket, Pear and Parmesan Salad

For a sophisticated start to an elaborate meal, try this simple salad of honey-rich pears, fresh Parmesan and aromatic leaves of rocket.

Serves 4

INGREDIENTS

3 ripe pears, Williams or Packhams
10 ml/2 tsp lemon juice
45 ml/3 tbsp hazelnut or walnut oil
115 g/4 oz rocket
75 g/3 oz Parmesan cheese
black pepper
open-textured bread, to serve

rocket

Parmesan cheese

pears

1 Peel and core the pears and slice thickly. Moisten with lemon juice to keep the flesh white.

2 Combine the nut oil with the pears. Add the rocket leaves and toss.

3 Turn the salad out on to 4 small plates and top with shavings of Parmesan cheese. Season with freshly ground black pepper and serve.

COOK'S TIP
If you are unable to buy rocket easily, you can grow your own from early spring to late summer.

New Spring Salad

This chunky salad makes a satisfying meal, use other spring vegetables, if you like.

Serves 4

INGREDIENTS

675 g/1½ lb small new
  potatoes, halved
400 g/14 oz can broad
  beans, drained
115 g/4 oz cherry tomatoes
50 g/2 oz/2½ cups walnut halves
30 ml/2 tbsp white wine vinegar
15 ml/1 tbsp wholegrain mustard
60 ml/4 tbsp olive oil
pinch of sugar
225 g/8 oz young asparagus
  spears, trimmed
6 spring onions, trimmed
salt and freshly ground black pepper
baby spinach leaves, to serve

*asparagus
spears*

*new
potatoes*

*wholegrain
mustard*

broad beans

*cherry
tomatoes*

*spring
onions*

walnut halves

1 Put the potatoes in a pan. Cover with cold water and bring to the boil. Cook for 10 –12 minutes, until tender. Meanwhile, tip the broad beans into a bowl. Cut the tomatoes in half and add them to the bowl with the walnuts.

2 Put the white wine vinegar, mustard, olive oil and sugar into a jar. Add salt and pepper to taste. Close the jar tightly and shake well.

3 Add the asparagus to the potatoes and cook for 3 minutes more. Drain the cooked vegetables well, cool under cold running water and drain again. Thickly slice the potatoes. Cut the spring onions into halves.

4 Add the asparagus, potatoes and spring onions to the bowl containing the broad bean mixture. Pour the dressing over the salad and toss well. Serve on a bed of baby spinach leaves.

Fresh Spinach and Avocado Salad

Young tender spinach leaves make a change from lettuce and are delicious served with avocado, cherry tomatoes and radishes in a tofu sauce.

Serves 2-3

INGREDIENTS
1 large avocado
juice of 1 lime
225 g/8 oz fresh baby spinach leaves
115 g/4 oz cherry tomatoes
4 spring onions, sliced
$^{1}/_{2}$ cucumber
50 g/2 oz radishes, sliced

FOR THE DRESSING
115 g/4 oz soft silken tofu
45 ml/3 tbsp milk
10 ml/2 tsp mustard
2.5 ml/$^{1}/_{2}$ tsp white wine vinegar
pinch of cayenne
salt and freshly ground black pepper

tofu   *spring onions*   *spinach leaves*

avocado

cherry tomatoes

cayenne   *white wine vinegar*   *mustard*   *lime*   *cucumber*

radishes   *milk*

1 Cut the avocado in half, remove the stone and strip off the skin. Cut the flesh into slices. Transfer to a plate, drizzle over the lime juice and set aside.

2 Wash and dry the spinach leaves. Put them in a mixing bowl.

COOK'S TIP
Use soft silken tofu rather than the firm block variety. It can be found in most supermarkets in long-life cartons.

3 Cut the larger cherry tomatoes in half and add all the tomatoes to the mixing bowl, with the spring onions. Cut the cucumber into chunks and add to the bowl with the sliced radishes.

4 Make the dressing. Put the tofu, milk, mustard, wine vinegar and cayenne in a food processor or blender. Add salt and pepper to taste. Process for 30 seconds until smooth. Scrape the dressing into a bowl and add a little extra milk if you like a thinner dressing. Sprinkle with a little extra cayenne and garnish with radish roses and herb sprigs, if liked.

Roquefort and Walnut Pasta Salad

This is a simple earthy salad, relying totally on the quality of the ingredients. There is no real substitute for the Roquefort – a blue-veined ewe's-milk cheese from south-western France.

Serves 4

INGREDIENTS
225 g/8 oz/2 cups pasta shapes
selection of salad leaves such as
   rocket, curly endive, lamb's lettuce
baby spinach or radicchio)
30 ml/2 tbsp walnut oil
60 ml/4 tbsp sunflower oil
30 ml/2 tbsp red wine vinegar or
   sherry vinegar
salt and ground black pepper
225 g/8 oz Roquefort cheese,
   roughly crumbled
115 g/4 oz/1 cup walnut halves

pasta shapes

Roquefort cheese   *walnuts*

salad leaves

1 Cook the pasta in plenty of boiling salted water according to the manufacturer's instructions. Drain well and cool. Wash and dry the salad leaves and place in a bowl.

2 Whisk together the walnut oil, sunflower oil, vinegar and salt and pepper to taste.

3 Pile the pasta in the centre of the leaves, scatter over the crumbled Roquefort and pour over the dressing.

4 Scatter over the walnuts. Toss just before serving.

COOK'S TIP
Try toasting the walnuts under the grill for a couple of minutes to release the flavour.

Chicory, Fruit and Nut Salad

Mildly bitter chicory is wonderful with sweet fruit, and is especially delicious when complemented by a creamy curry sauce.

Serves 4

INGREDIENTS
45 ml/3 tbsp mayonnaise
15 ml/1 tbsp Greek yogurt
15 ml/1 tbsp mild curry paste
90 ml/6 tbsp single cream
1/2 iceberg lettuce
2 heads of chicory
50 g/2 oz/1/2 cup cashew nuts
50 g/2 oz/1 1/4 cups flaked coconut
2 red apples
75 g/3 oz/1/2 cup currants

currants

iceberg lettuce

curry paste

mayonnaise

cashew nuts

red apples

single cream

flaked coconut

chicory

1 Mix the mayonnaise, Greek yogurt, curry paste and single cream in a small bowl. Cover and chill until required.

4 Toast the cashew nuts for 2 minutes until golden. Tip into a bowl and set aside. Spread out the coconut flakes on a baking sheet. Grill for 1 minute until golden.

2 Tear the iceberg lettuce into pieces and put into a mixing bowl.

3 Cut the root end off each head of chicory, separate the leaves and add them to the lettuce. Preheat the grill.

5 Quarter the apples and cut out the cores. Slice the apples and add to the lettuce with the coconut, cashew nuts and currants.

COOK'S TIP

Watch the coconut and cashew nuts very carefully when grilling, as they brown very fast.

6 Spoon the dressing over the salad, toss lightly and serve.

Avocado, Tomato and Mozzarella Pasta Salad with Pine Nuts

A salad made from ingredients representing the colours of the Italian flag – a sunny cheerful dish!

Serves 4

INGREDIENTS
175 g/6 oz/1½ cups pasta bows
6 ripe red tomatoes
225 g/8 oz mozzarella cheese
1 large ripe avocado
30 ml/2 tbsp pine nuts, toasted
1 sprig fresh basil, to garnish

DRESSING
90 ml/6 tbsp olive oil
30 ml/2 tbsp wine vinegar
5 ml/1 tsp balsamic vinegar (optional)
5 ml/1 tsp wholegrain mustard
pinch of sugar
salt and pepper
30 ml/2 tbsp chopped fresh basil

olive oil

avocado

tomatoes

basil

mozzarella cheese

pine nuts   *pasta bows*

1 Cook the pasta in plenty of boiling salted water according to the manufacturer's instructions. Drain well and cool.

2 Slice the tomatoes and mozzarella cheese into thin rounds.

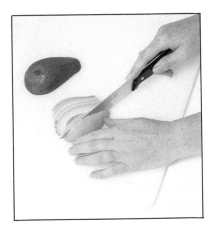

3 Halve the avocado, remove the stone and gently peel off the skin. Slice the flesh lengthways.

4 Whisk all the dressing ingredients together in a small bowl.

5 Arrange the tomato, mozzarella and avocado in overlapping slices around the edge of a flat plate.

6 Toss the pasta with half the dressing and the chopped basil. Pile into the centre of the plate. Pour over the remaining dressing, scatter over the pine nuts and garnish with a sprig of fresh basil. Serve immediately.

Tomato and Feta Cheese Salad

Sweet sun-ripened tomatoes are rarely more delicious than when served with feta cheese and olive oil. This salad, popular in Greece and Turkey, is enjoyed as a light meal with pieces of crispy bread.

Serves 4

INGREDIENTS
900 g/2 lb tomatoes
200 g/7 oz feta cheese
125 ml/4 fl oz/½ cup olive oil,
    preferably Greek
12 black olives
4 sprigs fresh basil
black pepper

COOK'S TIP
Feta cheese has a strong flavour and can be salty. The least salty variety is imported from Greece and Turkey, and is available from specialist delicatessens.

2 Slice the tomatoes thickly and arrange in a shallow dish.

3 Crumble the cheese over the tomatoes, sprinkle with olive oil, then strew with olives and fresh basil. Season with freshly ground black pepper and serve at room temperature.

1 Remove the tough cores from the tomatoes with a small knife.

tomatoes

basil

olives

feta cheese

Potato Salad with Egg and Lemon Dressing

Potato salads are a popular addition to any salad spread and are enjoyed with an assortment of cold meats and fish. This recipe draws on the contrasting flavours of egg and lemon. Chopped parsley provides a fresh finish.

Serves 4

INGREDIENTS

900 g/2 lb new potatoes, scrubbed or scraped
salt and pepper
1 medium onion, finely chopped
1 egg, hard-boiled
300 ml/10 fl oz/1¼ cups mayonnaise
1 clove garlic, crushed
finely grated zest and juice of 1 lemon
60 ml/4 tbsp chopped fresh parsley

COOK'S TIP

At certain times of the year potatoes are inclined to fall apart when boiled. This usually coincides with the end of a particular season when potatoes become starchy. Early-season varieties are therefore best for making salads.

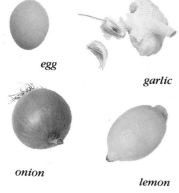

egg

garlic

onion

lemon

new potatoes

1 Bring the potatoes to the boil in a saucepan of salted water. Simmer for 20 minutes. Drain and allow to cool. Cut the potatoes into large dice, season well and combine with the onion.

2 Shell the hard-boiled egg and grate into a mixing bowl, then add the mayonnaise. Combine the garlic and lemon zest and juice in a small bowl and stir into the mayonnaise.

3 Fold in the chopped parsley, mix thoroughly into the potatoes and serve.

Grilled Pepper Salad

Grilled peppers are delicious served hot with a sharp dressing. You can also serve them cold.

Serves 2

INGREDIENTS
1 red pepper
1 green pepper
1 yellow or orange pepper
¹/₂ radicchio, separated into leaves
¹/₂ frisée, separated into leaves
7.5 ml/1¹/₂ tsp white wine vinegar
30 ml/2 tbsp extra virgin olive oil
175 g/6 oz goat's cheese
salt and freshly ground black pepper

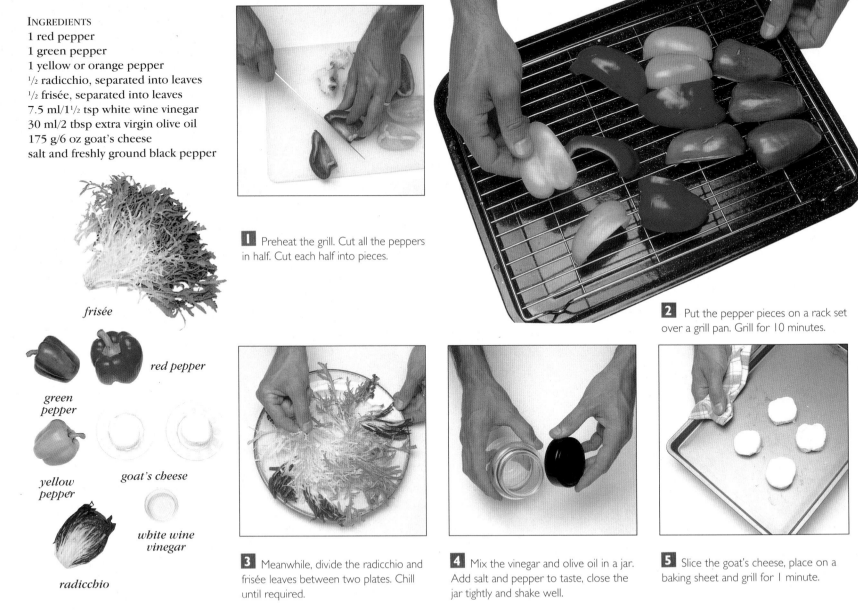

frisée

red pepper

green pepper

yellow pepper

goat's cheese

white wine vinegar

radicchio

1 Preheat the grill. Cut all the peppers in half. Cut each half into pieces.

2 Put the pepper pieces on a rack set over a grill pan. Grill for 10 minutes.

3 Meanwhile, divide the radicchio and frisée leaves between two plates. Chill until required.

4 Mix the vinegar and olive oil in a jar. Add salt and pepper to taste, close the jar tightly and shake well.

5 Slice the goat's cheese, place on a baking sheet and grill for 1 minute.

6 Arrange the peppers and grilled goat's cheese on the salads. Pour over the dressing and grind a little extra black pepper over each.

COOK'S TIP
Grill the peppers until they just start to blacken around the edges – don't let them burn.

Parmesan and Poached Egg Salad with Croûtons

Soft poached eggs, hot garlic croûtons and cool, crisp salad leaves make an unforgettable combination.

Serves 2

INGREDIENTS

¹/₂ small loaf white bread
75 ml/5 tbsp extra virgin olive oil
2 eggs
115 g/4 oz mixed salad leaves
2 garlic cloves, crushed
7.5 ml/¹/₂ tbsp white wine vinegar
25 g/1 oz Parmesan cheese

Parmesan cheese

mixed salad leaves

white bread

garlic cloves

eggs

1 Remove the crust from the bread. Cut the bread into 2.5 cm/1 in cubes.

2 Heat 30 ml/2 tbsp of the oil in a frying pan. Cook the bread for about 5 minutes, tossing the cubes occasionally, until they are golden brown.

3 Meanwhile, bring a pan of water to the boil. Carefully slide in the eggs, one at a time. Gently poach the eggs for 4 minutes until lightly cooked.

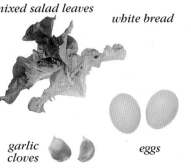

4 Divide the salad leaves between two plates. Remove the croûtons from the pan and arrange them over the leaves. Wipe the pan clean with kitchen paper.

5 Heat the remaining oil in the pan, add the garlic and vinegar and cook over high heat for 1 minute. Pour the warm dressing over each salad.

COOK'S TIP
Add a dash of vinegar to the water before poaching the eggs. This helps to keep the whites together. To ensure that a poached egg has a good shape, swirl the water with a spoon, whirlpool-fashion, before sliding in the egg.

6 Place a poached egg on each salad. Scatter with shavings of Parmesan and a little freshly ground black pepper, if liked.

Green Lentil and Cabbage Salad

This warm crunchy salad makes a satisfying meal if served with crusty French bread or wholemeal rolls.

Serves 4–6

INGREDIENTS
225 g/8 oz/1 cup puy lentils
1.3 litres/2¼ pints/6 cups cold water
1 garlic clove
1 bay leaf
1 small onion, peeled and studded
    with 2 cloves
15 ml/1 tbsp olive oil
1 red onion, finely sliced
2 garlic cloves, crushed
15 ml/1 tbsp thyme leaves
350 g/12 oz cabbage, finely shredded
finely grated rind and juice of 1 lemon
15 ml/1 tbsp raspberry vinegar
salt and freshly ground black pepper

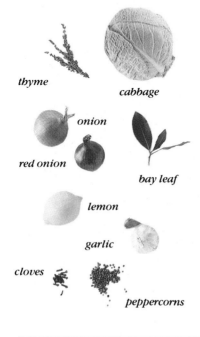

thyme

cabbage

onion

red onion

bay leaf

lemon

garlic

cloves

peppercorns

1 Rinse the lentils in cold water and place in a large pan with the water, peeled garlic clove, bay leaf and clove-studded onion. Bring to the boil and cook for 10 minutes. Reduce the heat, cover the pan and simmer gently for 15–20 minutes. Drain and remove the onion, garlic and bay leaf.

2 Heat the oil in a large pan. Add the red onion, garlic and thyme and cook for 5 minutes until softened.

3 Add the cabbage and cook for 3–5 minutes until just cooked but still crunchy.

4 Stir in the cooked lentils, lemon rind and juice and the raspberry vinegar. Season to taste and serve.

Wholemeal Pasta, Asparagus and Potato Salad with Parmesan

A meal in itself, this is a real treat when made with fresh asparagus just in season.

Serves 4

INGREDIENTS
225 g/8 oz/2 cups wholemeal
    pasta shapes
60 ml/4 tbsp extra virgin olive oil
salt and ground black pepper
350 g/12 oz baby new potatoes
225 g/8 oz fresh asparagus
115 g/4 oz piece fresh
    Parmesan cheese

olive oil

asparagus

Parmesan cheese

pasta shapes

new potatoes

1 Cook the pasta in boiling salted water according to the manufacturer's instructions. Drain well and toss with the olive oil, salt and pepper while still warm.

2 Wash the potatoes and cook in boiling salted water for 12–15 minutes or until tender. Drain and toss with the pasta.

3 Trim any woody ends off the asparagus and halve the stalks if very long. Blanch in boiling salted water for 6 minutes until bright green and still crunchy. Drain. Plunge into cold water to stop them cooking and allow to cool. Drain and dry on kitchen paper.

4 Toss the asparagus with the potatoes and pasta, season and transfer to a shallow bowl. Using a rotary vegetable peeler, shave the Parmesan over the salad.

Caesar Salad

There are many stories about the origin of Caesar Salad. The most likely is that it was invented by an Italian, Caesar Cardini, who owned a restaurant in Mexico in the 1920s. Simplicity is the key to its success.

Serves 4

INGREDIENTS
3 slices day-old bread, 1 cm/½ in thick
60 ml/4 tbsp garlic oil
salt and pepper
50 g/2 oz piece Parmesan cheese
1 cos lettuce

DRESSING
2 egg yolks, as fesh as possible
25 g/1 oz canned anchovy fillets, roughly chopped
½ tsp French mustard
120 ml/½ fl oz/½ cup olive oil, preferably Italian
15 ml/1 tbsp white wine vinegar

COOK'S TIP

The classic dressing for Caesar Salad is made with raw egg yolks. Ensure you use only the freshest eggs, bought from a reputable dealer. Expectant mothers, young children and the elderly are not advised to eat raw egg yolks. You could omit them from the dressing and grate hard-boiled yolks on top of the salad instead.

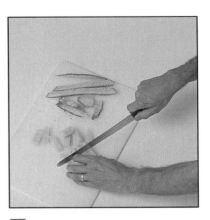

1 To make the dressing, combine the egg yolks, anchovies, mustard, oil and vinegar in a screw-top jar and shake well.

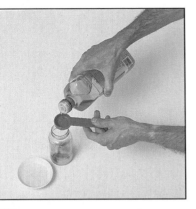

2 Remove the crusts from the bread with a serrated knife and cut into 2.5 cm/1 in fingers.

3 Heat the garlic oil in a large frying pan (skillet), add the pieces of bread and fry until golden. Sprinkle with salt and leave to drain on absorbent kitchen paper.

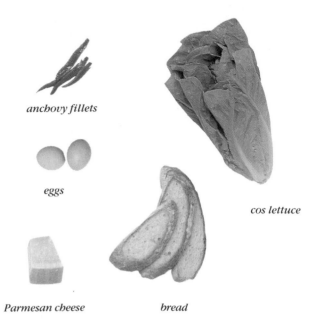

anchovy fillets

eggs

cos lettuce

Parmesan cheese

bread

4 Cut thin shavings from the Parmesan cheese with a vegetable peeler.

5 Wash the salad leaves and spin dry. Smother with the dressing, and scatter with garlic croûtons and Parmesan cheese. Season and serve.

Mediterranean Salad with Basil

A type of Salade Niçoise with pasta, conjuring up all the sunny flavours of the Mediterranean.

Serves 4

INGREDIENTS
225 g/8 oz/2 cups chunky pasta shapes
175 g/6 oz fine green beans
2 large ripe tomatoes
50 g/2 oz fresh basil leaves
200 g/7 oz can tuna fish in oil, drained
2 hard-boiled eggs, shelled and sliced
    or quartered
50 g/2 oz can anchovy fillets, drained
capers and black olives

DRESSING
90 ml/6 tbsp extra-virgin olive oil
30 ml/2 tbsp white wine vinegar or
    lemon juice
2 garlic cloves, crushed
2.5 ml/½ tsp Dijon mustard
30 ml/2 tbsp chopped fresh basil
salt and pepper

olive oil

tomatoes

garlic

basil

pasta shapes

egg

anchovy fillets

green beans

tuna fish

1 Whisk all the ingredients for the dressing together and leave to infuse while you make the salad.

2 Cook the pasta in plenty of boiling salted water according to the manufacturer's instructions. Drain well and cool.

3 Trim the beans and blanch in boiling salted water for 3 minutes. Drain and refresh in cold water.

4 Slice or quarter the tomatoes and arrange on the bottom of a bowl. Moisten with a little dressing and cover with a quarter of the basil leaves. Then cover with the beans. Moisten with a little more dressing and cover with a third of the remaining basil.

5 Cover with the pasta tossed in a little more dressing, half the remaining basil and the roughly flaked tuna.

6 Arrange the eggs on top, then finally scatter over the anchovy fillets, capers and black olives. Pour over the remaining dressing and garnish with the remaining basil. Serve immediately. Don't be tempted to chill this salad – all the flavour will be dulled.

Prawn and Mint Salad

Green prawns make all the difference to this salad, as the flavours marinate well into the prawns before cooking. Garnish with shavings of fresh coconut for a tropical topping.

Serves 4

INGREDIENTS
12 large green prawns
15 ml/1 tbsp unsalted butter
15 ml/1 tbsp fish sauce
juice of 1 lime
45 ml/3 tbsp thin coconut milk
5 ml/1 tsp caster sugar
1 garlic clove, crushed
2.5 cm/1 in piece of root ginger, peeled and grated
2 fresh red chillies, seeded and finely chopped
freshly ground black pepper
30 ml/2 tbsp fresh mint leaves
225 g/8 oz light green lettuce leaves, to serve

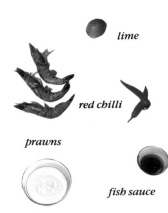
lime

red chilli

prawns

coconut milk

fish sauce

mint

ginger

lettuce

1 Peel the prawns leaving the tails intact.

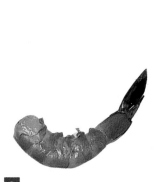

2 Remove the vein.

3 Melt the butter in a large frying pan and toss in the green prawns until they turn pink.

4 Mix the fish sauce, lime juice, coconut milk, sugar, garlic, ginger, chillies and pepper together.

5 Toss the warm prawns into the sauce with the mint leaves. Serve the prawn mixture on a bed of green lettuce leaves.

VARIATION
The prawns can be substituted with lobster tails if you are feeling extravagant.

Tuna Fish and Flageolet Bean Salad

Two cans of tuna fish form the basis of this delicious store cupboard salad.

Serves 4

INGREDIENTS
90 ml/6 tbsp mayonnaise
5 ml/1 tsp mustard
30 ml/2 tbsp capers
45 ml/3 tbsp chopped fresh parsley
pinch of celery salt
2 × 200 g/7 oz cans tuna fish in
   oil, drained
3 little gem lettuces
1 × 400 g/14 oz can flageolet
   beans, drained
1 × 400 g/14 oz can baby artichoke
   hearts, halved
12 cherry tomatoes, halved
toasted sesame bread, to serve

1 Combine the mayonnaise, mustard, capers and parsley in a mixing bowl. Season to taste with celery salt. Flake the tuna into the dressing and toss gently.

2 Arrange the lettuce leaves on four plates, then spoon the tuna mixture onto the leaves.

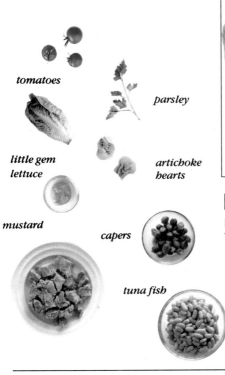

tomatoes

parsley

little gem lettuce

artichoke hearts

mustard

capers

tuna fish

flageolet beans

3 Spoon the flageolet beans to one side, followed by the tomatoes and artichoke hearts. Serve with slices of toasted sesame bread.

VARIATION

Flageolet beans are taken from the under-developed pods of haricot beans. They have a sweet creamy flavour and an attractive green colour. If not available, use white haricot or cannellini beans.

Thai Seafood Salad

This seafood salad with chilli, lemon grass and fish sauce is light and refreshing.

Serves 4

INGREDIENTS
225 g/8 oz ready-prepared squid
225 g/8 oz raw tiger prawns
8 scallops, shelled
225 g/8 oz firm white fish
30–45 ml/2–3 tbsp olive oil
small mixed lettuce leaves and
    coriander sprigs, to serve

FOR THE DRESSING
2 small fresh red chillies, seeded
    and finely chopped
5 cm/2 in piece lemon grass,
    finely chopped
2 fresh kaffir lime leaves,
    shredded
30 ml/2 tbsp Thai fish sauce
    (*nam pla*)
2 shallots, thinly sliced
30 ml/2 tbsp lime juice
30 ml/2 tbsp rice vinegar
10 ml/2 tsp caster sugar

white fish *squid*

scallops

tiger prawns *lemon grass*

Thai fish sauce

shallots *kaffir lime leaves*

1 Prepare the seafood: slit open the squid bodies, score the flesh with a sharp knife, then cut into square pieces. Halve the tentacles, if necessary. Peel and devein the prawns. Remove the dark beard-like fringe and tough muscle from the scallops. Cube the white fish.

2 Heat a wok until hot. Add the oil and swirl it around, then add the prawns and stir-fry for 2–3 minutes until pink. Transfer to a large bowl. Stir-fry the squid and scallops for 1–2 minutes until opaque. Remove and add to the prawns. Stir-fry the white fish for 2–3 minutes. Remove and add to the cooked seafood. Reserve any juices.

3 Put all the dressing ingredients in a small bowl with the reserved juices from the wok; mix well.

4 Pour the dressing over the seafood and toss gently. Arrange the salad leaves and coriander sprigs on four individual plates, then spoon the seafood on top. Serve at once.

Avocado, Crab and Coriander Salad

The sweet richness of crab combines especially well with ripe avocado, fresh coriander and tomato.

Serves 4

INGREDIENTS
700 g/1½ lb small new potatoes
1 sprig fresh mint
900 g/2 lb boiled crabs, or 275 g/10 oz frozen crab meat
1 Batavian endive or butterhead lettuce
175 g/6 oz lamb's lettuce or young spinach
1 large ripe avocado, peeled and sliced
175 g/6 oz cherry tomatoes
salt, pepper and nutmeg

DRESSING
75 ml/5 tbsp olive oil, preferably Tuscan
15 ml/1 tbsp lime juice
45 ml/3 tbsp chopped fresh coriander
½ tsp caster (superfine) sugar

crab

avocado

mint

cherry tomatoes

lamb's lettuce

coriander

new potatoes

1 Scrape or peel the potatoes. Cover with water, add a good pinch of salt and a sprig of mint. Bring to the boil and simmer for 20 minutes. Drain, cover and keep warm until needed.

2 Remove the legs and claws from each crab. Crack these open with the back of a chopping knife and then remove the white meat.

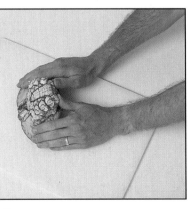

3 Turn the crab on its back and push the rear leg section away with the thumb and forefinger of each hand. Remove the flesh from inside the shell.

4 Discard the soft gills ('dead men's fingers'): the crab uses these gills to filter impurities in its diet. Apart from these and the shell, everything else is edible – white and dark meat.

5 Split the central body section open with a knife and remove the white and dark flesh with a pick or skewer.

COOK'S TIP

Young crabs offer the sweetest meat, but are more fiddly to prepare than older, larger ones. The hen crab carries more flesh than the cock which is considered to have a better overall flavour. The cock crab, shown here, is identified by his narrow apron flap at the rear. The hen has a broad flap under which she carries her eggs. Frozen crab meat is a good alternative to fresh and retains much of its original sweetness.

6 Combine the dressing ingredients in a screw-top jar and shake. Wash and spin the lettuces, then dress them. Distribute between 4 plates. Top with avocado, crab, tomatoes and warm new potatoes. Season with salt, pepper and freshly grated nutmeg and serve.

Chicken Liver Salad

This salad may be served as a first course on individual plates.

Serves 4

INGREDIENTS
mixed salad leaves, e.g. frisée and
   oakleaf lettuce or radicchio
1 avocado, diced
2 pink grapefruits, segmented
350 g/12 oz chicken livers
30 ml/2 tbsp olive oil
1 garlic clove, crushed
salt and freshly ground black pepper
crusty bread, to serve

FOR THE DRESSING
30 ml/2 tbsp lemon juice
60 ml/4 tbsp olive oil
2.5 ml/½ tsp wholegrain mustard
2.5 ml/½ tsp clear honey
15 ml/1 tbsp snipped fresh chives

chicken livers

grapefruit

olive oil

honey

avocado

mustard

lemon

chives

salad leaves

garlic

1 First prepare the dressing: put all the ingredients into a screw-topped jar and shake vigorously to emulsify. Taste and adjust the seasoning.

2 Wash and dry the salad. Arrange attractively on a serving plate with the avocado and grapefruit.

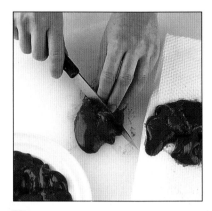

3 Dry the chicken livers on paper towels and remove any unwanted pieces. Cut the larger livers in half and leave the smaller ones whole.

4 Heat the oil in a large frying pan. Stir-fry the livers and garlic briskly until the livers are brown all over (they should be slightly pink inside).

5 Season with salt and freshly ground black pepper and drain on paper towels.

6 Place the liver on the salad and spoon over the dressing. Serve immediately with warm crusty bread.

Warm Stir-fried Salad

Warm salads are becoming increasingly popular because they are delicious and nutritious. Arrange the salad leaves on four individual plates, so the hot stir-fry can be served quickly on to them, ensuring the lettuce remains crisp and the chicken warm.

Serves 4

INGREDIENTS

15 ml/1 tbsp fresh tarragon
2 boneless, skinless chicken breasts, about 225 g/8 oz each
5 cm/2 in piece root ginger, peeled and finely chopped
45 ml/3 tbsp light soy sauce
15 ml/1 tbsp sugar
15 ml/1 tbsp sunflower oil
1 Chinese lettuce
½ frisée lettuce, torn into bite-size pieces
115 g/4 oz/cup unsalted cashews
2 large carrots, peeled and cut into fine strips
salt and freshly ground black pepper

chicken breast

carrot

ginger

cashews

1 Chop the tarragon.

2 Cut the chicken into fine strips and place in a bowl.

3 To make the marinade, mix together in a bowl the tarragon, ginger, soy sauce, sugar and seasoning.

4 Pour the marinade over the chicken strips and leave for a few minutes.

5 Strain the chicken from the marinade. Heat the wok, then add the oil. When the oil is hot, stir-fry the chicken for 3 minutes, add the marinade and bubble for 2–3 minutes.

6 Slice the Chinese lettuce and arrange on a plate with the frisée. Toss the cashews and carrots together with the chicken, pile on top of the bed of lettuce and serve immediately.

Chicken and Pasta Salad

This is a delicious way to use up left-over cooked chicken, and makes a filling meal.

Serves 4

INGREDIENTS
225 g/8 oz tri-coloured
 pasta twists
30 ml/2 tbsp bottled pesto sauce
15 ml/1 tbsp olive oil
1 beefsteak tomato
12 stoned black olives
225 g/8 oz cooked French beans
350 g/12 oz cooked chicken, cubed
salt and freshly ground black pepper
fresh basil, to garnish

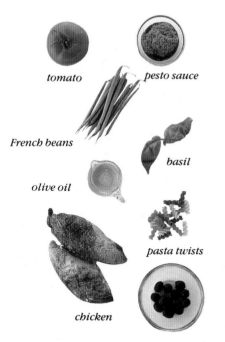

tomato

pesto sauce

French beans

basil

olive oil

chicken

pasta twists

black olives

1 Cook the pasta in plenty of boiling, salted water until *al dente* (about 12 minutes or as directed on the packet).

2 Drain the pasta and rinse in plenty of cold running water. Put into a bowl and stir in the pesto sauce and olive oil.

3 Skin the tomato by placing in boiling water for about 10 seconds and then into cold water, to loosen the skin.

4 Cut the tomato into small cubes and add to the pasta with the olives, seasoning and French beans cut into 4 cm/1 ½ in lengths. Add the cubed chicken. Toss gently together and transfer to a serving platter. Garnish with fresh basil.

Melon and Parma Ham Salad with Strawberry Salsa

Sections of cool fragrant melon wrapped with slices of air-dried ham make a delicious salad starter. If strawberries are in season, serve with a savoury-sweet strawberry salsa and watch it disappear.

Serves 4

INGREDIENTS
1 large melon, cantaloupe, galia or
 charentais
175 g/6 oz Parma or Serrano ham,
 thinly sliced

FOR THE SALSA
225 g/8 oz strawberries
5 ml/1 tsp caster sugar
30 ml/2 tbsp groundnut or
 sunflower oil
15 ml/1 tbsp orange juice
½ tsp finely grated orange zest
½ tsp finely grated fresh root ginger
salt and ground black pepper

1 Halve the melon and take the seeds out with a spoon. Cut the rind away with a paring knife, then slice the melon thickly. Chill until ready to serve.

2 To make the salsa, hull the strawberries and cut them into large dice. Place in a small mixing bowl with the sugar and crush lightly to release the juices. Add the oil, orange juice, zest and ginger. Season with salt and a generous twist of black pepper.

3 Arrange the melon on a serving plate, lay the ham over the top and serve with a bowl of salsa.

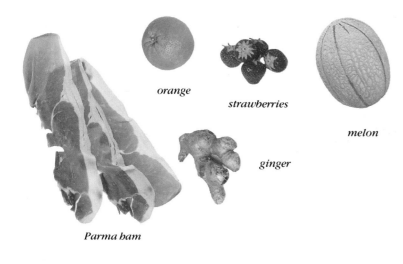

orange

strawberries

melon

ginger

Parma ham

Sweet Potato, Egg, Pork and Beetroot Salad

A delicious way to use up left-over roast pork. Sweet flavours balance well with the bitterness of the salad leaves.

Serves 4

INGREDIENTS
900 g/2 lb sweet potato, peeled and
  diced
salt
4 heads chicory
5 eggs, hard-boiled
450 g/1 lb pickled young beetroot
175 g/6 oz cold roast pork, sliced

DRESSING
75 ml/5 tbsp groundnut or
  sunflower oil
30 ml/2 tbsp white wine vinegar
10 ml/2 tsp Dijon mustard
5 ml/1 tsp fennel seeds, crushed

pork

sweet potato

eggs

beetroot

chicory

1 Bring the sweet potato to the boil in salted water and cook for 10–15 minutes or until soft. Drain and allow to cool.

2 To make the dressing, combine the oil, vinegar, mustard and fennel seeds in a screw-top jar and shake.

3 Separate the chicory leaves and arrange around the edge of 4 serving plates.

4 Dress the sweet potato and spoon over the salad leaves.

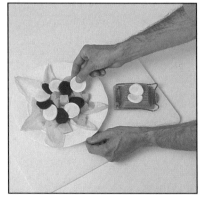

5 Shell the hard-boiled eggs. Slice the eggs and beetroot, and arrange to make an attractive border.

6 Cut the pork into 4 cm/1½ in fingers, moisten with dressing and pile into the centre. Season and serve.

Sesame Noodle Salad with Hot Peanuts

An orient-inspired salad with crunchy vegetables and a light soy dressing. The hot peanuts make a surprisingly successful union with the cold noodles.

Serves 4

INGREDIENTS

350 g/12 oz egg noodles
2 carrots, peeled and cut into fine julienne strips
½ cucumber, peeled and cut into 1 cm/½ in cubes
115 g/4 oz celeriac, peeled and cut into fine julienne strips
6 spring onions, finely sliced
8 canned water chestnuts, drained and finely sliced
175 g/6 oz beansprouts
1 small fresh green chilli, seeded and finely chopped
30 ml/2 tbsp sesame seeds, to serve
115 g/4 oz/1 cup peanuts, to serve

FOR THE DRESSING

15 ml/1 tbsp dark soy sauce
15 ml/1 tbsp light soy sauce
15 ml/1 tbsp runny honey
15 ml/1 tbsp rice wine or dry sherry
15 ml/1 tbsp sesame oil

2 Drain the noodles, refresh in cold water, then drain again.

3 Mix the noodles with all of the prepared vegetables.

1 Preheat the oven to 200°C/400°F/ Gas 6. Cook the egg noodles in boiling water, following the instructions on the side of the packet.

celeriac

beansprouts

green chilli

spring onion

sesame seeds

water chestnuts

cucumber

peanuts

carrot

noodles

4 Combine the dressing ingredients in a small bowl, then toss into the noodle and vegetable mixture. Divide the salad between 4 plates.

5 Place the sesame seeds and peanuts on separate baking trays and place in the oven. Take the sesame seeds out after 5 minutes and continue to cook the peanuts for a further 5 minutes until evenly browned.

6 Sprinkle the sesame seeds and peanuts evenly over each portion and serve at once.

Pasta is the **perfect** ingredient when it comes to serving food speedily. Fresh tagliatelle and linguine are **ready** as soon as they rise to the surface of the boiling water, and some oriental noodles **cook** even more **quickly.** Dried pasta takes only a little

longer, especially if you choose small shapes or the varieties made for soup. Sauces range from the **simple** – garlic and oil – to the **sophisticated**, with Fettuccine all'Alfredo, Double Tomato Tagliatelle, and Rigatoni with Spicy Sausage and Tomato Sauce among the **favourites**, old and new.

PASTA PRONTO

Penne with Spinach

Serves 4

INGREDIENTS

225 g/8 oz fresh spinach
1 garlic clove, crushed
1 shallot or small onion,
　finely chopped
½ small red pepper, seeded and
　finely chopped
1 small red chilli, seeded
　and chopped
150 ml/¼ pint/⅔ cup stock
350 g/12 oz penne
150 g/5 oz smoked turkey rashers
45 ml/3 tbsp low-fat crème fraîche
30 ml/2 tbsp grated
　Parmesan cheese
shavings of Parmesan cheese,
　to garnish

red pepper

grated
Parmesan cheese

red chilli

shallot

smoked turkey
rashers　*penne*

stock　*low-fat crème*
fraîche

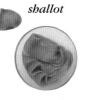

garlic

spinach

1 Wash the spinach and remove the hard central stalks. Shred finely.

2 Put the garlic, shallot or small onion, pepper and chilli into a large frying pan. Add the stock, cover and cook for about 5 minutes until tender. Add the prepared spinach and cook quickly for a further 2–3 minutes until it has wilted.

3 Cook the pasta in a large pan of boiling, salted water until *al dente*. Drain thoroughly.

4 Grill the smoked turkey rashers, cool a little, and chop finely.

5 Stir the crème fraîche and grated Parmesan into the pasta with the spinach, and toss carefully together.

6 Transfer to serving plates and sprinkle with chopped turkey and shavings of Parmesan cheese.

Green Pasta with Avocado Sauce

This is an unusual sauce with a pale green colour, studded with red tomato. It has a luxurious velvety texture. The sauce is rather rich, so you don't need too much of it.

Serves 6

INGREDIENTS
3 ripe tomatoes
2 large ripe avocados
25 g/1 oz/2 tbsp butter, plus extra for
    tossing the pasta
1 garlic clove, crushed
450 ml/12 fl oz/1½ cups
    double cream
salt and ground black pepper
dash of Tabasco sauce
450 g/1b green tagliatelle
freshly grated Parmesan cheese
60 ml/4 tbsp soured cream

tagliatelle

tomatoes

avocado

garlic

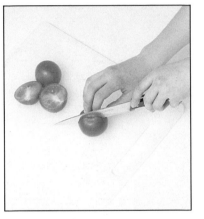

1 Halve the tomatoes and remove the cores. Squeeze out the seeds and cut the tomatoes into dice. Set aside.

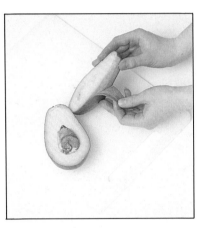

2 Halve the avocados, take out the stones and peel. Roughly chop up the flesh.

3 Melt the butter in a saucepan and add the garlic. Cook for 1 minute, then add the cream and chopped avocados. Raise the heat, stirring constantly to break up the avocados.

4 Add the diced tomatoes and season to taste with salt, pepper and a little Tabasco sauce. Keep warm.

5 Cook the pasta in plenty of boiling salted water according to the manufacturer's instructions. Drain well and toss with a knob of butter.

6 Divide the pasta between 4 warmed bowls and spoon over the sauce. Sprinkle with grated Parmesan and top with a spoonful of soured cream.

Mushroom Bolognese

A quick – and exceedingly tasty – vegetarian
version of the classic Italian meat dish.

Serves 4

INGREDIENTS
450 g/1 lb mushrooms
15 ml/1 tbsp olive oil
1 onion, chopped
1 garlic clove, crushed
15 ml/1 tbsp tomato purée
400 g/14 oz can chopped tomatoes
15 ml/1 tbsp chopped fresh oregano
450 g/1 lb fresh pasta
Parmesan cheese, to serve
chopped fresh oregano, to garnish

mushrooms

chopped tomatoes

oregano

garlic clove

pasta

onion

Parmesan cheese

tomato purée

1 Trim the mushroom stems neatly, then cut each mushroom into quarters.

2 Heat the oil in a large pan. Add the chopped onion and garlic and cook for 2–3 minutes.

3 Add the mushrooms to the pan and cook over a high heat for 3–4 minutes, stirring occasionally.

4 Stir in the tomato purée, chopped tomatoes and oregano. Lower the heat, cover and cook for 5 minutes.

5 Meanwhile, bring a large pan of salted water to the boil. Cook the pasta for 2–3 minutes until just tender.

COOK'S TIP

If you prefer to use dried pasta, make this the first thing that you cook. It will take 10–12 minutes, during which time you can make the mushroom mixture. Use 350 g/12 oz dried pasta.

6 Season the bolognese sauce with salt and pepper. Drain the pasta, tip it into a bowl and add the mushroom mixture. Toss to mix. Serve in individual bowls, topped with shavings of fresh Parmesan cheese and a sprinkling of chopped fresh oregano.

Fettuccine all'Alfredo

A classic dish from Rome, Fettuccine all'Alfredo is simply pasta tossed with double cream, butter and freshly grated Parmesan cheese. Popular additions are peas and strips of ham.

Serves 4

INGREDIENTS
25 g/1 oz/2 tbsp butter
150 ml/5 fl oz/⅔ cup double
    cream, plus 60 ml/4 tbsp extra
450 g/1 lb fettuccine
freshly grated nutmeg
salt and pepper
50 g/2 oz/½ cup freshly grated
    Parmesan cheese, plus extra to
    serve

fettuccine

nutmeg

Parmesan cheese

1 Place the butter and 150 ml/5 fl oz/ ⅔ cup cream in a heavy saucepan, bring to the boil and simmer for 1 minute until slightly thickened.

2 Cook the fettuccine in plenty of boiling salted water according to the manufacturer's instructions, but for 2 minutes' less time. The pasta should still be a little firm.

3 Drain very well and turn into the pan with the cream sauce.

4 Place on the heat and turn the pasta in the sauce to coat.

5 Add the extra 60 ml/4 tbsp cream, the cheese, salt and pepper to taste and a little grated nutmeg. Toss until well coated and heated through. Serve immediately with extra grated Parmesan cheese.

Spaghetti Olio e Aglio

This is another classic recipe from Rome. A quick and filling dish, originally the food of the poor involving nothing more than pasta, garlic and olive oil, but now fast becoming fashionable.

Serves 4

INGREDIENTS
2 garlic cloves
30 ml/2 tbsp fresh parsley
100 ml/4 fl oz/½ cup olive oil
450 g/1 lb spaghetti
salt and pepper

spaghetti

olive oil

parsley

garlic

1 Finely chop the garlic.

2 Chop the parsley roughly.

3 Heat the olive oil in a medium saucepan and add the garlic and a pinch of salt. Cook gently, stirring all the time, until golden. If the garlic becomes too brown, it will taste bitter.

4 Meanwhile cook the spaghetti in plenty of boiling salted water according to the manufacturer's instructions until *al dente*. Drain well.

5 Toss with the warm – not sizzling – garlic and oil and add plenty of black pepper and the parsley. Serve immediately.

Double Tomato Tagliatelle

Sun-dried tomatoes add pungency to this dish, while the grilled fresh tomatoes add bite.

Serves 4

INGREDIENTS
45 ml/3 tbsp olive oil
1 garlic clove, crushed
1 small onion, chopped
50 ml/2 fl oz/¼ cup dry white wine
6 sun-dried tomatoes, chopped
30 ml/2 tbsp chopped fresh parsley
50 g/2 oz/½ cup stoned black
  olives, halved
450 g/1 lb fresh tagliatelle
4 tomatoes, halved
Parmesan cheese, to serve
salt and freshly ground black pepper

tomatoes

parsley

garlic clove

sun-dried tomatoes

tagliatelle
dry white wine

onion

black olives

Parmesan cheese

COOK'S TIP

It is essential to buy Parmesan in a piece for this dish. Find a good source – fresh Parmesan should not be unacceptably hard – and shave or grate it yourself. The flavour will be much more intense than that of the ready-grated product.

1 Heat 30 ml/2 tbsp of the oil in a pan. Add the garlic and onion and cook for 2–3 minutes, stirring occasionally. Add the wine, sun-dried tomatoes and the parsley. Cook for 2 minutes. Stir in the black olives.

2 Bring a large pan of salted water to the boil. Add the fresh tagliatelle and cook for 2–3 minutes until just tender. Preheat the grill.

3 Put the tomatoes on a tray and brush with the remaining oil. Grill for 3–4 minutes.

4 Drain the pasta, return it to the pan and toss with the sauce. Serve with the grilled tomatoes, freshly ground black pepper and shavings of Parmesan.

Spaghetti with Black Olive and Mushroom Sauce

A rich pungent sauce topped with sweet cherry tomatoes.

Serves 4

INGREDIENTS
15 ml/1 tbsp olive oil
1 garlic clove, chopped
225 g/8 oz mushrooms, chopped
150 g/5 oz/generous ½ cup black
   olives, pitted
30 ml/2 tbsp chopped fresh parsley
1 fresh red chilli, seeded and chopped
450 g/1 lb spaghetti
225 g/8 oz cherry tomatoes
slivers of Parmesan cheese, to serve
   (optional)

garlic

mushrooms

red chillies

cherry tomatoes

black olives

spaghetti

parsley

1 Heat the oil in a large pan. Add the garlic and cook for 1 minute. Add the mushrooms, cover, and cook over a medium heat for 5 minutes.

2 Place the mushrooms in a blender or food processor with the olives, parsley and red chilli. Blend until smooth.

3 Cook the pasta following the instructions on the side of the packet until *al dente*. Drain well and return to the pan. Add the olive mixture and toss together until the pasta is well coated. Cover and keep warm.

4 Heat an ungreased frying pan and shake the cherry tomatoes around until they start to split (about 2–3 minutes). Serve the pasta topped with the tomatoes and garnished with slivers of Parmesan, if liked.

287

Pasta with Pesto Sauce

Don't stint on the fresh basil – this is the most wonderful sauce in the world! There are now good fresh pesto sauces in the chilled cabinets of large supermarkets. They taste completely different from the pesto sold in jars.

Serves 4

INGREDIENTS
2 garlic cloves
salt and pepper
50 g/2 oz/½ cup pine nuts
50 g/2 oz/1 cup fresh basil leaves
150 ml/5 fl oz/⅔ cup olive oil (not extra-virgin as it is too strong)
50 g/2 oz/4 tbsp unsalted butter, softened
60 ml/4 tbsp freshly grated Parmesan cheese
450 g/1 lb spaghetti

olive oil

spaghetti

pine nuts

Parmesan cheese

basil

1 Peel the garlic and process in a food processor with a little salt and the pine nuts until broken up. Add the basil leaves and continue mixing to a paste.

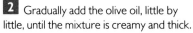

2 Gradually add the olive oil, little by little, until the mixture is creamy and thick.

3 Beat in the butter and season with pepper. Beat in the cheese. (Alternatively, you can make the pesto by hand using a pestle and mortar.)

4 Store the pesto in a jar (with a layer of olive oil on top to exclude the air) in the fridge until needed.

5 Cook the pasta in plenty of boiling salted water according to the manufacturer's instructions. Drain well.

COOK'S TIP

A good pesto can be made using parsley instead of basil and walnuts instead of pine nuts. To make it go further, add a spoonful or two of fromage frais. 'Red' pesto includes sun-dried tomato paste and pounded roasted red peppers.

6 Toss the pasta with half the pesto and serve in warm bowls with the remaining pesto spooned on top.

Pasta Shells with Tomatoes and Rocket

This pretty-coloured pasta dish relies for its success on rocket, a tasty salad green. Available in large supermarkets, it is a leaf easily grown in the garden or in a window box. Rocket has a slightly peppery taste.

Serves 4

INGREDIENTS
450 g/1 lb/4 cups pasta shells
salt and pepper
450 g/1 lb ripe cherry tomatoes
45 ml/3 tbsp olive oil
Parmesan cheese, to serve
75 g/3 oz fresh rocket

olive oil

pasta shells

cherry tomatoes

Parmesan cheese

rocket (arugula)

1 Cook the pasta in plenty of boiling salted water according to the manufacturer's instructions. Drain well.

2 Halve the tomatoes. Trim, wash and dry the rocket.

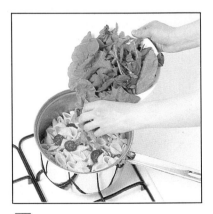

3 Heat the oil in a large saucepan, add the tomatoes and cook for barely 1 minute. The tomatoes should only just heat through and not disintegrate.

4 Shave the Parmesan cheese using a rotary vegetable peeler.

5 Add the pasta, then the rocket. Carefully stir to mix and heat through. Season well with salt and freshly ground black pepper. Serve immediately with plenty of shaved Parmesan cheese.

Spaghetti with Fresh Tomato Sauce

The heat from the pasta will release the delicious flavours of this sauce. Only use the really red and soft tomatoes – large ripe beefsteak or Marmande tomatoes are ideal. Don't be tempted to use small hard tomatoes: they have very little flavour.

Serves 4

INGREDIENTS
4 large ripe tomatoes
2 garlic cloves, finely chopped
60 ml/4 tbsp chopped fresh herbs
    such as basil, marjoram, oregano or
    parsley
150 ml/5 fl oz/⅔ cup olive oil
salt and pepper
450 g/1 lb spaghetti

olive oil

garlic

spaghetti

tomato

2 Lift out with a perforated spoon and plunge into a bowl of cold water. Peel off the skins, then dry the tomatoes on kitchen paper.

3 Halve the tomatoes and squeeze out the seeds. Chop into 6 mm/¼ in cubes and mix with the garlic, herbs, olive oil and seasoning in a non-metallic bowl.

1 Skin the tomatoes by placing in boiling water for 1 minute – no longer or they will become mushy.

4 Cook the pasta in plenty of boiling salted water.

5 Drain the pasta and mix with the sauce. Cover with a lid and leave for 2–3 minutes, toss again and serve immediately.

VARIATION

Mix 100 g/4 oz/¾ cup stoned (pitted) and chopped black Greek-style olives into the sauce just before serving.

Tagliatelle with Gorgonzola Sauce

Gorgonzola is a creamy Italian blue cheese. As an alternative you could use Danish Blue or Pipo Creme.

Serves 4

INGREDIENTS
25 g/1 oz/2 tbsp butter, plus extra for
  tossing the pasta
225 g/8 oz Gorgonzola cheese
150 ml/5 fl oz/⅔ cup double (heavy)
  or whipping cream
30 ml/2 tbsp dry vermouth
5 ml/1 tsp cornflour (cornstarch)
15 ml/1 tbsp chopped fresh sage
salt and pepper
450 g/1 lb tagliatelle

tagliatelle

Gorgonzola

sage

1 Melt 25 g/1 oz/2 tbsp butter in a heavy saucepan (it needs to be thick-based to prevent the cheese from burning). Stir in 175 g/6 oz crumbled Gorgonzola cheese and stir over a very gentle heat for 2–3 minutes until the cheese is melted.

2 Pour in the cream, vermouth and cornflour, whisking well to amalgamate. Stir in the chopped sage, then taste and season. Cook, whisking all the time, until the sauce boils and thickens. Set aside.

3 Boil the pasta in plenty of salted water according to the manufacturer's instructions. Drain well and toss with a little butter.

4 Reheat the sauce gently, whisking well. Divide the pasta between 4 serving bowls, top with the sauce and sprinkle over the remaining cheese. Serve immediately.

Pasta with Tomato and Cream Sauce

Here pasta is served with a deliciously rich version of ordinary tomato sauce.

Serves 4–6

INGREDIENTS
30 ml/2 tbsp olive oil
2 garlic cloves, crushed
400 g/14 oz canned chopped
    tomatoes
150 ml/5 fl oz/⅔ cup double (heavy)
    or whipping cream
30 ml/2 tbsp chopped fresh herbs
    such as basil, oregano or parsley
salt and pepper
450 g/1 lb/4 cups pasta, any variety

chopped tomatoes

olive oil

pasta

parsley

garlic

1 Heat the oil in a medium saucepan, add the garlic and cook for 2 minutes until golden.

2 Stir in the tomatoes, bring to the boil and simmer uncovered for 20 minutes, stirring occasionally to prevent sticking. The sauce is ready when you can see the oil separating on top.

3 Add the cream, bring slowly to the boil again and simmer until slightly thickened. Stir in the herbs, taste and season well.

4 Cook the pasta in plenty of boiling salted water according to the manufacturer's instructions. Drain well and toss with the sauce. Serve piping hot, sprinkled with extra herbs if liked.

COOK'S TIP

If you are really in a hurry, buy a good ready-made tomato sauce and simply stir in the cream and simmer until thickened.

Rigatoni with Spicy Sausage and Tomato Sauce

This is really a cheat's Bolognese sauce using the wonderful fresh spicy sausages sold in every Italian delicatessen.

Serves 4

INGREDIENTS
450 g/1 lb fresh spicy Italian sausage
30 ml/2 tbsp olive oil
1 medium onion, chopped
450 ml/15 fl oz/2 cups passata
    (strained crushed tomatoes)
150 ml/5 fl oz/⅔ cup dry red wine
6 sun-dried tomatoes in oil, drained
salt and pepper
450 g/1 lb/4 cups rigatoni or similar
    pasta
freshly grated Parmesan cheese, to
    serve

rigatoni

Italian sausage

Parmesan cheese

onion

sun-dried tomatoes

1 Squeeze the sausages out of their skins into a bowl and break up the meat.

2 Heat the oil in a medium saucepan and add the onion. Cook for 5 minutes until soft and golden. Stir in the sausagemeat, browning it all over and breaking up the lumps with a wooden spoon. Pour in the passata and the wine. Bring to the boil.

3 Slice the sun-dried tomatoes and add to the sauce. Simmer for 3 minutes until reduced, stirring occasionally. Season.

4 Cook the pasta in plenty of boiling salted water according to the manufacturer's instructions. Drain well and top with the sauce. Serve with grated Parmesan cheese.

Pasta with Fresh Tomato and Smoky Bacon Sauce

A wonderful sauce to prepare in mid-summer when the tomatoes are ripe and sweet.

Serves 4

INGREDIENTS
900 g/2 lb ripe tomatoes
6 rashers (slices) smoked streaky bacon
50 g/2 oz/4 tbsp butter
1 medium onion, chopped
salt and pepper
15 ml/1 tbsp chopped fresh oregano or 5 ml/1 tsp dried oregano
450 g/1 lb/4 cups pasta, any variety
freshly grated Parmesan cheese, to serve

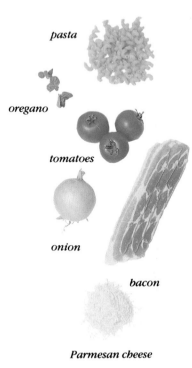

pasta

oregano

tomatoes

onion

bacon

Parmesan cheese

1 Plunge the tomatoes into boiling water for 1 minute, then into cold water to stop them from becoming mushy. Slip off the skins. Halve the tomatoes, remove the seeds and cores and roughly chop the flesh.

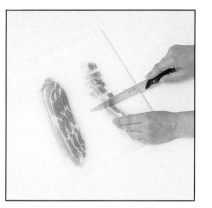

2 Remove the rind from the bacon and roughly chop.

3 Melt the butter in a saucepan and add the bacon. Fry until lightly brown, then add the onion and cook gently for 5 minutes until softened. Add the tomatoes, salt, pepper and oregano. Simmer gently for 10 minutes.

4 Cook the pasta in plenty of boiling salted water according to the manufacturer's instructions. Drain well and toss with the sauce. Serve with grated Parmesan cheese.

Tagliatelle with Prosciutto and Parmesan

A really simple dish, prepared in minutes from the best ingredients.

Serves 4

INGREDIENTS
100 g/4 oz prosciutto
450 g/1 lb tagliatelle
salt and pepper
75 g/3 oz/6 tbsp butter
50 g/2 oz/½ cup freshly grated
  Parmesan cheese
few fresh sage leaves, to garnish

tagliatelle

sage

prosciutto

Parmesan cheese

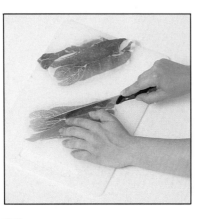

1 Cut the prosciutto into strips of the same width as the tagliatelle. Cook the pasta in plenty of boiling salted water according to manufacturer's instructions.

2 Meanwhile melt the butter gently in a saucepan, stir in the prosciutto strips and heat through, but do not fry.

3 Drain the tagliatelle well and pile into a warm serving dish.

4 Sprinkle over all the Parmesan cheese and pour over the buttery prosciutto. Season well with black pepper and garnish with the sage leaves.

Paglia e Fieno

The title of this dish translates as 'straw and hay' which refers to the yellow and green colours of the pasta when mixed together. Using fresh peas makes all the difference to this dish.

Serves 4

INGREDIENTS
50 g/2 oz/4 tbsp butter
350 g/12 oz/2 cups frozen petits pois (small peas) or 900 g/2 lb fresh peas, shelled
150 ml/5 fl oz/⅔ cup double (heavy) cream, plus 60 ml/4 tbsp extra
450 g/1 lb tagliatelle (plain and spinach mixed)
50 g/2 oz/½ cup freshly grated Parmesan cheese, plus extra to serve
salt and pepper
freshly grated nutmeg

tagliatelle

peas

Parmesan cheese

COOK'S TIP
Sautéed mushrooms and narrow strips of cooked ham also make a good addition.

1 Melt the butter in a heavy saucepan and add the peas. Sauté for 2–3 minutes, then add the cream, bring to the boil and simmer for 1 minute until slightly thickened.

2 Cook the fettuccine in plenty of boiling salted water according to the manufacturer's instructions, but for 2 minutes' less time. The pasta should still be *al dente*. Drain very well and turn into the pan with the cream and pea sauce.

3 Place on the heat and turn the pasta in the sauce to coat. Pour in the extra cream, the cheese, salt and pepper to taste and a little grated nutmeg. Toss until well coated and heated through. Serve immediately with extra Parmesan cheese.

Tagliatelle with Pea Sauce, Asparagus and Broad Beans

A creamy pea sauce makes a wonderful combination with the crunchy young vegetables.

Serves 4

INGREDIENTS
15 ml/1 tbsp olive oil
1 garlic clove, crushed
6 spring onions, sliced
225 g/8 oz/1 cup frozen peas, defrosted
350 g/12 oz fresh young asparagus
30 ml/2 tbsp chopped fresh sage, plus extra leaves to garnish
finely grated rind of 2 lemons
450 ml/¾ pint/1¾ cups vegetable stock or water
225 g/8 oz frozen broad beans, defrosted
450 g/1 lb tagliatelle
60 ml/4 tbsp low-fat yogurt

lemon

garlic

asparagus

broad beans

peas

yogurt

tagliatelle

sage

spring onion

1 Heat the oil in a pan. Add the garlic and spring onions and cook gently for 2–3 minutes until softened.

2 Add the peas and ⅓ of the asparagus, together with the sage, lemon rind and stock or water. Bring to the boil, reduce the heat and simmer for 10 minutes until tender. Purée in a blender until smooth.

3 Meanwhile remove the outer skins from the broad beans and discard.

5 Cook the tagliatelle following the instructions on the side of the packet until *al dente*. Drain well.

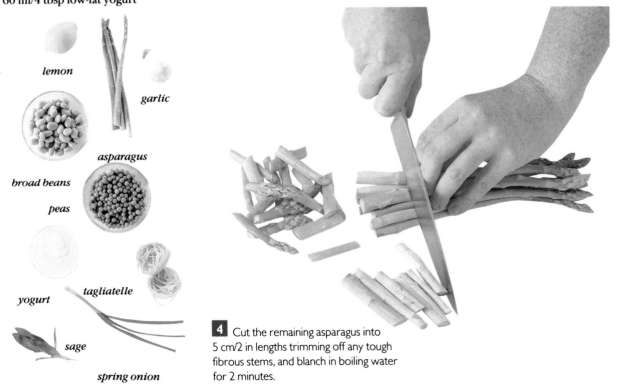

4 Cut the remaining asparagus into 5 cm/2 in lengths trimming off any tough fibrous stems, and blanch in boiling water for 2 minutes.

COOK'S TIP

Frozen peas and beans have been used here to cut down the preparation time, but the dish tastes even better if you use fresh young vegetables when in season.

6 Add the cooked asparagus and shelled beans to the sauce and reheat. Stir in the yogurt and toss into the tagliatelle. Garnish with a few extra sage leaves and serve.

Pasta Bows with Fennel and Walnut Sauce

A scrumptious blend of walnuts and crisp steamed fennel.

Serves 4

INGREDIENTS
75 g/3 oz/½ cup walnuts, roughly
    chopped
1 garlic clove
25 g/1 oz fresh flat-leaf parsley, picked
    from the stalks
115 g/4 oz/½ cup ricotta cheese
450 g/1 lb pasta bows
450 g/1 lb fennel bulbs
chopped walnuts, to garnish

garlic

pasta bows

ricotta

fennel

parsley

walnut halves

chopped walnuts

1 Place the chopped walnuts, garlic and parsley in a food processor. Pulse until roughly chopped. Transfer to a bowl and stir in the ricotta.

2 Cook the pasta following the instructions on the side of the packet until *al dente*. Drain well.

3 Slice the fennel thinly and steam for 4–5 minutes until just tender but still crisp.

4 Return the pasta to the pan and add the walnut mixture and the fennel. Toss well and sprinkle with the chopped walnuts. Serve immediately.

Pasta Rapido with Parsley Pesto

Pasta suppers can often be dull. Here's a fresh, lively sauce that will stir the appetite.

Serves 4

INGREDIENTS
450 g/1 lb dried pasta
75 g/3 oz/¾ cup whole almonds
50 g/2 oz/½ cup flaked almonds, toasted
25 g/1 oz/¼ cup freshly grated Parmesan cheese
pinch of salt

FOR THE SAUCE
35 g/1½ oz fresh parsley
2 garlic cloves, crushed
45 ml/3 tbsp olive oil
45 ml/3 tbsp lemon juice
5 ml/1 tsp sugar
250 ml/8 fl oz/1 cup boiling water

pasta

lemon

parsley

garlic

Parmesan cheese

flaked almonds

almonds

1 Bring a large saucepan of salted water to the boil. Toss in the pasta and cook according to the instructions on the packet. Toast the whole and flaked almonds separately under a moderate grill until golden brown. Put the flaked almonds aside until required.

2 For the sauce, chop the parsley finely in a food processor. Add the whole almonds and reduce to a fine consistency. Add the garlic, olive oil, lemon juice, sugar and water. Combine to make a sauce.

3 Drain the pasta and combine with half of the sauce. (The remainder of the sauce will keep in a screw-topped jar in the refrigerator for up to ten days.) Top with Parmesan and flaked almonds.

COOK'S TIP

To prevent pasta from sticking together during cooking, use plenty of water and stir well before the water returns to the boil.

Pasta with Prawns and Feta Cheese

This dish combines the richness of fresh prawns with the tartness of feta cheese. Goat's cheese could also be used.

Serves 4

INGREDIENTS
450 g/1 lb medium raw prawns
6 spring onions
50 g/2 oz/4 tbsp butter
225 g/8 oz feta cheese
small bunch fresh chives
450 g/1 lb/4 cups penne, garganelle
    or rigatoni
salt and ground black pepper

penne

spring onions

feta

chives

prawns

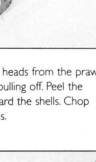

1 Remove the heads from the prawns by twisting and pulling off. Peel the prawns and discard the shells. Chop the spring onions.

2 Melt the butter in a frying pan and stir in the prawns. When they turn pink, add the spring onions and cook gently for 1 minute.

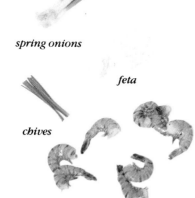

3 Cut the feta into 1 cm/½ in cubes.

4 Stir the feta cheese into the prawn mixture and season with black pepper.

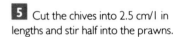

5 Cut the chives into 2.5 cm/1 in lengths and stir half into the prawns.

304

6 Cook the pasta in plenty of boiling salted water according to the manufacturer's instructions. Drain well, pile into a warmed serving dish and top with the sauce. Scatter with the remaining chives and serve.

Spaghetti alla Carbonara

It has been said that this dish was originally cooked by Italian coal miners or charcoal-burners, hence the name 'carbonara'. The secret of its creamy sauce is not to overcook the egg.

Serves 4

INGREDIENTS
175 g/6 oz unsmoked streaky bacon
1 garlic clove, chopped
3 eggs
450 g/1 lb spaghetti
salt and pepper
60 ml/4 tbsp freshly grated Parmesan
    cheese

bacon

garlic

spaghetti

eggs

Parmesan cheese

1 Cut the bacon into dice and place in a medium saucepan. Place over the heat and fry in its own fat with the garlic until brown. Keep warm until needed.

2 Whisk the eggs together in a bowl.

3 Cook the spaghetti in plenty of boiling salted water according to the manufacturer's instructions until *al dente*. Drain well.

4 Quickly turn the spaghetti into the pan with the bacon and stir in the eggs, a little salt, lots of pepper and half the cheese. Toss well to mix. The eggs should half-cook with the heat from the spaghetti. Serve in warm bowls with the remaining cheese.

Spaghetti with Tomato and Clam Sauce

Small sweet clams make this a delicately succulent sauce. Cockles would make a good substitute, or even mussels. Don't be tempted to use seafood pickled in vinegar – the result will be inedible!

Serves 4

INGREDIENTS

900 g/2 lb live small clams, or 2 ×
    400 g/14 oz cans clams in brine,
    drained
90 ml/6 tbsp olive oil
2 garlic cloves, crushed
600 g/1 lb 5 oz canned chopped
    tomatoes
45 ml/3 tbsp chopped fresh parsley
salt and pepper
450 g/1 lb spaghetti

olive oil   *spaghetti*

parsley

garlic

clams

I If using live clams, place them in a bowl of cold water and rinse several times to remove any grit or sand. Drain.

2 Heat the oil in a saucepan and add the clams. Stir over a high heat until the clams open. Throw away any that do not open. Transfer the clams to a bowl with a perforated spoon.

3 Reduce the clam juice left in the pan to almost nothing by boiling fast; this will also concentrate the flavour. Add the garlic and fry until golden. Pour in the tomatoes, bring to the boil and cook for 3–4 minutes until reduced. Stir in the clam mixture or canned clams and half the parsley and heat through. Season.

4 Cook the pasta in plenty of boiling salted water according to the manufacturer's instructions. Drain well and turn into a warm serving dish. Pour over the sauce and sprinkle with the remaining parsley.

Capellini with Rocket, Mangetout and Pine Nuts

A light but filling pasta dish with the added pepperiness of fresh rocket.

Serves 4

INGREDIENTS
250 g/9 oz capellini or angel-hair pasta
225 g/8 oz mangetout
175 g/6 oz rocket
50 g/2 oz/¼ cup pine nuts, roasted
30 ml/2 tbsp Parmesan cheese, finely
  grated (optional)
30 ml/2 tbsp olive oil (optional)

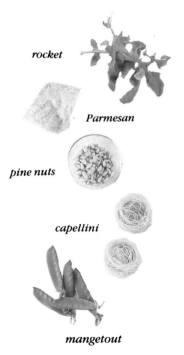

rocket

Parmesan

pine nuts

capellini

mangetout

1 Cook the capellini or angel-hair pasta following the instructions on the side of the packet until *al dente*.

2 Meanwhile, carefully top and tail the mangetout.

3 As soon as the pasta is cooked, drop in the rocket and mangetout. Drain immediately.

4 Toss the pasta with the roasted pine nuts, and Parmesan and olive oil if using. Serve at once.

Campanelle with Yellow Pepper Sauce

Roasted yellow peppers make a deliciously sweet and creamy sauce to serve with pasta.

Serves 4

INGREDIENTS
2 yellow peppers
50 g/2 oz/¼ cup soft goat's cheese
115 g/4 oz/½ cup low-fat fromage blanc
salt and freshly ground black pepper
450 g/1 lb short pasta such as campanelle or fusilli
50 g/2 oz/¼ cup flaked almonds, toasted, to serve

pepper

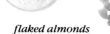
fromage blanc

flaked almonds

goat's cheese

campanelle

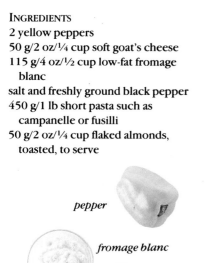

1 Place the whole yellow peppers under a preheated grill until charred and blistered. Place in a plastic bag to cool. Peel and remove the seeds.

2 Place the pepper flesh in a blender with the goat's cheese and fromage blanc. Blend until smooth. Season with salt and lots of black pepper.

3 Cook the pasta following the instructions on the side of the packet until *al dente*. Drain well.

4 Toss with the sauce and serve sprinkled with the toasted flaked almonds.

Spinach and Ricotta Conchiglie

Large pasta shells are designed to hold a variety of delicious stuffings. Few are more pleasing than this mixture of chopped spinach and ricotta cheese.

COOK'S TIP

Choose a large saucepan when cooking pasta and give it an occasional stir to prevent shapes from sticking together. If passata is not available, use a can of chopped tomatoes, sieved and puréed.

Serves 4

INGREDIENTS

350 g/12 oz large conchiglie
450 ml/¾ pint/scant 2 cups passata or tomato pulp
275 g/10 oz frozen chopped spinach, defrosted
50 g/2 oz crustless white bread, crumbled
120 ml/4 fl oz/½ cup milk
45 ml/3 tbsp olive oil
250 g/8 oz/2¼ cups Ricotta cheese
pinch of nutmeg
1 garlic clove, crushed
15 ml/1 tbsp olive oil
2.5 ml/½ tsp black olive paste (optional)
25 g/1 oz/¼ cup freshly grated Parmesan cheese
25 g/1 oz/2 tbsp pine nuts
salt and freshly ground black pepper

olive paste

pine nuts

Ricotta cheese

garlic

spinach

conchiglie

1 Bring a large saucepan of salted water to the boil. Toss in the pasta and cook according to the directions on the packet. Refresh under cold water, drain and reserve until needed.

2 Pour the passata or tomato pulp into a nylon sieve over a bowl and strain to thicken. Place the spinach in another sieve and press out any excess liquid with the back of a spoon.

3 Place the bread, milk and oil in a food processor and combine. Add the spinach and Ricotta and season with salt, pepper and nutmeg.

4 Combine the passata with the garlic, olive oil and olive paste if using. Spread the sauce evenly over the bottom of an ovenproof dish.

5 Spoon the spinach mixture into a piping bag fitted with a large plain nozzle and fill the pasta shapes (alternatively fill with a spoon). Arrange the pasta shapes over the sauce.

6 Preheat a moderate grill. Heat the pasta through in a microwave oven at high power (100%) for 4 minutes. Scatter with Parmesan cheese and pine nuts, and finish under the grill to brown the cheese.

Macaroni Cheese with Mushrooms

Macaroni cheese is an all-time classic from the mid-week menu. Here it is served in a light creamy sauce with mushrooms and topped with pine nuts.

Serves 4

INGREDIENTS
450 g/1 lb quick-cooking elbow
    macaroni
45 ml/3 tbsp olive oil
225 g/8 oz button mushrooms, sliced
2 fresh thyme sprigs
60 ml/4 tbsp plain flour
1 vegetable stock cube
600 ml/1 pint/2½ cups milk
2.5 ml/½ tsp celery salt
5 ml/1 tsp Dijon mustard
175 g/6 oz/1½ cups grated
    Cheddar cheese
25 g/1 oz/¼ cup freshly grated
    Parmesan cheese
25 g/1 oz/2 tbsp pine nuts
salt and freshly ground black pepper

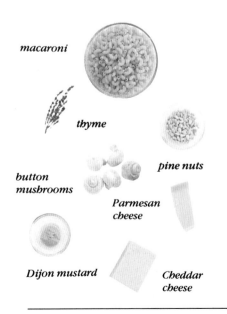

macaroni

thyme

pine nuts

button mushrooms

Parmesan cheese

Dijon mustard

Cheddar cheese

1 Bring a pan of salted water to the boil. Add the macaroni and cook according to the packet instructions.

2 Heat the oil in a heavy saucepan. Add the mushrooms and thyme, cover and cook over a gentle heat for 2–3 minutes. Stir in the flour and draw from the heat, add the stock cube and stir continuously until evenly blended. Add the milk a little at a time, stirring after each addition. Add the celery salt, mustard and Cheddar cheese and season. Stir and simmer briefly for 1–2 minutes until thickened.

3 Preheat a moderate grill. Drain the macaroni well, toss into the sauce and turn out into four individual dishes or one large flameproof gratin dish. Scatter with grated Parmesan cheese and pine nuts, then grill until brown and bubbly.

COOK'S TIP

Closed button mushrooms are best for white cream sauces. Open varieties can darken a pale sauce to an unattractive sludgy grey.

Singapore Noodles

A delicious supper dish with a stunning mix of flavours and textures.

Serves 4

INGREDIENTS
225 g/8 oz dried egg noodles
45 ml/3 tbsp groundnut oil
1 onion, chopped
2.5 cm/1 in piece fresh root
  ginger, finely chopped
1 garlic clove, finely chopped
15 ml/1 tbsp Madras
  curry powder
2.5 ml/½ tsp salt
115 g/4 oz cooked chicken or
  pork, finely shredded
115 g/4 oz cooked peeled prawns
115 g/4 oz Chinese cabbage
  leaves, shredded
115 g/4 oz beansprouts
60 ml/4 tbsp chicken stock
15–30 ml/1–2 tbsp dark soy sauce
1–2 fresh red chillies, seeded
  and finely shredded
4 spring onions, finely shredded

beansprouts

noodles

Chinese cabbage

ginger

curry powder

chicken

dark soy sauce

onion

stock

spring onions

red chillies

groundnut oil

prawns

1 Cook the noodles according to the packet instructions. Rinse thoroughly under cold water and drain well. Toss in 15 ml/1 tbsp of the oil and set aside.

2 Heat a wok until hot, add the remaining oil and swirl it around. Add the onion, ginger and garlic and stir-fry for about 2 minutes.

3 Add the curry powder and salt, stir-fry for 30 seconds, then add the egg noodles, chicken or pork and prawns. Stir-fry for 3–4 minutes.

4 Add the Chinese cabbage and beansprouts and stir-fry for 1–2 minutes. Sprinkle in the stock and soy sauce to taste and toss well until evenly mixed. Serve at once, garnished with the shredded red chillies and spring onions.

Oriental Vegetable Noodles

Thin Italian egg pasta is a good alternative to Oriental egg noodles; use it fresh or dried.

Serves 6

INGREDIENTS
500 g/1¼ lb thin tagliarini
1 red onion
115 g/4 oz shitake mushrooms
45 ml/3 tbsp sesame oil
45 ml/3 tbsp dark soy sauce
15 ml/1 tbsp balsamic vinegar
10 ml/2 tsp caster sugar
5 ml/1 tsp salt
celery leaves, to garnish

tagliarini

shitake mushrooms

red onion

balsamic vinegar

soy sauce

1 Boil the tagliarini in a large pan of salted boiling water, following the instructions on the pack.

2 Thinly slice the red onion and the mushrooms, using a sharp knife.

3 Heat the wok, then add 15 ml/1 tbsp of the sesame oil. When the oil is hot, stir-fry the onion and mushrooms for 2 minutes.

4 Drain the tagliarini, then add to the wok with the soy sauce, balsamic vinegar, sugar and salt. Stir-fry for 1 minute, then add the remaining sesame oil, and serve garnished with celery leaves.

Fried Singapore Noodles

Thai fish cakes vary in their size, and their hotness. You can buy them from Oriental supermarkets, but, if you cannot get hold of them, simply omit them from the recipe.

Serves 4

INGREDIENTS
175 g/6 oz rice noodles
60 ml/4 tbsp vegetable oil
2.5 ml/½ tsp salt
75 g/3 oz cooked prawns
175 g/6 oz cooked pork, cut
 into matchsticks
1 green pepper, seeded and chopped
 into matchsticks
2.5 ml/½ tsp sugar
10 ml/2 tsp curry powder
75 g/3 oz Thai fish cakes
10 ml/2 tsp dark soy sauce

rice noodles

pork

pepper

prawns

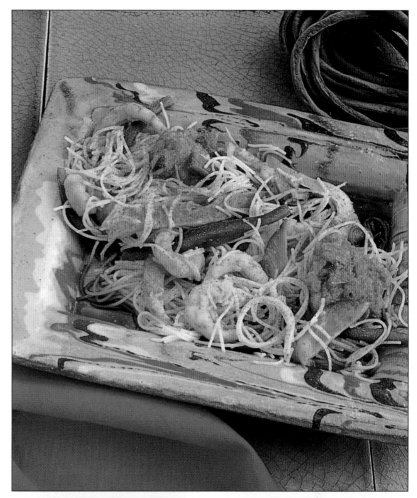

1 Soak the rice noodles in water for about 10 minutes, drain well, then pat dry with kitchen towels.

2 Heat the wok, then add half the oil. When the oil is hot, add the noodles and salt and stir-fry for 2 minutes. Transfer to a heated serving dish to keep warm.

3 Heat the remaining oil and add the prawns, pork, pepper, sugar, curry powder and remaining salt. Stir-fry the ingredients for 1 minute.

4 Return the noodles to the pan and stir-fry with the Thai fish cakes for 2 minutes. Stir in the soy sauce and serve.

Mixed Rice Noodles

A delicious noodle dish made extra special by adding avocado and garnishing with prawns.

Serves 4

INGREDIENTS

15 ml/1 tbsp sunflower oil
2.5 cm/1 in piece root ginger, peeled
    and grated
2 cloves garlic, crushed
45 ml/3 tbsp dark soy sauce
225 g/8 oz peas, thawed if frozen
450 g/1 lb rice noodles
450 g/1 lb fresh spinach, coarse
    stalks removed
30 ml/2 tbsp smooth peanut butter
30 ml/2 tbsp tahini
150 ml/¼ pint/⅔ cup milk
1 ripe avocado, peeled and stoned
roasted peanuts and peeled prawns,
    to garnish

rice noodles

ginger

peas

peanut butter

spinach

1 Heat the wok, then add the oil. When the oil is hot, stir-fry the ginger and garlic for 30 seconds. Add 15 ml/1 tbsp of the soy sauce and 150 ml/¼ pint/⅔ cup boiling water.

2 Add the peas and noodles, then cook for 3 minutes. Stir in the spinach. Remove the vegetables and noodles, drain and keep warm.

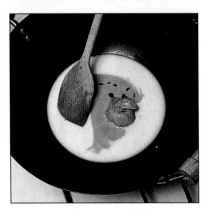

3 Stir the peanut butter, remaining soy sauce, tahini and milk together in the wok, and simmer for 1 minute.

4 Add the vegetables and noodles, slice in the avocado and toss together. Serve piled on individual plates. Spoon some sauce over each portion and garnish with peanuts and prawns.

Mee Krob

This delicious dish makes a filling meal. Take care when frying vermicelli as it has a tendency to spit when added to hot oil.

Serves 4

INGREDIENTS
125 ml/4 fl oz/½ cup vegetable oil
225 g/8 oz rice vermicelli
150 g/5 oz French beans, topped,
    tailed and halved lengthwise
1 onion, finely chopped
2 boneless, skinless chicken breasts,
    about 175 g/6 oz each, cut
    into strips
5 ml/1 tsp chilli powder
225 g/8 oz cooked prawns
45 ml/3 tbsp dark soy sauce
45 ml/3 tbsp white wine vinegar
10 ml/2 tsp caster sugar
fresh coriander sprigs, to garnish

chicken
breast

rice vermicelli

onion

French beans

prawns

1 Heat the wok, then add 60 ml/4 tbsp of the oil. Break up the vermicelli into 7.5 cm/3 in lengths. When the oil is hot, fry the vermicelli in batches. Remove from the heat and keep warm.

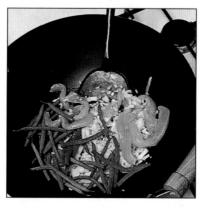

2 Heat the remaining oil in the wok, then add the French beans, onion and chicken and stir-fry for 3 minutes until the chicken is cooked.

3 Sprinkle in the chilli powder. Stir in the prawns, soy sauce, vinegar and sugar, and stir-fry for 2 minutes.

4 Serve the chicken, prawns and vegetables on the vermicelli, garnished with sprigs of fresh coriander.

PIZZA PRESTO

It isn't **surprising** that pizza has become the world's favourite food. What could be more delicious? The vast range of toppings means that there's a **flavour** to suit every palate, from a simple sprinkling of fresh herbs to the classic **combination** of prosciutto, mushrooms and artichokes. Making pizza used to be a protracted affair: the dough needed to be kneaded, then left to rise before being baked. Fortunately we have **swift** solutions today – ready-made bases, pizza mixes and doughs that can be **baked** as soon as they are mixed.

Margherita

(Tomato, Basil and Mozzarella)
This classic pizza is simple to prepare. The sweet flavour of sun-ripe tomatoes works wonderfully with the basil and mozzarella.

Serves 2–3

INGREDIENTS
1 pizza base, about 25–30 cm/10–12 in diameter
30 ml/2 tbsp olive oil
1 quantity Tomato Sauce
150 g/5 oz mozzarella
2 ripe tomatoes, thinly sliced
6–8 fresh basil leaves
30 ml/2 tbsp freshly grated Parmesan
black pepper

basil

mozzarella

Parmesan

olive oil

Tomato Sauce

tomatoes

1 Preheat the oven to 220°C/425°F/Gas 7. Brush the pizza base with 15 ml/1 tbsp of the oil and then spread over the Tomato Sauce.

2 Cut the mozzarella into thin slices.

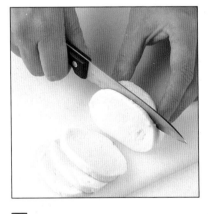

3 Arrange the sliced mozzarella and tomatoes on top of the pizza base.

4 Roughly tear the basil leaves, add and sprinkle with the Parmesan. Drizzle over the remaining oil and season with black pepper. Bake for 15–20 minutes until crisp and golden. Serve immediately.

Marinara

(Tomato and Garlic)
The combination of garlic, good quality olive oil and
oregano give this pizza an unmistakably Italian flavour.

Serves 2–3

INGREDIENTS
60 ml/4 tbsp olive oil
675 g/1½ lb plum tomatoes, peeled,
  seeded and chopped
1 pizza base, about 25–30 cm/10–12 in
  diameter
4 garlic cloves, cut into slivers
15 ml/1 tbsp chopped fresh oregano
salt and black pepper

olive oil

oregano

plum tomatoes

garlic

1 Preheat the oven to 220°C/425°F/
Gas 7. Heat 30 ml/2 tbsp of the oil in a
pan. Add the tomatoes and cook, stirring
frequently for about 5 minutes until soft.

2 Place the tomatoes in a sieve and
leave to drain for about 5 minutes.

3 Transfer the tomatoes to a food
processor or blender and purée until
smooth.

4 Brush the pizza base with half the
remaining oil. Spoon over the tomatoes
and sprinkle with garlic and oregano.
Drizzle over the remaining oil and season.
Bake for 15–20 minutes until crisp and
golden. Serve immediately.

Napoletana

(Tomato, Mozzarella and Anchovies)
This pizza is a speciality of Naples. It is both one of the simplest to prepare and the most tasty.

Serves 2–3

INGREDIENTS
1 pizza base, about 25–30 cm/10–12 in
diameter
30 ml/2 tbsp olive oil
6 plum tomatoes
2 garlic cloves, chopped
115 g/4 oz mozzarella, grated
50 g/2 oz can anchovy fillets, drained
and chopped
15 ml/1 tbsp chopped fresh oregano
30 ml/2 tbsp freshly grated Parmesan
black pepper

Parmesan

mozzarella

anchovy fillets

olive oil

plum tomatoes

garlic

oregano

1 Preheat the oven to 220°C/425°F/
Gas 7. Brush the pizza base with 15 ml/
1 tbsp of the oil. Put the tomatoes in a
bowl and pour over boiling water. Leave
for 30 seconds, then plunge into cold
water.

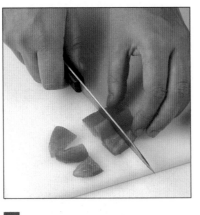

2 Peel, seed and roughly chop the
tomatoes. Spoon the tomatoes over the
pizza base and sprinkle over the garlic.

3 Mix the mozzarella with the
anchovies and scatter over.

4 Sprinkle over the oregano and
Parmesan. Drizzle over the remaining oil
and season with black pepper. Bake for
15–20 minutes until crisp and golden.
Serve immediately.

Quattro Formaggi

(Four Cheeses)
Rich and cheesey, these individual pizzas are quick to
assemble, and the aroma of melting cheese is
irresistible.

Serves 4

INGREDIENTS
1 quantity Superquick Pizza Dough
15 ml/1 tbsp Garlic Oil
½ small red onion, very thinly sliced
50 g/2 oz Dolcelatte
50 g/2 oz mozzarella
50 g/2 oz Gruyère, grated
30 ml/2 tbsp freshly grated Parmesan
15 ml/1 tbsp chopped fresh thyme
black pepper

mozzarella

red onion

Parmesan

Garlic Oil

Dolcelatte

Gruyère

thyme

1 Preheat the oven to 220°C/425°F/
Gas 7. Divide the dough into four pieces
and roll out each one on a lightly floured
surface into a 13 cm/5 in circle. Place well
apart on two greased baking sheets, then
push up the dough edges to make a thin
rim. Brush with Garlic Oil and top with
the red onion.

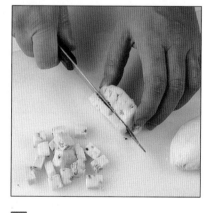

2 Cut the Dolcelatte and mozzarella
into cubes and scatter over the bases.

3 Mix together the Gruyère, Parmesan
and thyme and sprinkle over.

4 Grind over plenty of black pepper.
Bake for 15–20 minutes until crisp and
golden and the cheese is bubbling. Serve
immediately.

Fiorentina

Spinach is the star ingredient of this pizza. A grating of nutmeg to heighten its flavour gives this pizza its unique character.

Serves 2–3

INGREDIENTS
175 g/6 oz fresh spinach
45 ml/3 tbsp olive oil
1 small red onion, thinly sliced
1 pizza base, about 25–30 cm/10–12 in diameter
1 quantity Tomato Sauce
freshly grated nutmeg
150 g/5 oz mozzarella
1 size 3 egg
25 g/1 oz Gruyère, grated

mozzarella

Gruyère

Tomato Sauce

spinach

red onion

nutmeg

egg

1 Preheat the oven to 220°C/425°F/Gas 7. Remove the stalks from the spinach and wash the leaves in plenty of cold water. Drain well and pat dry with kitchen paper.

2 Heat 15 ml/1 tbsp of the oil and fry the onion until soft. Add the spinach and continue to fry until just wilted. Drain off any excess liquid.

3 Brush the pizza base with half the remaining oil. Spread over the Tomato Sauce, then top with the spinach mixture. Grate over some nutmeg.

4 Thinly slice the mozzarella and arrange over the spinach. Drizzle over the remaining oil. Bake for 10 minutes, then remove from the oven.

5 Make a small well in the centre and drop the egg into the hole.

6 Sprinkle over the Gruyère and return to the oven for a further 5–10 minutes until crisp and golden. Serve immediately.

Sun-dried Tomatoes, Basil and Olive Pizza Bites

This quick and easy recipe uses scone pizza dough with the addition of chopped fresh basil.

Makes 24

INGREDIENTS
18–20 fresh basil leaves
1 quantity Scone Pizza Dough
30 ml/2 tbsp tomato oil (from jar of sun-dried tomatoes)
1 quantity Tomato Sauce
115 g/4 oz (drained weight) sun-dried tomatoes in oil, chopped
10 pitted black olives, chopped
50 g/2 oz mozzarella, grated
30 ml/2 tbsp freshly grated Parmesan
shredded basil leaves, to garnish

mozzarella

black olives

Parmesan

Tomato Sauce

tomato oil

basil

sun-dried tomatoes

1 Preheat the oven to 220°C/425°F/ Gas 7. Tear the basil leaves into small pieces. Add half to the scone mix before mixing to a soft dough. Set aside the remainder.

2 Knead the dough gently on a lightly floured surface until smooth. Roll out and use to line a 30 × 18 cm/12 × 7 in Swiss-roll tin. Push up the edges to make a thin rim.

3 Brush the base with 15 ml/1 tbsp of the tomato oil, then spread over the Tomato Sauce. Scatter over the sun-dried tomatoes, olives and remaining basil.

4 Mix together the mozzarella and Parmesan and sprinkle over. Drizzle over the remaining tomato oil. Bake for about 20 minutes. Cut lengthways and across into 24 bite-size pieces. Garnish with extra shredded basil leaves and serve immediately.

Mini Pizzas

For a quick supper dish try these delicious little pizzas made with fresh and sun-dried tomatoes.

Makes 4

INGREDIENTS

1 × 150 g/5 oz packet pizza mix
8 halves sun-dried tomatoes in olive
    oil, drained
50 g/2 oz/½ cup black olives, pitted
225 g/8 oz ripe tomatoes, sliced
50 g/2 oz/¼ cup goat's cheese
30 ml/2 tbsp fresh basil leaves

basil

tomatoes

*sun-dried
tomatoes*

black olives

goat's cheese

1 Preheat the oven to 200°C/400°F/ Gas 6. Make up the pizza base following the instructions on the side of the packet.

2 Divide the dough into 4 and roll each piece out to a 13 cm/5 in disc. Place on a lightly oiled baking sheet.

3 Place the sun-dried tomatoes and olives in a blender or food processor and blend until smooth. Spread the mixture evenly over the pizza bases.

4 Top with the tomato slices and crumble over the goat's cheese. Bake for 10–15 minutes. Sprinkle with the fresh basil and serve.

New Potato, Rosemary and Garlic

New potatoes, smoked mozzarella, rosemary and garlic make the flavour of this pizza unique. For a delicious variation, use sage instead of rosemary.

Serves 2–3

INGREDIENTS
350 g/12 oz new potatoes
45 ml/3 tbsp olive oil
2 garlic cloves, crushed
1 pizza base, 25–30 cm/10–12 in
    diameter
1 red onion, thinly sliced
150 g/5 oz smoked mozzarella, grated
10 ml/2 tsp chopped fresh rosemary
salt and black pepper
30 ml/2 tbsp freshly grated Parmesan,
    to garnish

olive oil

Parmesan

smoked mozzarella

new potatoes

rosemary

red onion

garlic

1 Preheat the oven to 200°C/425°F/ Gas 7. Cook the potatoes in boiling salted water for 5 minutes. Drain well. When cool, peel and slice thinly.

2 Heat 30 ml/2 tbsp of the oil in a frying pan. Add the sliced potatoes and garlic and fry for 5–8 minutes until tender.

3 Brush the pizza base with the remaining oil. Scatter over the onion, then arrange the potatoes on top.

4 Sprinkle over the mozzarella and rosemary. Grind over plenty of black pepper and bake for 15–20 minutes until crisp and golden. Remove from the oven and sprinkle over the Parmesan to serve.

Fresh Herb

Cut this pizza into thin wedges and serve as part of a mixed antipasti.

Serves 8

INGREDIENTS
115 g/4 oz mixed fresh herbs, such as
  parsley, basil and oregano
3 garlic cloves, crushed
120 ml/4 fl oz/½ cup double cream
1 pizza base, 25–30 cm/10–12 in
  diameter
15 ml/1 tbsp Garlic Oil
115 g/4 oz Pecorino, grated
salt and black pepper

double cream

Garlic Oil

Pecorino

basil

parsley

garlic

1 Preheat the oven to 220°C/425°F/
Gas 7. Chop the herbs, in a food
processor if you have one.

2 In a bowl mix together the herbs,
garlic, cream and seasoning.

3 Brush the pizza base with the Garlic
Oil, then spread over the herb mixture.

4 Sprinkle over the Pecorino. Bake for
15–20 minutes until crisp and golden and
the topping is still moist. Cut into thin
wedges and serve immediately.

Spinach and Ricotta Panzerotti

These make great party food to serve with drinks or as tasty appetizers for a crowd.

Makes 20–24

INGREDIENTS

115 g/4 oz frozen chopped spinach,
  defrosted and squeezed dry
50 g/2 oz ricotta
50 g/2 oz freshly grated Parmesan
generous pinch freshly grated nutmeg
2 quantities Superquick Pizza Dough
1 egg white, lightly beaten
vegetable oil for deep-frying
salt and black pepper

nutmeg

ricotta

vegetable oil

egg

frozen spinach

Parmesan

1 Place the spinach, ricotta, Parmesan, nutmeg and seasoning in a bowl and beat until smooth.

2 Roll out the dough on a lightly floured surface to about 3 mm/⅛ in thick. Using a 7.5 cm/3 in plain round cutter stamp out 20–24 circles.

3 Spread a teaspoon of spinach mixture over one half of each circle.

4 Brush the edges of the dough with a little egg white.

5 Fold the dough over the filling and press the edges firmly together to seal.

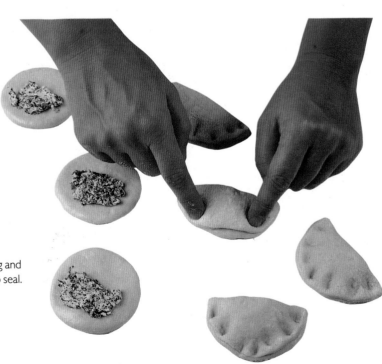

COOK'S TIP

Do serve these as soon as possible after frying, they will become much less appetizing if left to cool.

6 Heat the oil in a large heavy-based pan or deep-fat fryer to 180°C/350°F. Deep-fry the panzerotti a few at a time for 2–3 minutes until golden. Drain on kitchen paper and serve immediately.

Aubergine, Shallot and Sun-dried Tomato Calzone

Aubergines, shallots and sun-dried tomatoes make an unusual filling for calzone. Add more or less red chilli flakes, depending on personal taste.

Serves 2

INGREDIENTS
45 ml/3 tbsp olive oil
2 shallots, chopped
4 baby aubergines
1 garlic clove, chopped
50 g/2 oz (drained weight) sun-dried
  tomatoes in oil, chopped
1.25 ml/¼ tsp dried red chilli flakes
10 ml/2 tsp chopped fresh thyme
1 quantity Superquick Pizza Dough
75 g/3 oz mozzarella, cubed
salt and black pepper
15–30 ml/1–2 tbsp freshly grated
  Parmesan, to serve

Parmesan

mozzarella

thyme

olive oil

baby aubergines

shallots

red chilli flakes

1 Preheat the oven to 220°C/425°F/ Gas 7. Trim the aubergines, then cut into small cubes.

2 Cook the shallots until soft in a frying pan. Add the aubergines, garlic, sun-dried tomatoes, red chilli flakes, thyme and seasoning. Cook for 4–5 minutes, stirring frequently, until the aubergine is beginning to soften.

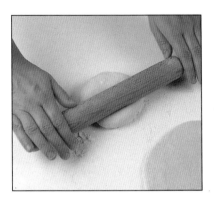

3 Divide the dough in half and roll out each piece on a lightly floured surface to an 18 cm/7 in circle.

4 Spread the aubergine mixture over half of each circle, leaving a 2.5 cm/1 in border, then scatter over the mozzarella.

5 Dampen the edges with water, then fold over the other half of dough to enclose the filling. Press the edges firmly together to seal. Place on two greased baking sheets.

6 Brush with half the remaining oil and make a small hole in the top of each to allow the steam to escape. Bake for 15–20 minutes until golden. Remove from the oven and brush with the remaining oil. Sprinkle over the Parmesan and serve immediately.

Tomato, Fennel and Parmesan

This pizza relies on the winning combination of tomatoes, fennel and Parmesan. The fennel adds both a crisp texture and a distinctive flavour.

Serves 2–3

INGREDIENTS
1 fennel bulb
45 ml/3 tbsp Garlic Oil
1 pizza base, 25–30 cm/10–12 in
   diameter
1 quantity Tomato Sauce
30 ml/2 tbsp chopped fresh flat-leaf
   parsley
50 g/2 oz mozzarella, grated
50 g/2 oz Parmesan, grated
salt and black pepper

flat-leaf parsley

mozzarella

Parmesan

Tomato Sauce

fennel bulb

Garlic Oil

1 Preheat the oven to 220°C/425°F/ Gas 7. Trim and quarter the fennel lengthways. Remove the core and slice thinly.

2 Heat 30 ml/2 tbsp of the Garlic Oil in a frying pan and sauté the fennel for 4–5 minutes until just tender. Season.

3 Brush the pizza base with the remaining Garlic Oil and spread over the Tomato Sauce. Spoon the fennel on top and scatter over the flat-leaf parsley.

4 Mix together the mozzarella and Parmesan and sprinkle over. Bake for 15–20 minutes until crisp and golden. Serve immediately.

Red Onion, Gorgonzola and Sage

This topping combines the richness of Gorgonzola with the earthy flavours of sage and sweet red onions.

Serves 4

INGREDIENTS
1 quantity Superquick Pizza Dough
30 ml/2 tbsp Garlic Oil
2 small red onions
150 g/5 oz Gorgonzola *piccante*
2 garlic cloves
10 ml/2 tsp chopped fresh sage
black pepper

sage

Gorgonzola

garlic

Garlic Oil

red onions

1 Preheat the oven to 220°C/425°F/ Gas 7. Divide the dough into eight pieces and roll out each one on a lightly floured surface to a small oval about 5 mm/¼ in thick. Place well apart on two greased baking sheets and prick with a fork. Brush the bases well with 15 ml/1 tbsp of the Garlic Oil.

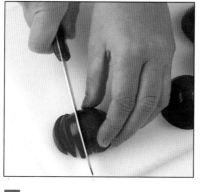

2 Halve, then slice the onions into thin wedges. Scatter over the pizza bases.

3 Remove the rind from the Gorgonzola. Cut the cheese into small cubes, then scatter it over the onions.

4 Cut the garlic lengthways into thin strips and sprinkle over, along with the sage. Drizzle the remaining oil on top and grind over plenty of black pepper. Bake for 10–15 minutes until crisp and golden. Serve immediately.

Spring Vegetable and Pine Nuts

This colourful pizza is well worth the time it takes to prepare. You can vary the ingredients according to availability.

Serves 2–3

INGREDIENTS
1 pizza base, 25–30 cm/10–12 in diameter
45 ml/3 tbsp Garlic Oil
1 quantity Tomato Sauce
4 spring onions
2 courgettes
1 leek
115 g/4 oz asparagus tips
15 ml/1 tbsp chopped fresh oregano
30 ml/2 tbsp pine nuts
50 g/2 oz mozzarella, grated
30 ml/2 tbsp freshly grated Parmesan
black pepper

Parmesan

mozzarella

Tomato Sauce

spring onions

leek

courgette

asparagus

pine nuts

1 Preheat the oven to 220°C/425°F/ Gas 7. Brush the pizza base with 15 ml/1 tbsp of the Garlic Oil then spread over the Tomato Sauce.

2 Slice the spring onions, courgettes, leek and asparagus.

3 Heat half the remaining Garlic Oil in a frying pan and stir-fry the vegetables for 3–5 minutes.

4 Arrange the vegetables over the Tomato Sauce.

5 Sprinkle the oregano and pine nuts over the pizza.

6 Mix together the mozzarella and Parmesan and sprinkle over. Drizzle over the remaining Garlic Oil and season with black pepper. Bake for 15–20 minutes until crisp and golden. Serve immediately.

Quattro Stagioni

(Four Seasons)

This traditional pizza is divided into quarters, each with a different topping to depict the four seasons of the year.

Serves 2–4

INGREDIENTS
45 ml/3 tbsp olive oil
50 g/2 oz button mushrooms, sliced
1 pizza base, about 25–30 cm/10–12 in
    diameter
1 quantity Tomato Sauce
50 g/2 oz Parma ham
6 pitted black olives, chopped
4 bottled artichoke hearts in oil,
    drained
3 canned anchovy fillets, drained
50 g/2 oz mozzarella, thinly sliced
8 fresh basil leaves, shredded
black pepper

artichoke hearts

mozzarella

olive oil

Tomato Sauce

Parma ham

basil

black olives

button mushrooms

anchovy fillets

1 Preheat the oven to 220°C/425°F/ Gas 7. Heat 15 ml/1 tbsp of the oil in a frying pan and fry the mushrooms until all the juices have evaporated. Leave to cool.

2 Brush the pizza base with half the remaining oil. Spread over the Tomato Sauce and mark into four equal sections with a knife.

3 Arrange the mushrooms over one section of the pizza.

4 Cut the Parma ham into strips and arrange with the olives on another section.

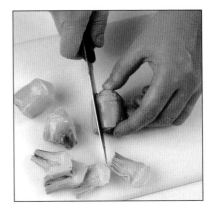

5 Thinly slice the artichoke hearts and arrange over a third section. Halve the anchovies lengthways and arrange with the mozzarella over the fourth section.

6 Scatter over the basil. Drizzle over the remaining oil and season with black pepper. Bake for 15–20 minutes until crisp and golden. Serve immediately.

Pancetta, Leek and Smoked Mozzarella

Smoked mozzarella with its brownish smoky-flavoured skin, pancetta and leeks make this an extremely tasty and easy-to-prepare pizza, ideal for a light lunch.

Serves 4

INGREDIENTS
30 ml/2 tbsp freshly grated Parmesan
1 quantity Superquick Pizza Dough
30 ml/2 tbsp olive oil
2 medium leeks
8–12 slices pancetta
150 g/5 oz smoked mozzarella
black pepper

pancetta

leeks

smoked mozzarella

olive oil

Parmesan

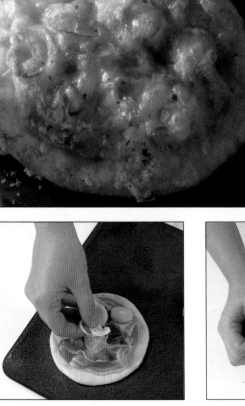

1 Preheat the oven to 220°C/425°F/ Gas 7. Dust the work surface with the Parmesan, then knead into the dough. Divide the dough into four pieces and roll out each one to a 13 cm/5 in circle. Place well apart on two greased baking sheets, then push up the edges to make a thin rim. Brush with 15 ml/1 tbsp of the oil.

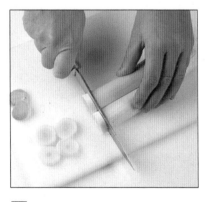

2 Trim and thinly slice the leeks.

3 Arrange the pancetta and leeks on the pizza bases.

4 Grate the smoked mozzarella and sprinkle over. Drizzle over the remaining oil and season with black pepper. Bake for 15–20 minutes until crisp and golden. Serve immediately.

Ham and Mozzarella Calzone

A calzone is a kind of "inside-out" pizza – the dough is on the outside and the filling on the inside. For a vegetarian version replace the ham with sautéed mushrooms or chopped cooked spinach.

Serves 2

INGREDIENTS
1 quantity Superquick Pizza Dough
115 g/4 oz ricotta
30 ml/2 tbsp freshly grated Parmesan
1 egg yolk
30 ml/2 tbsp chopped fresh basil
75 g/3 oz cooked ham, finely chopped
75 g/3 oz mozzarella, cut into small
  cubes
olive oil for brushing
salt and black pepper

basil

ricotta

egg

mozzarella

Parmesan

cooked ham

1 Preheat the oven to 220°C/425°F/ Gas 7. Divide the dough in half and roll out each piece on a lightly floured surface to an 18 cm/7 in circle.

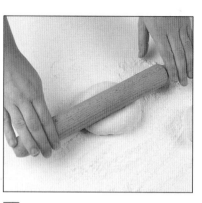

2 In a bowl mix together the ricotta, Parmesan, egg yolk, basil and seasoning.

3 Spread the mixture over half of each circle, leaving a 2.5 cm/1 in border, then scatter the ham and mozzarella on top. Dampen the edges with water, then fold over the other half of dough to enclose the filling.

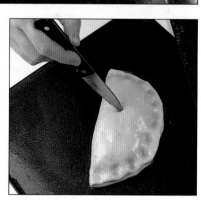

4 Press the edges firmly together to seal. Place on two greased baking sheets. Brush with oil and make a small hole in the top of each to allow the steam to escape. Bake for 15–20 minutes until golden. Serve immediately.

Prosciutto, Mushroom and Artichoke

Here is a pizza full of rich and varied flavours. For a delicious variation use mixed cultivated mushrooms.

Serves 2–3

INGREDIENTS
1 bunch spring onions
60 ml/4 tbsp olive oil
225 g/8 oz mushrooms, sliced
2 garlic cloves, chopped
1 pizza base, about 25–30 cm/10–12 in
  diameter
8 slices prosciutto *di speck*
4 bottled artichoke hearts in oil,
  drained and sliced
60 ml/4 tbsp freshly grated Parmesan
salt and black pepper
thyme sprigs, to garnish

Parmesan

spring onions

mushrooms

prosciutto

olive oil

artichoke hearts

1 Preheat the oven to 220°C/425°F/ Gas 7. Trim the spring onions, then chop all the white and some of the green stems.

2 Heat 30 ml/2 tbsp of the oil in a frying pan. Add the spring onions, mushrooms and garlic and fry over a moderate heat until all the juices have evaporated. Season and leave to cool.

3 Brush the pizza base with half the remaining oil. Arrange the prosciutto, mushrooms and artichoke hearts on top.

4 Sprinkle over the Parmesan, then drizzle over the remaining oil and season. Bake for 15–20 minutes. Garnish with thyme sprigs and serve immediately.

Ham and Pineapple French Bread Pizza

French bread makes a great pizza base. For a really speedy recipe use ready-prepared pizza topping instead of the Tomato Sauce.

Serves 4

INGREDIENTS
2 small baguettes
1 quantity Tomato Sauce
75 g/3 oz sliced cooked ham
4 rings canned pineapple, drained
    well and chopped
½ small green pepper, seeded and cut
    into thin strips
75 g/3 oz mature Cheddar
salt and black pepper

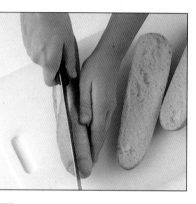

mature Cheddar

green pepper

pineapple

cooked ham

baguette

Tomato Sauce

1 Preheat the oven to 200°C/400°F/Gas 6. Cut the baguettes in half lengthways and toast the cut sides until crisp and golden.

2 Spread the Tomato Sauce over the toasted baguettes.

3 Cut the ham into strips and arrange on the baguettes with the pineapple and pepper. Season.

4 Grate the Cheddar and sprinkle on top. Bake or grill for 15–20 minutes until crisp and golden.

Parma Ham, Roasted Peppers and Mozzarella Ciabatta Pizzas

Succulent roasted peppers, salty Parma ham and creamy mozzarella – the delicious flavours of these easy pizzas are hard to beat.

Serves 2

INGREDIENTS
½ loaf ciabatta bread
1 red pepper, roasted and peeled
1 yellow pepper, roasted and peeled
4 slices Parma ham, cut into thick strips
75 g/3 oz mozzarella
black pepper
tiny basil leaves, to garnish

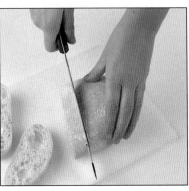

ciabatta

basil

mozzarella

Parma ham

red and yellow peppers

1 Cut the ciabatta bread into four thick slices and toast both sides until golden.

2 Cut the roasted peppers into thick strips and arrange on the toasted bread with the Parma ham.

3 Thinly slice the mozzarella and arrange on top. Grind over plenty of black pepper. Place under a hot grill for 2–3 minutes until the cheese is bubbling.

4 Arrange the basil leaves on top and serve immediately.

Chorizo and Sweetcorn

The combination of spicy chorizo and sweet, tender corn works well in this hearty and colourful pizza. For a simple variation you could use chopped fresh basil instead of flat-leaf parsley.

Serves 2–3

INGREDIENTS

1 pizza base, about 25–30 cm/10–12 in
   diameter
15 ml/1 tbsp Garlic Oil
1 quantity Tomato Sauce
175 g/6 oz chorizo sausages
175 g/6 oz (drained weight) canned
   sweetcorn kernels
30 ml/2 tbsp chopped fresh flat-leaf
   parsley
50 g/2 oz mozzarella, grated
30 ml/2 tbsp freshly grated Parmesan

Tomato Sauce

flat-leaf parsley

mozzarella

chorizo sausages

Garlic Oil

Parmesan

sweetcorn

1 Preheat the oven to 220°C/425°F/ Gas 7. Brush the pizza base with Garlic Oil and spread over the Tomato Sauce.

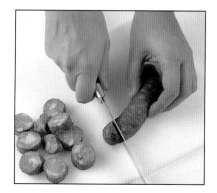

2 Skin and cut the chorizo sausages into chunks and scatter over the Tomato Sauce. Bake for 10 minutes then remove from the oven.

3 Sprinkle over the sweetcorn and flat-leaf parsley.

4 Mix together the mozzarella and Parmesan and sprinkle over. Bake for a further 5–10 minutes until crisp and golden. Serve immediately.

American Hot

This popular pizza is spiced with green chillies and pepperoni.

Serves 2–3

INGREDIENTS
1 pizza base, about 25–30 cm/10–12 in
 diameter
15 ml/1 tbsp olive oil
115 g/4 oz can peeled and chopped
 green chillies in brine, drained
1 quantity Tomato Sauce
75 g/3 oz sliced pepperoni
6 pitted black olives
15 ml/1 tbsp chopped fresh oregano
115 g/4 oz mozzarella, grated
oregano leaves, to garnish

mozzarella

oregano

Tomato Sauce

pepperoni

olive oil

green chillies

black olives

1 Preheat the oven to 220°C/425°F/ Gas 7. Brush the pizza base with the oil.

2 Stir the chillies into the sauce, and spread over the base.

3 Scatter over the pepperoni.

4 Halve the olives lengthways and scatter over, with the oregano.

5 Sprinkle over the grated mozzarella and bake for 15–20 minutes until the pizza is crisp and golden.

VARIATION

You can make this pizza as hot as you like. For a really fiery version use fresh red or green chillies, cut into thin slices, in place of the chillies in brine.

6 Garnish with oregano leaves and serve immediately.

Spicy Sausage

This is a tasty and substantial pizza. You may substitute fresh Italian spicy sausages, available from good Italian delicatessens, if you prefer.

Serves 3–4

INGREDIENTS
225 g/8 oz good quality pork sausages
5 ml/1 tsp mild chilli powder
2.5 ml/½ tsp freshly ground black
  pepper
30 ml/2 tbsp olive oil
2–3 garlic cloves
1 pizza base, about 25–30 cm/10–12 in
  diameter
1 quantity Tomato Sauce
1 red onion, thinly sliced
15 ml/1 tbsp chopped fresh oregano
15 ml/1 tbsp chopped fresh thyme
50 g/2 oz mozzarella, grated
50 g/2 oz freshly grated Parmesan

Tomato Sauce

thyme and oregano

red onion   *Parmesan*

mozzarella

olive oil

pork sausages

mild chilli powder

1 Preheat the oven to 220°C/425°F/ Gas 7. Skin the sausages by running a sharp knife down the side of the skins. Place the sausagemeat in a bowl and add the chilli powder and black pepper; mix well. Break the sausagemeat into walnut-sized balls.

2 Heat 15 ml/1 tbsp of the oil in a frying pan and fry the sausage balls for 2–3 minutes until evenly browned.

3 Using a slotted spoon remove the sausage balls from the pan and drain on kitchen paper.

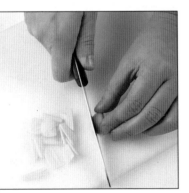

4 Thinly slice the garlic cloves.

5 Brush the pizza base with the remaining oil, then spread over the Tomato Sauce. Scatter over the sausages, garlic, onion and herbs.

6 Sprinkle over the mozzarella and Parmesan and bake for 15–20 minutes until crisp and golden. Serve immediately.

Caramelized Onion, Salami and Black Olive

The flavour of the sweet caramelized onion is offset by the salty black olives and herbes de Provence in the pizza base and the sprinkling of Parmesan to finish.

Serves 4

INGREDIENTS
700 g/1½ lb red onions
60 ml/4 tbsp olive oil
12 pitted black olives
1 quantity Superquick Pizza Dough
5 ml/1 tsp dried herbes de Provence
6–8 slices Italian salami, quartered
30–45 ml/2–3 tbsp freshly grated
  Parmesan
black pepper

Italian salami

red onions

black olives

olive oil

Parmesan

herbes de Provence

1 Preheat the oven to 220°C/425°F/ Gas 7. Thinly slice the onions.

2 Heat 30 ml/2 tbsp of the oil in a pan and add the onions. Cover and cook gently for 10 minutes, stirring occasionally until the onions are soft and very lightly coloured. Leave to cool.

3 Finely chop the black olives.

4 Knead the dough on a lightly floured surface, adding the black olives and herbes de Provence. Roll out the dough and use to line a 30 × 18 cm/12 × 7 in Swiss-roll tin. Push up the dough edges to make a thin rim and brush with half the remaining oil.

5 Spoon half the onions over the base, top with the salami and the remaining onions.

6 Grind over plenty of black pepper and drizzle over the remaining oil. Bake for 15–20 minutes until crisp and golden. Remove from the oven and sprinkle over the Parmesan to serve.

Pepperoni Pan Pizza

This pizza is made using a scone base which happily does not require proving! The topping can be varied to include whatever you like best – tuna fish, prawns, ham or salami are all good alternatives to the pepperoni.

Serves 2–3

INGREDIENTS

15 ml/1 tbsp chopped fresh mixed herbs
1 quantity Scone Pizza Dough
30 ml/2 tbsp tomato purée
400 g/14 oz can chopped tomatoes, drained well
50 g/2 oz button mushrooms, thinly sliced
75 g/3 oz sliced pepperoni
6 pitted black olives, chopped
50 g/2 oz Edam, grated
50 g/2 oz mature Cheddar, grated
15 ml/1 tbsp chopped fresh basil, to garnish

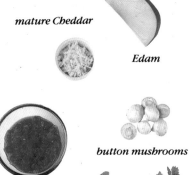

mature Cheddar

Edam

button mushrooms

chopped tomatoes

black olives

basil

fresh mixed herbs

pepperoni

tomato purée

1 Add the herbs to the scone mix before mixing to a soft dough.

2 Turn the dough on to a lightly floured surface and knead lightly until smooth. Roll out to fit a well-greased frying pan, about 22 cm/8½ in diameter.

3 Cook the dough in the pan over a low heat for about 5 minutes until the base is golden. Lift carefully with a palette knife to check.

4 Turn the base on to a baking sheet, then slide it back into the pan, with the cooked side uppermost.

5 Mix together the tomato purée and drained tomatoes and spread over the pizza base. Scatter over the mushrooms, pepperoni, olives and cheeses. Continue to cook for about 5 minutes until the underside is golden.

6 When it is ready, transfer the pan to a preheated moderate grill for 4–5 minutes to melt the cheese. Scatter over the basil and serve immediately.

Chilli Beef

Minced beef, red kidney beans and smoky cheese combined with oregano, cumin and chillies give this pizza a Mexican character.

Serves 4

INGREDIENTS
30 ml/2 tbsp olive oil
1 red onion, finely chopped
1 garlic clove, crushed
½ red pepper, seeded and finely
   chopped
175 g/6 oz lean minced beef
2.5 ml/½ tsp ground cumin
2 fresh red chillies, seeded and
   chopped
115 g/4 oz (drained weight) canned
   red kidney beans
1 quantity Superquick Pizza Dough
1 quantity Tomato Sauce
15 ml/1 tbsp chopped fresh oregano
50 g/2 oz mozzarella, grated
75 g/3 oz oak-smoked Cheddar, grated
salt and black pepper

Tomato Sauce

red onion

minced beef

mozzarella

oak-smoked Cheddar

red chillies

oregano

olive oil

red kidney beans

red pepper

1 Preheat the oven to 220°C/425°F/ Gas 7. Heat 15 ml/1 tbsp of the oil in a frying pan, add the onion, garlic and pepper and gently fry until soft. Increase the heat, add the beef and brown well, stirring constantly.

2 Add the cumin and chillies and continue to cook, stirring, for about 5 minutes. Add the beans and seasoning.

3 Roll out the dough on a surface dusted with cornmeal and use to line a 30 × 18 cm/12 × 7 in greased Swiss-roll tin. Push up the dough edges to make a rim.

4 Spread over the Tomato Sauce.

5 Spoon over the beef mixture then scatter over the oregano.

6 Sprinkle over the cheeses and bake for 15–20 minutes until crisp and golden. Serve immediately.

VARIATION

If you prefer a milder version of this spicy pizza, reduce the amount of fresh chillies or leave them out altogether.

Chicken, Shiitake Mushroom and Coriander

The addition of shiitake mushrooms adds an earthy flavour to this colourful pizza, while fresh red chilli adds a hint of spiciness.

Serves 3–4

INGREDIENTS
45 ml/3 tbsp olive oil
350 g/12 oz chicken breast fillets, skinned and cut into thin strips
1 bunch spring onions, sliced
1 fresh red chilli, seeded and chopped
1 red pepper, seeded and cut into thin strips
75 g/3 oz fresh shiitake mushrooms, wiped and sliced
45–60 ml/3–4 tbsp chopped fresh coriander
1 pizza base, about 25–30 cm/10–12 in diameter
15 ml/1 tbsp Chilli Oil
150 g/5 oz mozzarella
salt and black pepper

chicken breast fillets

spring onions

coriander

red chilli

red pepper

Chilli Oil

olive oil

shiitake mushrooms

1 Preheat the oven to 220°C/425°F/Gas 7. Heat 30 ml/2 tbsp of the olive oil in a wok or large frying pan. Add the chicken, spring onions, chilli, pepper and mushrooms and stir-fry over a high heat for 2–3 minutes until the chicken is firm but still slightly pink within. Season.

2 Pour off any excess oil, then set aside the chicken mixture to cool.

3 Stir the fresh coriander into the chicken mixture.

4 Brush the pizza base with the chilli oil.

5 Spoon over the chicken mixture and drizzle over the remaining olive oil.

6 Grate the mozzarella and sprinkle over. Bake for 15–20 minutes until crisp and golden. Serve immediately.

Smoked Chicken, Yellow Pepper and Sun-dried Tomato Pizzettes

These ingredients complement each other perfectly and make a really delicious topping.

Serves 4

INGREDIENTS
1 quantity Superquick Pizza Dough
45 ml/3 tbsp olive oil
60 ml/4 tbsp sun-dried tomato paste
2 yellow peppers, seeded and cut into thin strips
175 g/6 oz sliced smoked chicken or turkey, chopped
150 g/5 oz mozzarella, cubed
30 ml/2 tbsp chopped fresh basil
salt and black pepper

basil

mozzarella

yellow peppers

olive oil

smoked chicken

sun-dried tomato paste

1 Preheat the oven to 220°C/425°F/Gas 7. Divide the dough into four pieces and roll out each one on a lightly floured surface to a 13 cm/5 in circle. Place well apart on two greased baking sheets, then push up the dough edges to make a thin rim. Brush with 15 ml/1 tbsp of the oil.

2 Brush the pizza bases generously with the sun-dried tomato paste.

3 Stir-fry the peppers in half the remaining oil for 3–4 minutes.

4 Arrange the chicken and peppers on top of the sun-dried tomato paste.

5 Scatter over the mozzarella and basil. Season with salt and black pepper.

VARIATION

For a vegetarian pizza with a similar smokey taste, omit the chicken, roast the yellow peppers and remove the skins before using, and replace the mozzarella with Bavarian smoked cheese.

6 Drizzle over the remaining oil and bake for 15–20 minutes until crisp and golden. Serve immediately.

Mixed Seafood

Here is a pizza that gives you the full flavour of the Mediterranean, ideal for a summer evening supper!

Serves 3–4

INGREDIENTS

1 pizza base, 25–30 cm/10–12 in diameter
30 ml/2 tbsp olive oil
1 quantity Tomato Sauce
400 g/14 oz bag frozen mixed cooked seafood (including mussels, prawns and squid), defrosted
3 garlic cloves
30 ml/2 tbsp chopped fresh parsley
30 ml/2 tbsp freshly grated Parmesan, to garnish

1 Preheat the oven to 220°C/425°F/Gas 7. Brush the pizza base with 15 ml/1 tbsp of the oil.

2 Spread over the Tomato Sauce. Bake for 10 minutes. Remove from the oven.

3 Pat the seafood dry using kitchen paper, then arrange on top.

mixed seafood

garlic

olive oil

parsley

Tomato Sauce

Parmesan

4 Chop the garlic and scatter over.

5 Sprinkle over the parsley, then drizzle over the remaining oil.

VARIATION

If you prefer, this pizza can be made with mussels or prawns on their own, or any combination of your favourite seafood.

6 Bake for a further 5–10 minutes until the seafood is warmed through and the base is crisp and golden. Sprinkle with Parmesan and serve immediately.

Salmon and Avocado

Smoked and fresh salmon make a delicious pizza topping when mixed with avocado. Smoked salmon trimmings are cheaper than smoked salmon slices and could be used instead.

Serves 3–4

INGREDIENTS

150 g/5 oz salmon fillet
120 ml/4 fl oz/½ cup dry white wine
1 pizza base, 25–30 cm/10–12 in
   diameter
15 ml/1 tbsp olive oil
400 g/14 oz can chopped tomatoes,
   drained well
115 g/4 oz mozzarella, grated
1 small avocado
10 ml/2 tsp lemon juice
30 ml/2 tbsp crème fraîche
75 g/3 oz smoked salmon, cut into
   strips
15 ml/1 tbsp capers
30 ml/2 tbsp snipped fresh chives, to
   garnish
black pepper

lemon

chopped tomatoes

dry white wine

mozzarella

avocado

smoked salmon

salmon fillet

crème fraîche

1 Preheat the oven to 220°C/425°F/ Gas 7. Place the salmon fillet in a frying pan, pour over the wine and season with black pepper. Bring slowly to the boil, remove from the heat, cover and cool. (The fish will cook in the cooling liquid.) Skin and flake the salmon into small pieces, removing any bones.

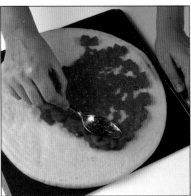

2 Brush the pizza base with the oil and spread over the drained tomatoes. Sprinkle over 50 g/2 oz of the mozzarella. Bake for 10 minutes, then remove from the oven.

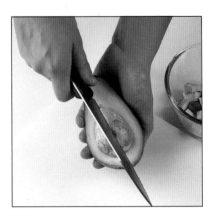

3 Meanwhile, halve, stone and peel the avocado. Cut the flesh into small cubes and toss carefully in the lemon juice.

4 Dot teaspoonsful of the crème fraîche over the pizza base.

5 Arrange the fresh and smoked salmon, avocado, capers and remaining mozzarella on top. Season with black pepper. Bake for a further 5–10 minutes until crisp and golden.

6 Sprinkle over the chives and serve immediately.

Mussel and Leek Pizzettes

Serve these tasty seafood pizzettes with a crisp green salad for a light lunch.

Serves 4

INGREDIENTS
450 g/1 lb live mussels
120 ml/4 fl oz/½ cup dry white wine
1 quantity Superquick Pizza Dough
15 ml/1 tbsp olive oil
50 g/2 oz Gruyère
50 g/2 oz mozzarella
2 small leeks
salt and black pepper

olive oil

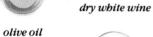

dry white wine

mussels

mozzarella

Gruyère

leeks

1 Preheat the oven to 220°C/425°F/Gas 7. Place the mussels in a bowl of cold water to soak, and scrub well. Remove the beards and discard any mussels that are open.

2 Place the mussels in a pan. Pour over the wine, cover and cook over a high heat, shaking the pan occasionally, for 5–10 minutes until the mussels have opened.

3 Drain off the cooking liquid. Remove the mussels from their shells, discarding any that remain closed. Leave to cool.

4 Divide the dough into four pieces and roll out each one on a lightly floured surface to a 13 cm/5 in circle. Place well apart on two greased baking sheets, then push up the dough edges to form a thin rim. Brush the pizza bases with the oil. Grate the cheeses and sprinkle half evenly over the bases.

5 Thinly slice the leeks, then scatter over the cheese. Bake for 10 minutes, then remove from the oven.

VARIATION

Frozen or canned mussels can also be used, but will not have the same flavour and texture. Make sure you defrost the mussels properly.

6 Arrange the mussels on top. Season and sprinkle over the remaining cheese. Bake for a further 5–10 minutes until crisp and golden. Serve immediately.

Prawn, Sun-dried Tomato and Basil Pizzettes

Sun-dried tomatoes with their concentrated caramelized tomato flavour make an excellent topping for pizzas. Serve these pretty pizzettes as an appetizer or snack.

Serves 4

INGREDIENTS
1 quantity Superquick Pizza Dough
30 ml/2 tbsp Chilli Oil
75 g/3 oz mozzarella, grated
1 garlic clove, chopped
½ small red onion, thinly sliced
4–6 pieces sun-dried tomatoes, thinly sliced
115 g/4 oz cooked prawns, peeled
30 ml/2 tbsp chopped fresh basil
salt and black pepper
shredded basil leaves, to garnish

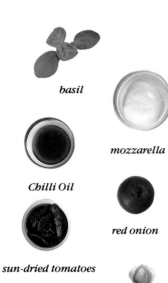

basil

mozzarella

Chilli Oil

red onion

sun-dried tomatoes

garlic

1 Preheat the oven to 220°C/425°F/ Gas 7. Divide the dough into eight pieces.

2 Roll out each one on a lightly floured surface to a small oval about 5 mm/¼ in thick. Place well apart on two greased baking sheets. Prick all over with a fork.

3 Brush the pizza bases with 15 ml/ 1 tbsp of the chilli oil and top with the mozzarella, leaving a 1 cm/½ in border.

4 Divide the garlic, onion, sun-dried tomatoes, prawns and basil between the pizza bases. Season and drizzle over the remaining chilli oil. Bake for 8–10 minutes until crisp and golden. Garnish with basil leaves and serve immediately.

Crab and Parmesan Calzonelli

These miniature calzone owe their popularity to their impressive presentation. If preferred, you can use prawns instead of crab.

Makes 10–12

INGREDIENTS

1 quantity Superquick Pizza Dough
115 g/4 oz mixed prepared crab meat, defrosted if frozen
15 ml/1 tbsp double cream
30 ml/2 tbsp freshly grated Parmesan
30 ml/2 tbsp chopped fresh parsley
1 garlic clove, crushed
salt and black pepper
parsley sprigs, to garnish

Parmesan

double cream

crab meat

parsley

garlic

1 Preheat the oven to 200°C/400°F/ Gas 6. Roll out the dough on a lightly floured surface to 3 mm/⅛ in thick. Using a 7.5 cm/3 in plain round cutter stamp out 10–12 circles.

2 In a bowl mix together the crab meat, cream, Parmesan, parsley, garlic and seasoning.

3 Spoon a little of the filling on to one half of each circle. Dampen the edges with water and fold over to enclose filling.

4 Seal the edges by pressing with a fork. Place well apart on two greased baking sheets. Bake for 10–15 minutes until golden. Garnish with parsley sprigs.

Tuna, Anchovy and Caper

This pizza makes a substantial supper dish which will provide two to three generous portions accompanied by a simple salad.

Serves 2–3

INGREDIENTS
1 quantity Scone Pizza Dough
30 ml/2 tbsp olive oil
1 quantity Tomato Sauce
1 small red onion
200 g/7 oz can tuna, drained
15 ml/1 tbsp capers
12 pitted black olives
45 ml/3 tbsp freshly grated Parmesan
50 g/2 oz can anchovy fillets, drained
   and halved lengthways
black pepper

Tomato Sauce

olive oil

Parmesan

black olives

tuna

red onion

capers

1 Preheat the oven to 220°C/425°F/ Gas 7. Roll out the dough on a lightly floured surface to a 25 cm/10 in circle. Place on a greased baking sheet and brush with 15 ml/1 tbsp of the oil. Spread the Tomato Sauce evenly over the dough.

2 Cut the onion into thin wedges and arrange on top.

3 Roughly flake the tuna with a fork and scatter over the onion.

4 Sprinkle over the capers, black olives and Parmesan.

5 Lattice the anchovy fillets over the top of the pizza.

6 Drizzle over the remaining oil, then grind over plenty of black pepper. Bake for 15–20 minutes until crisp and golden. Serve immediately.

DASHING

Happy endings are only a moment away with this superb selection of sweet **treats**. Not surprisingly, **fresh** fruit features strongly. Who could resist Pineapple Wedges with Rum Butter Glaze, Ginger and Banana Brûlée or the **warm** promise of Kentucky Fried Peaches? Nectarines with Marzipan and

Mascarpone can be made in a **jiffy**, yet are stylish enough to serve after the grandest meal. For children of all ages, from six to sixty-six, **Fruit** Kebabs with Chocolate and Marshmallow Fondue provide the **perfect** finale to any meal.

DESSERTS

Caramelized Apples

A sweet, sticky dessert which is very quickly made,
and usually very quickly eaten!

Serves 4

INGREDIENTS
675 g/1½ lb dessert apples
115 g/4 oz/½ cup unsalted butter
25 g/1 oz fresh white breadcrumbs
50 g/2 oz/½ cup ground almonds
rind of 2 lemons, finely grated
60 ml/4 tbsp golden syrup
60 ml/4 tbsp thick Greek yogurt,
    to serve

lemon

golden syrup

*ground
almonds*

apple

1 Peel and core the apples.

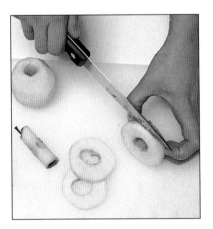

2 Carefully cut the apples into 1 cm/
½ in-thick rings.

3 Heat the wok, then add the butter.
When the butter has melted, add the
apple rings and stir-fry for 4 minutes until
golden and tender. Remove from the
wok, reserving the butter. Add the
breadcrumbs to the hot butter and stir-
fry for 1 minute.

4 Stir in the ground almonds and lemon
rind and stir-fry for a further 3 minutes,
stirring constantly. Sprinkle the
breadcrumb mix over the apples, then
drizzle warmed golden syrup over the
top. Serve with thick Greek yogurt.

Char-grilled Apples on Cinnamon Toasts

This simple, scrumptious dessert is best made with an enriched bread such as brioche, but any light, sweet bread will do.

Serves 4

4 sweet dessert apples
juice of ½ lemon
4 individual brioches or muffins
60 ml/4 tbsp melted butter
30 ml/2 tbsp golden caster
  sugar
5 ml/1 tsp ground cinnamon
cream or Greek-style yogurt, to
  serve

sweet dessert apples

golden caster sugar

lemon

brioches

melted butter

ground cinnamon

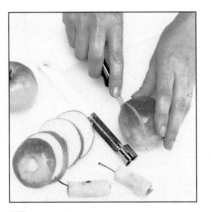

1 Core the apples and then cut them horizontally in 3–4 thick slices. Sprinkle with lemon juice.

2 Cut the brioches or muffins into thick slices. Brush with melted butter on both sides.

3 Mix together the sugar and cinnamon.

4 Place the apple and brioche slices on the hot barbecue and cook them for ·3–4 minutes, turning once, until they are beginning to turn golden brown.

5 Sprinkle half the cinnamon sugar over the apple slices and toasts and cook for a further minute, until they are a rich golden brown.

6 To serve, arrange the apple slices over the toasts and sprinkle them with the remaining cinnamon sugar. Serve hot, with cream or yogurt.

Fruit Kebabs with Chocolate and Marshmallow Fondue

Children love these treats – and with supervision they can help to make them.

Serves 4

2 bananas
2 kiwi fruit
12 strawberries
15 ml/1 tbsp melted butter
15 ml/1 tbsp lemon juice
5 ml/1 tsp ground cinnamon

FOR THE FONDUE
225 g/8 oz plain chocolate
100 ml/4 fl oz/½ cup single cream
8 marshmallows
2.5 ml/½ tsp vanilla essence

plain chocolate

vanilla essence

bananas

lemon juice
ground cinnamon

melted butter

single cream

marshmallows

kiwi fruit

strawberries

1 Peel the bananas and cut each into six thick chunks. Peel the kiwi fruit thinly and quarter them. Thread the bananas, kiwi fruit and strawberries on to four wooden or bamboo skewers.

2 Mix together the butter, lemon juice and cinnamon and brush the mixture over the fruits.

3 For the fondue, place the chocolate, cream and marshmallows in a small pan and heat gently on the barbecue, without boiling, stirring until the mixture has melted and is smooth.

4 Cook the kebabs on the barbecue for 2–3 minutes, turning once, or until golden. Stir the vanilla essence into the fondue and serve it with the kebabs.

Barbecued Strawberry Croissants

A deliciously simple, sinful dessert, which is like eating warm cream cakes!

Serves 4

4 croissants
115 g/4 oz/¹/₂ cup ricotta cheese
115 g/4 oz/¹/₂ cup strawberry
   conserve or jam

croissants

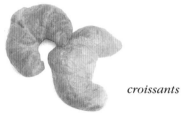

ricotta cheese

strawberry conserve

1 Split the croissants in half and open them out on a board.

2 Spread the bottom half of each croissant with ricotta cheese.

3 Top with a generous spoonful of strawberry conserve and replace the top half of the croissant.

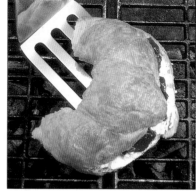

4 Place the croissants on a hot barbecue and cook for 2–3 minutes, turning once.

COOK'S TIP

As an alternative to croissants, try fresh scones or muffins, toasted on the barbecue.

Pineapple Wedges with Rum Butter Glaze

Fresh pineapple is even more full of flavour when grilled; this spiced rum glaze makes it into a very special dessert.

Serves 4

1 medium pineapple
30 ml/2 tbsp dark muscovado
   sugar
5 ml/1 tsp ground ginger
60 ml/4 tbsp melted butter
30 ml/2 tbsp dark rum

pineapple

melted butter

dark muscovado sugar

ground ginger   *dark rum*

1 With a large, sharp knife, cut the pineapple lengthways into four wedges. Cut out and discard the centre core.

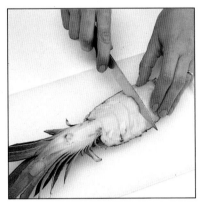

2 Cut between the flesh and skin, to release the flesh, but leave the skin in place. Slice the flesh across, into chunks.

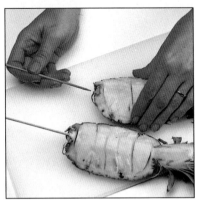

3 Push a bamboo skewer lengthways through each wedge and into the stalk, to hold the chunks in place.

4 Mix together the sugar, ginger, melted butter and rum and brush over the pineapple. Cook the wedges on a hot barbecue for 3–4 minutes; pour the remaining glaze over the top and serve.

COOK'S TIP

For an easier version, simply cut off the skin and then slice the whole pineapple into thick slices and cook as above.

Nectarines with Marzipan and Mascarpone

A luscious dessert that no one can resist – dieters may like to use low-fat soft cheese or ricotta instead of mascarpone.

Serves 4

4 firm, ripe nectarines or
 peaches
75 g/3 oz marzipan
75 g/3 oz/5 tbsp mascarpone
 cheese
3 macaroon biscuits, crushed

mascarpone cheese

nectarines

marzipan

macaroon biscuits

1 Cut the nectarines or peaches in half, removing the stones.

2 Cut the marzipan into eight pieces and press one piece into the stone cavity of each nectarine half.

3 Spoon the mascarpone on top. Sprinkle the crushed macaroons over the mascarpone.

4 Place the half-fruits on a hot barbecue for 3–5 minutes, until they are hot and the mascarpone starts to melt.

COOK'S TIP

Either peaches or nectarines can be used for this recipe. If the stone does not pull out easily when you halve the fruit, use a small, sharp knife to cut around it.

Mango and Coconut Stir-fry

Choose a ripe mango for this recipe. If you buy one
that is a little under-ripe, leave it in a warm place for
a day or two before using.

Serves 4

INGREDIENTS
¼ coconut
1 large, ripe mango
juice of 2 limes
rind of 2 limes, finely grated
15 ml/1 tbsp sunflower oil
15 g/½ oz/1 tbsp butter
30 ml/1½ tbsp clear honey
crème fraîche, to serve

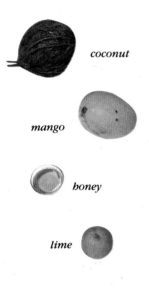

coconut

mango

honey

lime

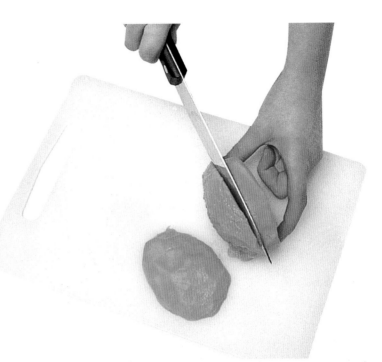

1 Prepare the coconut flakes by
draining the milk from the coconut and
peeling the flesh with a vegetable peeler.

2 Peel the mango. Cut the stone out of
the middle of the fruit. Cut each half of the mango into slices.

COOK'S TIP

Because of the delicate taste of
desserts, always make sure your wok
has been scrupulously cleaned so
there is no transference of flavours –
a garlicky mango isn't quite the effect
you want to achieve!

3 Place the mango slices in a bowl and
pour over the lime juice and rind, to
marinate them.

4 Meanwhile, heat the wok, then add
10 ml/2 tsp of the oil. When the oil is hot,
add the butter. When the butter has
melted, stir in the coconut flakes and
stir-fry for 1–2 minutes until the coconut
is golden brown. Remove and drain on
kitchen towels. Wipe out the wok. Strain
the mango slices, reserving the juice.

5 Heat the wok and add the remaining
oil. When the oil is hot, add the mango
and stir-fry for 1–2 minutes, then add the
juice and allow to bubble and reduce for
1 minute. Then stir in the honey, sprinkle
on the coconut flakes and serve with
crème fraîche.

Apples and Raspberries in Rose Pouchong Syrup

Inspiration for this dessert stems from the fact that the apple and the raspberry belong to the rose family. The subtle flavours are shared here in an infusion of rose-scented tea.

Serves 4

INGREDIENTS
5 ml/1 tsp rose pouchong tea
5 ml/1 tsp rose water (optional)
50 g/2 oz/¼ cup sugar
5 ml/1 tsp lemon juice
5 dessert apples
175 g/6 oz/1½ cups fresh raspberries

tea

apples

sugar

raspberries

COOK'S TIP
If fresh raspberries are out of season, use the same weight of frozen fruit or a 400 g/14 oz can of well drained fruit.

1 Warm a large tea pot. Add the rose pouchong tea and 900 ml/1½ pints/3¾ cups of boiling water together with the rose water, if using. Allow to stand and infuse for 4 minutes.

2 Measure the sugar and lemon juice into a stainless steel saucepan. Strain in the tea and stir to dissolve the sugar.

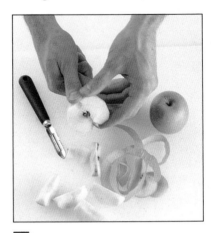

3 Peel and core the apples, then cut into quarters.

4 Poach the apples in the syrup for about 5 minutes.

5 Transfer the apples and syrup to a large metal tray and leave to cool to room temperature.

6 Pour the cooled apples and syrup into a bowl, add the raspberries and mix to combine. Spoon into individual dishes or bowls and serve warm.

Apricot and Almond Bake

This dessert consists of a few apricots, either fresh or canned, strewn over an almond batter. Hot from the oven, this dessert is bound to please with a scoop or two of best vanilla ice cream.

Serves 4

INGREDIENTS
50 g/2 oz/4 tbsp butter, softened, plus extra for greasing
50 g/2 oz/¼ cup caster sugar
50 g/2 oz/¾ ground almonds
15 ml/1 tbsp self-raising flour
1 egg
2.5 ml/½ tsp almond essence
175 g/6 oz/1 cup fresh apricots or 1 × 400 g/14 oz can apricots in syrup
icing sugar, for dusting
vanilla ice cream, custard or cream, to serve

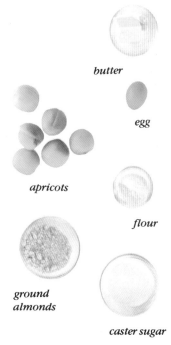

butter

egg

apricots

flour

ground almonds

caster sugar

1 Preheat the oven to 200°C/400°F/Gas 6. Lightly grease a 23 cm/9 in enamel pie plate with butter and set aside.

4 Add the egg and almond essence, then combine into a smooth batter.

2 Soften the butter if necessary in a microwave oven for 20 seconds at 100% high power. Combine the butter and sugar in a mixing bowl.

5 Turn the batter into a pie plate and spread it to the edge. Split the apricots, discard the stones if using fresh fruit, and arrange over the batter. Bake in the preheated oven for 15–20 minutes until springy to the touch.

3 Mix the ground almonds and flour together and add to the butter.

6 Dust with icing sugar and serve hot with vanilla ice cream, cream or custard.

Kentucky Fried Peaches

Never mind your diet, when peaches are this good, it's time for a break!

Serves 4

INGREDIENTS
5 large ripe peaches
50 g/2 oz/4 tbsp butter
30 ml/2 tbsp soft brown sugar
45 ml/3 tbsp Kentucky bourbon
1.2 litres/2 pints/5 cups vanilla
    ice cream
50 g/2 oz/½ cup pecan nuts, toasted

pecan nuts

vanilla ice cream

bourbon

peaches

butter

brown sugar

COOK'S TIP
Peaches that ripen after they are picked will not release their skins when blanched in boiling water.

1 Place the peaches in a large bowl and cover with boiling water to loosen their skins. Drain, refresh under cold running water and slice.

2 Heat the butter in a large frying pan until it foams and begins to brown. Add the sugar, peaches and bourbon, turn up the heat and cook until soft and syrupy. Spoon the hot peaches over the ice cream and decorate with pecan nuts.

Grilled Pineapple with Rum-custard Sauce

Freshly ground black pepper may seem an unusual ingredient to put with pineapple, until you realise that peppercorns are the fruit of a tropical vine. If the idea does not appeal, make the sauce without pepper.

Serves 4

INGREDIENTS
1 ripe pineapple
25 g/1 oz/2 tbsp butter
fresh strawberries, sliced, to serve

FOR THE SAUCE
1 egg
2 egg yolks
30 ml/2 tbsp caster sugar
30 ml/2 tbsp dark rum
2.5 ml/½ tsp freshly ground
   black pepper

butter

rum

eggs

pineapple

black pepper

caster sugar

1 Remove the top and bottom from the pineapple with a serrated knife. Pare away the outer skin from top to bottom, remove the core and cut into slices.

2 Preheat a moderate grill. Dot the pineapple slices with butter and grill for about 5 minutes.

3 To make the sauce, place all the ingredients in a bowl. Set over a saucepan of simmering water and whisk with a hand-held mixer for about 3–4 minutes or until foamy and cooked. Scatter the strawberries over the pineapple and serve with the sauce.

COOK'S TIP
The sweetest pineapples are picked and exported when ripe. Contrary to popular belief, pineapples do not ripen well after picking. Choose fruit that smells sweet and yields to firm pressure from your thumbs.

Cherry Pancakes

These pancakes are virtually fat-free, and lower in calories and higher in fibre than traditional ones. Serve with a spoonful of natural yogurt or fromage frais.

Serves 4

INGREDIENTS
FOR THE PANCAKES
50 g/2 oz/½ cup plain flour
50 g/2 oz/⅓ cup plain wholemeal
   flour
pinch of salt
1 egg white
150 ml/¼ pint/⅔ cup skimmed milk
150 ml/¼ pint/⅔ cup water
a little oil for frying

FOR THE FILLING
425 g/15 oz can black cherries in juice
7.5 ml/1½ tsp arrowroot

skimmed milk

wholemeal flour

plain flour

black cherries

arrowroot

egg

1 Sift the flours and salt into a bowl, adding any bran left in the sieve to the bowl at the end.

2 Make a well in the centre of the flour and add the egg white. Gradually beat in the milk and water, whisking hard until all the liquid is incorporated and the batter is smooth and bubbly.

3 Heat a non-stick pan with a small amount of oil until the pan is very hot. Pour in just enough batter to cover the base of the pan, swirling the pan to cover the base evenly.

4 Cook until the pancake is set and golden, and then turn to cook the other side. Remove to a sheet of absorbent paper and then cook the remaining batter, to make about eight pancakes.

5 Drain the cherries, reserving the juice. Blend about 30 ml/2 tbsp of the juice from the can of cherries with the arrowroot in a saucepan. Stir in the rest of the juice. Heat gently, stirring, until boiling. Stir over a moderate heat for about 2 minutes, until thickened and clear.

COOK'S TIP

If fresh cherries are in season, cook them gently in enough apple juice just to cover them, and then thicken the juice with arrowroot as in Step 5.

The basic pancakes will freeze very successfully. Interleave them with non-stick or absorbent paper, overwrap them in polythene and seal. Freeze for up to six months. Thaw at room temperature.

6 Add the cherries and stir until thoroughly heated. Spoon the cherries into the pancakes and fold them in quarters.

Crispy Cinnamon Toasts

This recipe is based on a sweet version of French toast. You can use fancy cutters to create a pretty dessert or, if you do not have cutters, simply cut the crusts off the bread and cut it into little fingers.

Serves 4

INGREDIENTS
50 g/2 oz raisins
45 ml/3 tbsp Grand Marnier
4 medium slices white bread
3 × size 4 eggs, beaten
15 ml/1 tbsp ground cinnamon
2 large oranges
20 ml/1½ tbsp sunflower oil
25 g/1 oz/2 tbsp unsalted butter
15 ml/1 tbsp demerara sugar
thick Greek yogurt, to serve

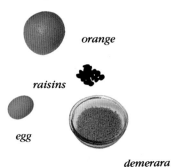

orange

raisins

egg

demerara sugar

bread

1 Soak the raisins in the Grand Marnier for 10 minutes.

2 Cut the bread into shapes with a cutter. Place the shapes in a bowl with the eggs and cinnamon to soak.

3 Peel the oranges. Remove any excess pith from the peel, then cut it into fine strips and blanch. Refresh it in cold water, then drain.

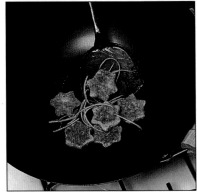

4 Strain the raisins. Heat the wok, then add the oil. When the oil is hot, stir in the butter until melted, then add the bread and fry, turning once, until golden brown. Stir in the raisins and orange rind, and sprinkle with sugar. Serve warm with thick Greek yogurt.

Apple Soufflé Omelette

Apples sautéed until they are slightly caramelized make a delicious filling for an omelette dredged with icing sugar and branded with a hot skewer.

Serves 2

INGREDIENTS
4 eggs, separated
30 ml/2 tbsp single cream
15 ml/1 tbsp caster sugar
15 g/½ oz/1 tbsp butter
icing sugar, for dredging

FOR THE FILLING
25 g/1 oz/2 tbsp butter
1 eating apple, peeled, cored
    and sliced
30 ml/2 tbsp soft light brown sugar
45 ml/3 tbsp single cream

eggs

single cream

caster sugar

butter

icing sugar

eating apple

soft light brown sugar

1 Make the filling. Melt the butter in a frying pan. Add the apples and sprinkle them with the brown sugar. Sauté until the apples are just tender and have caramelized a little. Stir in the cream and keep warm while making the omelette.

2 Place the egg yolks in a bowl. Add the cream and sugar and beat well. In a grease-free bowl whisk the egg whites until they hold soft peaks, then fold them into the yolk mixture.

3 Preheat the grill. Melt the butter in a large, heavy-based frying pan. Pour in the soufflé mixture and spread evenly. Cook for 1 minute until golden underneath, then place the pan under the hot grill to brown the top of the omelette.

4 Heat a metal skewer. Slide the omelette on to a plate, add the apple mixture, then fold it over. Sift the icing sugar over thickly, then mark in a criss-cross pattern with a hot metal skewer. Serve immediately.

Red Berry Sponge Tart

When soft berry fruits are in season, try making this delicious sponge tart. Serve warm from the oven with scoops of vanilla ice cream.

Serves 4

INGREDIENTS
softened butter, for greasing
450 g/1 lb/4 cups soft berry fruits
    such as raspberries, blackberries,
    blackcurrants, redcurrants,
    strawberries or blueberries
2 eggs, at room temperature
50 g/2 oz/¼ cup caster sugar, plus
    extra to taste (optional)
15 ml/1 tbsp plain flour
50 g/2 oz/¾ cup ground almonds
vanilla ice cream, to serve

1 Preheat the oven to 190°C/375°F/Gas 5. Brush a 23 cm/9 in flan tin with softened butter and line the bottom with a circle of non-stick baking paper. Scatter the fruit in the bottom of the tin with a little sugar if the fruits are tart.

eggs

ground almonds

flour

caster sugar

redcurrants

blackcurrants

raspberries

strawberries

2 Whisk the eggs and sugar together for about 3–4 minutes or until they leave a thick trail across the surface. Combine the flour and almonds, then fold into the egg mixture with a spatula – retaining as much air as possible.

3 Spread the mixture on top of the fruit base and bake in the preheated oven for 15 minutes. Turn out onto a serving plate and serve with vanilla ice cream.

VARIATION

When berry fruits are out of season, use bottled fruits, but ensure that they are well drained before use.

Orange Yogurt Brûlées

A luxurious treat, but one that is much lower in fat than the classic brûlées, which are made with cream, eggs and large amounts of sugar.

Serves 4

INGREDIENTS
2 medium-size oranges
150 g/5 oz/⅔ cup Greek yogurt
50 g/2 oz/¼ cup crème fraîche
45 ml/3 tbsp golden caster sugar
30 ml/2 tbsp light muscovado sugar

golden caster sugar

light muscovado sugar

crème fraîche

oranges

Greek yogurt

1 With a sharp knife, cut away all the peel and white pith from the oranges and chop the fruit. Or, if there's time, segment the oranges, removing all the membrane.

2 Place the fruit in the bottom of four individual flameproof dishes. Mix together the yogurt and crème fraîche and spoon the mixture over the oranges.

COOK'S TIP

For a lighter version, simply use 200 g/7 oz/⅞ cup low-fat natural yogurt instead of the Greek yogurt and crème fraîche.

3 Mix together the two sugars and sprinkle them evenly over the tops of the dishes.

4 Place the dishes under a preheated, very hot grill for 3–4 minutes or until the sugar melts and turns to a rich golden brown. Serve warm or cold.

Raspberry and Passion Fruit Chinchillas

Few desserts are so strikingly easy to make as this one: beaten egg whites and sugar baked in a dish, turned out and served with a handful of soft fruit.

VARIATION

If raspberries are out of season, use either fresh, bottled or canned soft berry fruit such as strawberries, blueberries or redcurrants.

Serves 4

INGREDIENTS
25 g/1 oz/2 tbsp butter, softened
5 egg whites
150 g/5 oz/⅔ cup caster sugar
2 passion fruit
250 ml/8 fl oz/1 cup ready-made
   custard from a carton or can
milk, as required
675 g/1½ lb/6 cups fresh raspberries
icing sugar, for dusting

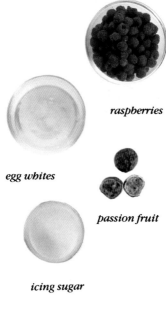

raspberries

egg whites

passion fruit

icing sugar

1 Preheat the oven to 180°C/350°F/ Gas 4. Brush four 300 ml/½ pint soufflé dishes with a visible layer of soft butter.

2 Whisk the egg whites in a mixing bowl until firm. (You can use an electric whisk.) Add the sugar a little at a time and whisk into a firm meringue.

3 Halve the passion fruit, take out the seeds with a spoon and fold them into the meringue.

4 Turn the meringue out into the prepared dishes, stand in a deep roasting pan which has been half-filled with boiling water and bake for 10 minutes. The meringue will rise above the tops of the soufflé dishes.

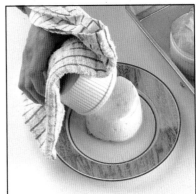

5 Turn the chinchillas out upside-down onto a serving plate. Thin the custard with a little milk and pour around the edge.

6 Top with raspberries, dredge with icing sugar and serve warm or cold.

Ginger and Banana Brûlée

Desserts don't have to be elaborate to achieve excellent results. The proof of the pudding is this simple ginger and banana brûlée.

Serves 6–8

INGREDIENTS
4 thick slices ginger cake
6 bananas, sliced
30 ml/2 tbsp lemon juice
300 ml/½ pint/1¼ cups whipping cream or fromage frais
60 ml/4 tbsp fruit juice
30–45 ml/3–4 tbsp soft light brown sugar

ginger cake

bananas

lemon

whipping cream

fruit juice

soft light brown sugar

1 Cut the cake into chunks and arrange in an ovenproof dish. Slice the bananas and toss in the lemon juice.

2 Preheat the grill. Whip the cream until firm, then gently whip in the fruit juice. (If using fromage frais, just gently stir in the juice.) Drain the bananas and fold them into the mixture; spoon over the ginger cake.

3 Sprinkle over the sugar in an even layer. Place under the hot grill for 2–3 minutes to caramelize. Serve at once, or allow to cool, then chill for a crisp topping.

VARIATION

For a delicious alternative try chocolate cake and pears instead of ginger cake and bananas. You could also drizzle a little liqueur or sherry over the chocolate cake for a touch of luxury.

Quick Apricot Blender Whip

One of the quickest desserts you could make – and also one of the prettiest.

Serves 4

INGREDIENTS
400 g/14 oz can apricot halves in juice
15 ml/1 tbsp Grand Marnier or brandy
175 g/6 oz/¾ cup Greek yogurt
30 ml/2 tbsp flaked almonds

Greek yogurt

Grand Marnier

apricot halves

flaked almonds

1 Drain the juice from the apricots and place the fruit and liqueur in a blender or food processor.

2 Process the apricots until smooth.

3 Spoon the fruit purée and yogurt in alternate spoonfuls into four tall glasses or glass dishes, swirling them together slightly to give a marbled effect.

4 Lightly toast the almonds until they are golden. Let them cool slightly and then sprinkle them on top.

COOK'S TIP

For an even lighter dessert, use low-fat instead of Greek yogurt, and, if you prefer to omit the liqueur, add a little of the fruit juice from the can.

Brazilian Coffee Bananas

Rich, lavish and sinful-looking, this dessert takes only about 2 minutes to make!

Serves 4

INGREDIENTS
4 small ripe bananas
15 ml/1 tbsp instant coffee granules or
   powder
15 ml/1 tbsp hot water
30 ml/2 tbsp dark muscovado sugar
250 g/9 oz/1⅛ cups Greek yogurt
15 ml/1 tbsp toasted flaked almonds

bananas

Greek yogurt

flaked almonds

instant coffee

dark muscovado sugar

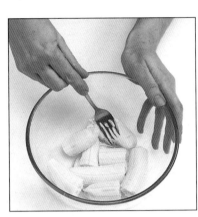

1 Peel and slice one banana and mash the remaining three with a fork.

2 Dissolve the coffee in the hot water and stir into the mashed bananas.

3 Spoon a little of the mashed banana mixture into four serving dishes and sprinkle with sugar. Top with a spoonful of yogurt, then repeat until all the ingredients are used up.

4 Swirl the last layer of yogurt for a marbled effect. Finish with a few banana slices and flaked almonds. Serve cold. Best eaten within about an hour of making.

VARIATION

For a special occasion, add a dash – just a dash – of dark rum or brandy to the bananas for extra richness.

Raspberry Muesli Layer

As well as being a delicious, low-fat, high-fibre dessert, this can also be served for a quick, healthy breakfast.

Serves 4

INGREDIENTS
225 g/8 oz/2¼ cups fresh or frozen and thawed raspberries
225 g/8 oz/1 cup low-fat natural yogurt
75 g/3 oz/½ cup Swiss-style muesli

raspberries

Swiss-style muesli

natural yogurt

COOK'S TIP
This recipe can be made in advance and stored in the fridge for several hours, or overnight if you're serving it for breakfast.

1 Reserve four raspberries for decoration, and then spoon a few raspberries into four stemmed glasses or glass dishes.

2 Top the raspberries with a spoonful of yogurt in each glass.

3 Sprinkle a layer of muesli over the yogurt.

4 Repeat with the raspberries and other ingredients. Top each with a whole raspberry.

Mixed Melon Salad with Wild Strawberries

Ice-cold melon is a delicious way to end a meal. Here several varieties are combined with strongly flavoured wild or woodland strawberries. If wild berries are not available, use ordinary strawberries or raspberries.

Serves 4

INGREDIENTS
1 cantaloupe or charentais melon
1 galia melon
900 g/2 lb water melon
175 g/6 oz wild strawberries
4 sprigs fresh mint

wild strawberries

galia melon

mint

cantaloupe melon

water melon

COOK'S TIP

Ripe melons should give slightly when pressed at the base, and should give off a fruity, melony scent. Buy carefully if you plan to use the fruit on the day.

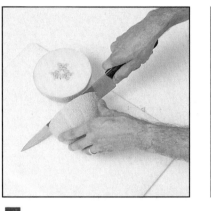

1 Halve the cantaloupe, galia and water melons.

2 Remove the seeds from the cantaloupe and galia with a spoon.

3 With a melon scoop, take out as many balls as you can from all 3 melons. Combine in a large bowl and refrigerate.

4 Add the wild strawberries and turn out into 4 stemmed glass dishes.

5 Decorate with sprigs of mint.

Passion-fruit and Apple Foam

Passion-fruit have an exotic, scented flavour that makes this simple apple dessert very special; if passion-fruit are not available, use two finely chopped kiwi fruit instead.

Serves 4

INGREDIENTS
500 g/1 lb cooking apples
90 ml/6 tbsp apple juice
3 passion-fruit
3 egg whites
1 red-skinned apple, to decorate
lemon juice

apple juice

lemon

cooking apples

red-skinned apple

eggs

passion-fruit

1 Peel, core and roughly chop the cooking apples and place them in a pan, with the apple juice.

2 Bring to the boil, and then reduce the heat and cover the pan. Cook gently, stirring occasionally, until the apple is very tender.

3 Remove from the heat and beat the apple mixture with a wooden spoon until it becomes a fairly smooth purée (or purée the apple in a food processor).

4 Cut the passion-fruit in half and scoop out the flesh. Stir the flesh into the apple purée.

5 Place the egg whites in a clean, dry bowl and whisk them until they form soft peaks. Fold the egg whites into the apple mixture. Spoon the apple foam into four serving dishes.

COOK'S TIP

It's important to use a good cooking apple, such as a Bramley, for this recipe, because the fluffy texture of a cooking apple breaks down easily to a purée. You can use dessert apples, but you will find it easier to purée them in a food processor.

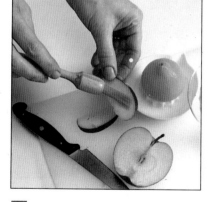

6 Thinly slice the red-skinned apple and brush the slices with lemon juice, to prevent them from browning. Arrange the slices on top of the apple foam and serve cold.

Prune and Orange Pots

A simple, storecupboard dessert, made in minutes.
It can be served straight away, but it's best chilled
for about half an hour before serving.

Serves 4

INGREDIENTS
225 g/8 oz/1½ cups ready-to-eat dried
   prunes
150 ml/¼ pint/⅔ cup orange juice
225 g/8 oz/1 cup low-fat natural
   yogurt
shreds of orange rind, to decorate

orange juice

natural yogurt

orange rind

prunes

1 Remove the stones from the prunes and roughly chop them. Place them in a pan with the orange juice.

2 Bring the juice to the boil, stirring. Reduce the heat, cover and leave to simmer for 5 minutes, until the prunes are tender and the liquid is reduced by half.

3 Remove from the heat, allow to cool slightly and then beat well with a wooden spoon, until the fruit breaks down to a rough purée.

4 Transfer mixture to a bowl. Stir in the yogurt, swirling the yogurt and fruit purée together lightly, to give an attractive marbled effect.

5 Spoon the mixture into stemmed glasses or individual dishes, smoothing the tops.

6 Top each pot with a few shreds of orange rind, to decorate. Chill before serving.

VARIATION

This dessert can also be made with other ready-to-eat dried fruit, such as apricots or peaches. For a special occasion, add a dash of brandy or Cointreau with the yogurt.

Peach Melba

In the original dish created by Escoffier for the opera singer Dame Nellie Melba, peaches and ice cream were served upon an ice swan.

Serves 4

· INGREDIENTS
300 g/11 oz hulled raspberries
squeeze of lemon juice
icing sugar, to taste
2 large ripe peaches or 425 g/15 oz
    can sliced peaches
8 scoops vanilla ice cream

raspberries

lemon

peaches

icing sugar

vanilla ice cream

1 Press the raspberries through a fine-mesh nylon strainer set over a bowl. Stir in a little lemon juice and sweeten to taste with icing sugar.

2 If using fresh peaches, dip them in boiling water for 4–5 seconds, then slip off the skins. Cut them in half along the indented line, then slice them. If using canned peaches, drain them well.

3 Place two scoops of ice cream in each individual glass dish, top with peach slices, then pour over the raspberry purée. Serve immediately.

COOK'S TIP
If you'd like to prepare this ahead of time, scoop the ice cream on to a cold baking sheet and freeze until ready to serve, then transfer the scoops to the dishes.

Ice Cream Strawberry Shortcake

This American classic couldn't be easier to make. Fresh, juicy strawberries, shop-bought flan cases and rich vanilla ice cream are all you need to create a feast of a dessert.

Serves 4

INGREDIENTS
3 x 15 cm/6 in sponge flan cases, or shortbread rounds
1.2 litres/2 pints/5 cups vanilla or strawberry ice cream
675 g/1½ lb hulled fresh strawberries, halved if large

strawberries

vanilla ice cream

flan case

1 If using flan cases, trim the raised edges with a serrated knife.

2 Set aside a third of the ice cream and strawberries for the topping. Place half the remaining ice cream and strawberries on one flan case or shortbread.

3 Place a second flan case on top and cover with a second layer of ice cream and fruit.

4 Top with the third flan case, the reserved ice cream and strawberries and serve.

COOK'S TIP

Don't worry if the shortcake falls apart when you cut into it. Messy cakes are best. Ice Cream Strawberry Shortbread can be assembled up to 1 hour in advance and kept in the freezer without spoiling the fruit.

Chocolate Mousse on the Loose

Super-light, dark, creamy and delicious; the chocolate mousse is always popular and should maintain a high profile on any dessert menu.

Serves 4

INGREDIENTS
200 g/7 oz best quality plain
    chocolate, plus extra for flaking
3 eggs
30 ml/2 tbsp dark rum or whisky
50 g/2 oz/¼ cup caster sugar
300 ml/½ pint/1¼ cups
    whipping cream
icing sugar, for dusting

plain chocolate

whipping cream

eggs

caster sugar

1 Break the chocolate into a bowl, stand over a saucepan of simmering water and melt. Separate the egg whites into a large mixing bowl, remove the chocolate from the heat and stir in the egg yolks and alcohol.

2 Whisk the egg whites until firm, gradually add the sugar and whisk until stiff peaks form.

3 Whip the cream to a dropping consistency and set aside until required.

4 Give the egg whites a final beating with a rubber spatula, add the chocolate and fold all the ingredients together gently, retaining as much air as possible.

5 Fold in the loosely whipped cream, turn into four glasses or bowls. If time permits, chill until ready to serve.

COOK'S TIP

It is a false economy to use inexpensive chocolate. Choose the best quality dark chocolate you can find and enjoy it!

6 Decorate with flaked chocolate and dust with icing sugar.

Black Forest Sundae

There's more than one way to enjoy the classic Black Forest Gateau. Here the traditional ingredients are layered in a sundae glass to make a superb cold sweet.

Serves 4

INGREDIENTS
400 g/14 oz can stoned black cherries in syrup
15 ml/1 tbsp cornflour
45 ml/3 tbsp Kirsch
150 ml/¼ pint/⅔ cup whipping cream
15 ml/1 tbsp icing sugar
600 ml/1 pint/2½ cups chocolate ice cream
115 g/4 oz chocolate cake
8 fresh cherries
vanilla ice cream, to serve

canned black cherries

cornflour

whipping cream

chocolate ice cream

chocolate cake

fresh cherries

icing sugar

Kirsch

Bottled black cherries often have a better flavour than canned ones, especially if the stones are left in. You needn't remove the stones – just remember to warn your guests.

1 Strain the cherry syrup from the can into a saucepan. Spoon the cornflour into a small bowl and stir in 30 ml/2 tbsp of the strained cherry syrup.

2 Bring the syrup in the saucepan to the boil. Stir in the cornflour and syrup mixture. Simmer briefly, stirring, until the syrup thickens.

3 Add the drained canned cherries, stir in the Kirsch and spread on a metal tray to cool.

4 Whip the cream with the icing sugar.

5 Place a spoonful of the cherry mixture in the bottom of four sundae glasses. Continue with layers of ice cream, chocolate cake, whipped cream and more cherry mixture until the glasses are full.

6 Finish with a piece of chocolate cake, two scoops of ice cream and more cream. Decorate with the fresh cherries.

INDEX